Understanding crime prevention
Social control, risk and
late modernity

£15-99
6/06

CRIME AND JUSTICE
Series editor: Mike Maguire
University College of Wales, College of Cardiff

Crime and Justice is a series of short introductory texts on central topics in criminology. The books in this series are written for students by internationally renowned authors. Each book tackles a key area within criminology, providing a concise and up-to-date overview of the principal concepts, theories, methods and findings relating to the area. Taken as a whole, the *Crime and Justice* series will cover all the core components of an undergraduate criminology course.

Current and forthcoming titles

Understanding youth and crime
Sheila Brown

Understanding crime data
Clive Coleman and Jenny Moynihan

Understanding social exclusion, crime and justice
Loraine Gelsthorpe

Understanding justice
Barbara A. Hudson

Understanding crime prevention
Gordon Hughes

Understanding criminal justice and the penal system
Mike Maguire

Understanding criminology
Sandra Walklate

Understanding crime prevention
Social control, risk and late modernity

Gordon Hughes

Open University Press
Buckingham · Philadelphia

In memory of my parents, Ada and Booey, and
for Tan and Lizzie

Open University Press
Celtic Court
22 Ballmoor
Buckingham
MK18 1XW

email: enquiries@openup.co.uk
world wide web: http://www.openup.co.uk

and
325 Chestnut Street
Philadelphia, PA 19106, USA

First Published 1998

A catalogue record of this book is available from the British Library

ISBN   0 335 19940 2 (pb)   0 335 19941 0 (hb)

Library of Congress Cataloging-in-Publication Data
Hughes, Gordon, 1952–
    Understanding crime prevention: social control, risk, and late
modernity/Gordon Hughes.
        p.   cm. – (Crime and justice)
    Includes bibliographical references and index.
    ISBN 0-335-19941-0 (hardcover). – ISBN 0-335-19940-2 (pbk.)
    1. Crime prevention.   2. Criminology.   3. Social control.   4. Risk
management.   I. Title.   II. Series: Crime and justice (Buckingham, England)
HV7431.H84   1998
364.4–dc21   98-13169   CIP

Typeset by Type Study, Scarborough
Printed in Great Britain by Biddles Ltd, Guildford and Kings Lynn

Contents

Series editor's foreword

This is the fifth in a series of textbooks – all of whose titles begin with the word *Understanding* – which cover important areas of debate within the fields of criminology, criminal justice and penology. The aim of the series is to provide relatively short and accessible texts, written by experienced lecturers and researchers, which will give undergraduates or postgraduates a solid grounding in the relevant area and, hopefully, a taste for the subject which will lead them to explore the literature further. Although aimed primarily at students new to the field, and although written as far as possible in plain language, the books do not give the false impression that they are dealing with a simple subject, easily mastered. On the contrary, all the authors aim to 'stretch' readers and to encourage them to approach criminological knowledge and theory in a critical and questioning frame of mind. Moreover, they do not simply summarize the relevant literature, but where appropriate express their own views and explain how and why they differ with other authors.

Gordon Hughes deals with a subject which has come more and more to the fore in criminological writing over recent years – that of crime prevention. Strictly speaking, of course, this covers a huge variety of strategies – from imprisoning or 'rehabilitating' offenders to installing locks on property – many of which have a very long history. Indeed, the first three chapters provide a useful overview of historical shifts in how crime prevention has been perceived and practised. However, the main focus of the book is upon relatively new approaches to crime prevention and on the reasons for their emergence and rapid spread in many different countries. In Britain, since the early 1980s, terms like 'situational crime prevention', 'neighbourhood watch', 'multi-agency partnership' and 'community safety' have become buzzwords in many government departments, local authority areas and voluntary agencies. There has also been a massive expansion in the use of closed-circuit television (CCTV) systems in town centre streets and even residential areas. In the United States, and increasingly elsewhere, privatization of the control of the public and semi-public areas has become commonplace, with greatly reduced freedom of access to 'outsiders' and reduced tolerance of even minor deviant behaviour. Taken together, such developments have potentially enormous implications for the nature of relations between individuals and between different kinds of social groups. They reflect new ways of thinking about the notion of 'community'. They appear also to represent a more general shift in the dominant modes of social control, which can be linked to other major social and economic changes, at a global as well as a national level. Gordon Hughes offers a broad sociological account and explanation of these changes, which leads him into discussion of important theoretical concepts such as late modernity, risk and globalization. A particular strength of the book – one of the first student texts to present the topic of crime prevention in this way – is that care is taken to explain these complex theoretical ideas as far as possible in simple language and to ground them in concrete examples.

The first four books in the Crime and Justice series covered penal theory (Barbara A. Hudson), crime data and statistics (Clive Coleman and Jenny Moynihan), modern criminological theory (Sandra Walklate) and youth and crime (Sheila Brown). Others in the pipeline include sentencing and the penal system (Mike Maguire) and crime and social exclusion (Loraine Gelsthorpe). All are central topics in the growing field of crime-related studies in universities, and each book makes an ideal foundation text for core courses or modules. As an aid to understanding, clear summaries are provided at regular intervals, and a glossary of key terms and concepts is a feature of every book. In addition, to help students expand their knowledge in specific areas, recommendations for further reading are given at the end of each chapter.

Finally, I must again record my gratitude to Roy Light and John Skelton for the original suggestion that I become involved in editing a series of this nature, as well as to Jacinta Evans, Nick Evans, Justin Vaughan, Joan Malherbe, Pat Lee and Gaynor Clements (past and present staff of Open University Press) for their help in bringing it to fruition. Most of all, I thank the authors, who have all made my job as series editor both simple and pleasurable.

Mike Maguire
Professor of Crime and Criminal Justice, University of Wales, Cardiff

Acknowledgements

Many thanks to Mike Maguire for inviting me to write this book, and for his helpful comments during its production. Thanks also to the editorial staff at the Open University Press for their support throughout the last year. A huge debt is owed to the members of the Applied Social Sciences discipline group at the Open University. Working at the Open University really is a collective enterprise and I couldn't ask for a more supportive group with which to be involved. Your imprint's here although you'll spot my idiosyncrasies for which I take full responsibility!

Most particularly, I am indebted to several friends and colleagues for their many helpful and critical comments on all or parts of the manuscript. Many thanks go to John Clarke, Adrian Little, Eugene McLaughlin, Rob Mears, John Muncie and Kevin Stenson.

Thanks to Sylv and Derek for encouraging me way back in Liverpool. And cheers Lizzie for sharing this project and lots more.

Introduction

Beyond the paradigm of technicist evaluation

To a large degree, the vision of crime prevention as a fully-fledged professional discipline is a grail for the future – but this is surely an irresistible
challenge to practitioners, researchers, evaluators, and policy-makers.
(Ekblom, 1996: 87)

Reducing crime: crime is caused by the lack of integrity in a nation.
Crime is the outburst of stress. A group of 7000 people practising the
Maharishi's Transcendental Meditation and Yogic Flying will eliminate
stress and maintain orderliness in the collective consciousness of
Europe. This will reduce crime dramatically . . . Crime rate in Mersey-
side has fallen by 60% compared to national trends since 1988 when a
group of Yogic Flyers was set up nearby.
(Natural Law Party manifesto in European elections 1995)

A fellow is walking down the street in London wearing a suit of protective armour and waving a large club over his head, all the while
shouting 'Get back! Get back!' So a policeman comes along and says,
'Excuse me Sir, but what exactly are you doing?' The guy says, 'I'm
doing tiger prevention. I'm doing this to keep tigers away'. The puzzled
cop scratches his head and says, 'But sir, no tigers have been seen on the
streets of London in my lifetime'. And the guy says, 'See, it works!'
(Currie, 1996: 13)

It is difficult to ignore the contemporary clamour surrounding, and hive of activity and industry around, that notoriously amorphous phenomenon of crime prevention in Western societies like the UK. For supporters of the bandwagon around 'new' crime prevention strategies, it is clearly a 'big idea' whose time has come. No one can deny that there has been a growth industry of late around crime prevention, employing *inter alia* academic researchers, business 'consultants', evaluators, politicians, policy makers, professional practitioners, media pundits and, not least, a new 'volunteer army' made up of 'responsible' and 'active' citizens. More sober or sceptical commentators point out that crime prevention is as old as the first lock and key and, of course, in an important sense the prevention of crime has been an aim of every correctional ideology concerned with the control of crime. Despite this important corrective to the 'talking up' of crime prevention as 'the new kid on the criminological block', there does appear to be something significant, specific and different about the prominent place occupied in the last decades of the twentieth century by the plethora of strategies and practices collectively known as crime prevention across many Western societies. Collectively the new politics of crime prevention may represent a new form of governance of crime control as well as claiming to offer a way out of the 'failed' traditional criminal sanctions such as incarceration. As the two leading criminologists, Tonry and Farrington (1995: vii) note: 'Crime bedevils Western societies and criminal sanctions are increasingly understood to have only modest effects on crime rates or patterns' and arising out of this crisis, 'preventive approaches to crime as distinguished from law enforcement or criminal justice approaches, are receiving new and renewed emphasis in many countries'. Crime prevention thinking and strategies are clearly now an important part of the broad debate concerning 'what is to be done about law and order'.

In our present times, there are often inflated claims made for crime prevention initiatives. These may take the bizarre form of the Natural Law Party's mystical link between yogic flying and reduced crime on the banks of the Mersey (see p. 1). However, more mainstream politicians have also been prone to hyperbole about new crime prevention initiatives, as in the then Home Secretary, Michael Howard's call in the mid-1990s for citizens to go out and 'walk with a purpose' in order to combat crime. It is also clear that social scientists are at times prone to make inflated claims for a new expertise about crime prevention. The opening statement to this introduction by Paul Ekblom, a leading Home Office researcher, appears to smack of a form of positivistic utopianism as well as new empire-building (with its talk of a 'grail' based on a distinct 'discipline' of crime prevention). Not all commentators are enamoured by this 'holy grail' of scientific evaluation and Elliot Currie's comic vignette at the start of this introduction may represent a valuable corrective to bear in mind when thinking about 'what works' in crime prevention. It is wise therefore to be wary of the quest for a 'pure', self-contained, scientific and technical discipline of crime prevention (and criminology). The cult of 'what works' and 'how to measure success' appears to smack of what Poggi (quoted in Sparks, 1997: 45) has wittily termed the 'unrequited crush on the natural sciences' among some social scientists.

It is important to note that crime prevention is a notoriously difficult notion to define. In this book I offer a critical introduction to this essentially contested field and place both current and past discourses on crime prevention in a new 'frame': namely that opened up by the insights of critical social theory and in particular historical sociology. There has never been a time when there was a uniform consensus over the question of what is to be done about crime and its control. Proponents and critics of crime prevention will continue to disagree as to the 'success' of crime prevention. This noted, the developments in criminal justice during the last decades of the twentieth century make it impossible for any study of crime and disorder to ignore the debate around the slippery concept of crime prevention. This book will aim to guide you through the competing claims for crime prevention among academic commentators, policy makers and politicians. What is clear is that within both academic and political circles in contemporary societies like the UK, a higher profile has been given to crime prevention measures, or at least the rhetoric of crime prevention, than at any previous time. And yet crime prevention remains a topic largely segregated from critical social theory, remaining the province for modest theorizing at best, and more often seemingly technical and pragmatic work. Put briefly, there has been an obsession with the closely-tied questions 'what works?' and 'how is what works to be measured?'

In the following chapters I will explain and contextualize both the current 'growth industry' around crime prevention and crime prevention discourses in terms of their wider socio-historical contexts. This analysis will move beyond the realm of the technicist and theoretically modest theorizing of most current criminological work in this field by developing a theoretical framework which focuses on the changing historical, cultural and institutional expressions of crime prevention and social control. On the surface it may seem that the interest in crime prevention is new. In fact this is far from the truth. What is new are governments' current uses of the term crime prevention for their promotion of multi-agency, situational and social strategies and 'partnerships' against crime; that is, an agenda for crime prevention beyond a police-driven agenda. During the last decade in both criminology and policy circles, crime prevention has become connoted with a particular reading of what it involves and the kind of 'species' of policy and practice through which it is constituted. A main aim of this book is to help foster a broader and more critical understanding of what crime prevention has been in the past and may become in the future.

Towards a sociology of crime prevention

Traditionally in the social sciences there has been much more theoretical and empirical interest in studying the underlying causes of crime than in understanding and explaining forms of crime prevention and control (McLaughlin and Muncie, 1996). Similarly, compared to the study of punishment (addressed by Barbara Hudson in a companion text on justice in this series; Hudson, 1996), crime prevention has been of little interest to philosophers, historians and sociologists. Instead, until recently, it has been largely left to the more administratively oriented studies of policy evaluation. In the work of critical criminologists during the 1970s and 1980s crime prevention was noticeable for its absence. It was possibly deemed irrelevant to the wider theoretical and political questions of determinism versus voluntarism in human action, history and class struggle, power and inequality, structure and agency, all of which were given renewed importance by radical criminologists (see, for example, Taylor *et al.*, 1973). Paul Rock (1989) has argued that in practice, much of criminology is dominated by empirical problems and policy questions about such matters as how crime can be measured, predicted and controlled and that only a very minor part is taken up with the separate activity called theorizing. If this is an accurate depiction of criminology as a discipline, it is even more applicable to traditional criminological activity around crime prevention. Theorizing about crime control and prevention is not as clearly focused as theorizing about crime causation. At the risk of some exaggeration, the predominant literature on crime prevention has been of a 'technicist' and 'administrative' nature (see Tonry and Farrington, 1995). In other words, we have witnessed the development of a body of technical and pragmatic knowledge aimed at helping those in power to put their ideas into practice through technical evaluations (an example of what Foucault, 1977, termed 'knowledge-power' practices). This 'technicist' orientation thus sees crime as a technical and practical problem needing an administrative and apolitical 'solution'. This 'administrative' aim has been prioritized over the broader critical questioning of the main assumptions, principles and social consequences of the different approaches to crime prevention associated with the state and (increasingly) the private sector. As a consequence, there has been an absence of a critical body of work on the wider politics of the phenomenon. First and foremost, this book aims to correct this neglect. I would argue in particular that the critical understanding of crime prevention philosophies and strategies (which together I term 'discourses') is a prerequisite for explaining past, present and future policies and trends in social control. Discourse is the concept now widely used (and often abused) to capture the complex interconnections between forms of knowledge, power relations and institutionalized practices at specific times and in specific places.

This book addresses some broad questions about the complex ways in

which societies are structured and subject to transformations in their dominant formations, and how such processes are both reflected in, and articulated by, the extent to which 'prevention' is entertained as a viable crime
control strategy. The book draws largely on UK data but this is informed by
a comparative perspective. The UK focus does not preclude comparisons
with other countries or within itself. Chapter 7 in particular focuses on
global trends in crime prevention (or what might be more appropriately
termed 'risk management'). Particular attention is given to developments in
Western Europe, Australasia and North America.The particular focus of this
book is therefore on the placing of the theories, policies and practices of
crime prevention in their socio-political and ideological contexts. It is
important to see theory in its social context and to note that theories have
real consequences. As Lilly *et al.* (1995: 5) have argued, 'social context plays
a critical role in nourishing certain ways of theorizing about crime'. On the
basis of historical research on crime, Lilly *et al.* go on to contend that it is
clear that the approach to crime control and prevention that characterizes a
particular era is inextricably linked to contemporary notions about crime
causation. This claim informs the detailed analysis of comparative discourses of crime prevention over history which I present in Chapters 2 to 7.
It is therefore crucial that the interconnections between social context,
criminological theory, criminal justice policy making, specific institutional
practices and wider strategies of social control are employed as the framework for analysis.

From this starting point, certain key questions emerge:

- What is the relationship of crime prevention to the maintenance and
transformation, more broadly, of social order?
- Why do we find different strategies of crime prevention in different places
and at different times?

To put things more concretely, why did the appeal and strategy of the
'bobby on the beat' (the uniformed beat police officer presence on the
street) wane in mainland Britain in the late 1970s and 1980s and re-emerge,
at least rhetorically, again as a powerful crime prevention 'icon' in the
1990s? Similarly, why has the apparently 'pre-modern' notion of public
shaming re-emerged as an appealing strategy in some variants of
community-based crime prevention across contemporary late-modern
societies? Are we seeing the renaissance of a neo-medieval conception of the
'fortress city' in the major metropolises of the world in general and in the
USA in particular? Why are there changing strategies of crime prevention
such as the emergence of multi-agency, 'community safety' initiatives –
rather than police-driven initiatives – in many Western societies in the late
twentieth century?

The exploration of the complex connections between such specific
instances and the wider social forces and transformations unleashed by what

Anthony Giddens (1990, 1991) has termed 'late modernity' will be the key focus of this book. It will also be argued that a critical grasp of the competing definitions, models and philosophies of crime prevention, together with an understanding of the often contradictory nature of crime prevention policies and initiatives are vital to an adequate grasp of the wider politics of law and order in contemporary 'risk society' (Beck, 1992). Indeed, it will be suggested that the very images of the 'good society' may be discerned through the lens of crime prevention. At the same time, I will argue that the history of crime prevention, and the history of theorizing about crime prevention, cannot be seen as a story of linear progress. This non-evolutionist approach to the trends in crime prevention is given further credence both by the current celebration of 'emotive' and 'traditional' deterrent forms of prevention through punitive incarceration and the rise of retributive vigilantism (Christie, 1993) and the 'resurfacing' of intellectual support for rehabilitation of offenders through treatment programmes among some psychologists in the UK and USA in the mid-1990s (McGuire, 1995; see also Chapter 3). What is striking is the multiplicity of competing discourses. The historical sociologist Norbert Elias (1956) wisely cautioned against using the study of history as a source of 'blame attribution' although it is difficult to deny that there is much human misery and 'blood on the tracks' of past crime control practices. That noted, it is important to maintain a degree of both detachment and empathy (or what Max Weber (1949) termed *verstehen*) towards the motives, hopes and consequences of past conceptual frames. Blame attribution has often come too easily in radical writing on the 'past sins' of history. Although it is psychologically satisfying, it is sociologically unproductive.

It may already be evident that this book attempts to offer the student of crime prevention a sociological understanding of the phenomenon. However, in so doing, I wish to depart from the standard textbook approach to studying social issues. This usually delineates and comments on the major perspectives or schools of thought in sociology (from functionalism to Marxism and feminism and now to postmodernism). Instead the aim here is to understand crime prevention chiefly in terms of two major, closely linked analytical frames in contemporary social theory: namely the late modern risk society thesis and the debate around communitarianism.

The late modern risk society thesis, communitarianism and crime control

Modernity may be understood as the period approximately from the mid-eighteenth century through to the latter decades of the twentieth century. In the West it has been a period characterized by capitalist industrialization and imperialism, urbanization, secularization, the gradual establishment of constitutional government (normally a limited form of democracy) and the welfare state. Intellectually, it has been a period characterized by the dominant belief in progress and order and the solution of problems through science and rationality. According to this intellectual project, the scientific application of knowledge held out the possibility of our understanding and *controlling* both the social and physical environment in a way which broke with all past traditions. The late modern risk society thesis has emerged from recent sociological theorizing on the changing nature of society in the late twentieth century and, in particular, the gradual shift away from the certainties of modernity and the growth of fears of 'new' risks. The growing concern over the problem of what is to be done about crime and its control may be viewed as indicative of such growing uncertainties. The late modern risk society thesis alerts us to the centrality of concerns over risk and insecurity (for example the fears over, and effects of, crime and violence) and their 'management' in the late twentieth century. Behind such new cultural forms lies the process of 'globalization' which refers to 'the intensification of world-wide social relations which link distant localities in such a way that local happenings are shaped by events occurring many miles away and vice versa' (Giddens, 1990: 64). However, as Doreen Massey (1997) notes, the term 'globalization' is more accurately referring to a particular type of development which she terms 'neo-liberal globalization'. The latter refers to a particular project based on neo-liberal, free market assumptions by which the privileged and capital have the freedom to both roam the world and defend their fortress homes. In this type of globalization, there is a mix of openness to capital and closedness to people. The emphasis of the globalization debate on the idea that the world is becoming more interconnected should not make us lose sight of the crucial developments whereby greater inequalities are being generated. A growth of massive divides has arisen within the 'global' world order and there have been massive exclusions from it due to the dominant free market form which globalization has taken (Massey, 1997: 9–10).

According to proponents of the late modernity and risk society thesis, previous traditional institutions are viewed as being increasingly destabilized in the last decades of the twentieth century. Concomitantly there is also much greater critical and reflexive scepticism about expert knowledge and authority among increasing numbers of the population (whether it be about the causes of food contamination, the most effective way to control pollution, or the control of crime). At the same time risk society appears to be obsessed with the quest for security and safety, not least through the appeal to community and belonging. In the context of crime, increasing emphasis is placed on the management of risk rather than the prevention of crime *per se*. The idea that crime can be effectively prevented thus seems to be in the process of being replaced by a widespread recognition that at best crime, given its routine social normality and presence, may be better understood as a risk to be managed (see Chapter 7 for a full discussion of the late modern risk society thesis).

In apparent contrast to the scepticism of proponents of the late modern risk society thesis, 'communitarianism' is a philosophical and sociological tradition in which there is an emphasis on the centrality of communal bonds and networks for the maintenance of social order. In the context of crime prevention, communitarian commentators, on both the ideological 'right' and 'left', suggest that 'most social control is communitarian control rather than state control and that most of the day-to-day successes are achieved by dialogic regulation, with state regulation stepping in to mop up the failures' (Braithwaite, 1995: 302). In other words, it is the routine activities of ordinary people in the mundane contexts of shared social life which are the key to successful crime prevention specifically and to social control more generally. Communitarians support a move away from the top-down, 'statist' solutions to crime control of the nineteenth and twentieth centuries to bottom-up communal solutions, invoking notions of 'social beings' rather than 'atomized individuals'. 'Statism' for our purposes may be understood as the theory and practice of concentrating power in the state resulting in a 'weak' position for the individual or community with respect to government (for a fuller discussion of communitarianism see Chapter 6).

The late modernity thesis and recent communitarian theories of social order will be employed as the two major theoretical frames informing this text. In particular, they offer a clear means of making sense of crime prevention and contextualizing crime prevention in relation to broader social transformations. When discussed and used in tandem, the two frames of analysis offer the reader a sociologically stimulating journey through the complex terrain of the politics of crime prevention at the end of the present century.

Some initiatives in crime prevention are associated with the informal social relations between people in communities, while others are more obviously 'top-down' approaches emanating from the state, both locally and centrally. In this book I will explore how these different approaches and strategies of crime prevention (and social control more generally) may be best explained in terms of their social, historical and ideological contexts. The modern statist definition of crime prevention is most conveniently dated from the eighteenth and nineteenth centuries in Western European societies. However, mechanisms for the control of 'antisocial' behaviours (however such behaviours may be defined) are arguably a universal feature of all human societies (Durkheim, 1893). It is important to note that successive fashions in crime prevention associated with the state since the nineteenth century may be discerned and explained. The same lesson is true of the history of penal thinking and practice (see Hudson, 1996), although on both fronts (penality and crime prevention) it is vital to be deeply sceptical about viewing such successive 'fashions' as necessarily implying a series of progressive stages.

Chapter 1 introduces the notoriously 'slippery' concept of crime prevention by mapping the competing definitions of the term in contemporary criminology. It is argued that there is no clear conceptual consensus as to what the boundaries of crime prevention are although there is an important settlement about 'crime' as the object of prevention discourses. Accordingly, this chapter examines critically the dominant definitions and attempted 'typologies' of crime prevention in criminology, not least for what they leave out ('absences') as for what they include in their conceptual building programme. The dominance of a pragmatic, 'what works' discourse is noted together with a neglect of the wider political and normative issues surrounding the talk and practice of crime control. In the course of this discussion, I address the related questions of why there has been a discernible 'growth industry' in crime prevention across Western societies in recent decades, and how this development might be understood in the context of the wider Draconian politics of 'law and order' and penal incapacitation in these same societies.

Chapters 2 and 3 focus on the two most influential discourses on crime prevention to emerge during the era of modernity: namely classicism and positivism. Chapter 2 presents the key intellectual tenets of the classical school of criminology and its theory of prevention. This body of work is contextualized as a product of modernity and a reaction against 'traditional' practices of retributive punishment. I then examine how this 'reformist' discourse helped initiate and realize the new institutional practices of the nineteenth century state around the preventive notions of deterrence and reform. The conceptual flaws in this discourse are examined next together with the recognition of its abiding influence on, and importance to, the workings of contemporary criminal justice and crime prevention.

Chapter 3 plots the main features of the positivist discourse on crime prevention since the late nineteenth century. This lengthy chapter examines the past and present 'traces' of this historically dominant criminological discourse and explores the question of why positivist discourses will not go away in the contemporary politics and practices of crime prevention. The chapter begins with an outline of the 'Lombrosian project' before focusing on twentieth-century developments around both psychological and sociological positivisms. Particular attention is given to the chequered history of rehabilitation as prevention.

In Chapters 4, 5 and 6 the closely interrelated strategies and philosophies of situational, multi-agency and communitarian crime prevention are examined. In their different ways, each of these developments may be understood in the context of the 'master narrative' of the social transformations associated with late modernity. Chapter 4 examines the main tenets and 'effects' of the situational discourse which focuses on controlling the opportunities to commit crime and the management of individualized risks. Particular attention is given to exploring the elective affinity between this theory and technique of crime prevention and the hegemonic ideology of 'neo-liberalism' across many Western societies in the last decades of the twentieth century. Chapter 5 focuses on the emergence of the strategy of 'managerialist', multi-agency crime prevention – epitomized by powerful appeals to 'partnerships' and 'community safety' – and how this development may be best understood. It is suggested that this new form of 'governance' of crime, drawing on both 'situational' and 'social' interventions, offers both regressive and progressive potentialities. Chapter 6 discusses the competing discourses of communitarian crime prevention. In particular, I examine the conservative, and currently dominant, appeal of moral communitarianism. This conservative, moralizing discourse is seen to involve the call for a nostalgic return to a moral authoritarian community of the 'past', not least as a reaction to the uncertainties brought by late modernity. The chapter then examines what I term radical/progressive variants of communitarianism, focusing on left pluralist, social democratic and abolitionist work. The consequences of both conservative and progressive discourses of communitarianism for crime prevention in particular and social justice in general are critically explored.

Chapter 7 discusses the implications of the dominant trends in late modernity for the futures of crime control across much of the world. A detailed examination of the work of both Giddens and Beck is provided before three possible 'models' of social control for the future are introduced. I term these models (1) 'fortress cities', privatism and social exclusion; (2) 'high trust' societies and authoritarian communitarianism; (3) civic and inclusive 'safe' cities. This chapter concludes by arguing that these dystopian and utopian scenarios are not likely to be realized in the 'pure' form presented in these heuristic models or what Max Weber (1949) termed 'ideal types'. Instead I argue that elements from all three are likely to resurface and converge in specific situations and locales. Furthermore, I argue that it is impossible to understand adequately the changing modes of crime control without a close and critical engagement with the wider politics of social order in late modernity.

The book concludes, in the Postscript, by arguing that we may be moving beyond the paradigm of crime prevention to that of *risk management* and *community safety* in the globalizing/localizing trends of the social control of populations. It is contended that this Janus-faced, probable future, holding both regressive and progressive potentialities for social order, makes the task of critical engagement with the politics of social control from social scientists even more pressing. Not least, it is argued that a 'replacement discourse' (van Swaaningen, 1997) to that of privatized actuarialism, regressive communitarianism and penal populism needs to be articulated. In particular, I suggest that a positive set of imaginings around human rights, social justice, social inclusion and the re-figuring of the 'public' as a positive good may move us beyond the suffocating embrace of both moral authoritarianism and hyper-individualism. In the process, the debate will have to move beyond the traditional and hegemonic crime control agenda.

Further reading

Lilly, J., Cullen, F. and Ball, R. (1995) *Criminological Theory: Context and Consequences*. London: Sage.

Morrison, W. (1995) *Theoretical Criminology: From Modernity to Post-modernism*. London: Cavendish Publishing Ltd.

Muncie, J., McLaughlin, E. and Langan, M. (1996) *Criminological Perspectives: A Reader*. London: Sage.

chapter one

Mapping the terrain
of crime prevention

Crime prevention: a recent growth industry

The last decades of the twentieth century have witnessed a growth of interest in crime prevention across the varied constituencies of academic
researchers, practitioners in the criminal justice system, private sector knowledge brokers, politicians and the public at large. Indeed crime prevention
has become what may be termed a 'buzzword' in policy circles across most
countries of the world. It has been claimed by some criminologists that crime
prevention has become a major organizing principle of almost all Western
criminal justice systems (Roberts and Grossman, 1990: 76). Bottoms and
Wiles have claimed more modestly that during the last 20 to 30 years in
many Western societies there has been a general government-led movement
for the development of an organized set of activities under the general heading of crime prevention (Bottoms and Wiles, 1996: 1). It also needs to be
emphasized that there has been a massive increase in the production of, and
trade in, private security, anti-risk techniques of crime prevention, from
locks and alarms to the use of capitalist companies, such as the security corporation of Group 4 for crime control functions previously set aside for state
agencies. The acknowledgement of such an international development

would seem difficult to refute. It is certainly the case that of late there has been a mini boom industry in criminological writing concerned with the plethora of policy and practice initiatives centred around crime prevention.

Meanings of crime prevention

Let's begin with a seemingly simple question: what specific activities do you think of when you hear the words crime prevention? I expect that different readers may come up with quite a number of different examples of activities which could be placed under the umbrella term of crime prevention, not least depending on where they live and who they are (in terms of gender, 'race', age, class etc.). Perhaps the image of the notion of the (English-specific?) 'bobby on the beat' came to mind, or the activities of your street's local neighbourhood watch group. Alternatively you may have thought of the installation of one of the oldest of all techniques of crime prevention, the household lock. Others may have envisaged the ever more popular 'hi-tech fix' of closed-circuit television (CCTV) which is now commonly found in shopping malls, on motorways, in car parks and in city centres. Given the renewed emphasis on the individual citizen looking out to protect him or herself, some readers may have thought about the 'self-help' preventive strategy of not walking out alone at night. Finally, in the light of the cross-party political consensus in the UK on 'getting tough' on offenders, some of you may have seen the locking up of criminals in prison as the most obvious form of preventing crime. Probably and tellingly, it is doubtful that many people would come up with examples of crime prevention initiatives targeted at business and corporate crime (that is, crimes chiefly *by* business or corporations rather than crimes against them), or crimes between intimates (such as domestic violence and child abuse), or crimes of the state (such as crimes by states against the human rights of their citizens or those of other peoples). It may be helpful to bear in mind Sandra Walklate's important distinction between what she terms 'crime of the streets', 'crime of the suites' and 'crime behind closed doors' (Walklate, 1996: 296). It is understandable then that business crime ('crime of the suites'), crime between intimates ('crime behind closed doors') and, I would add, 'crime by states' rarely get onto our everyday, commonsensical 'agenda' of what crime prevention is because the simple truth is that crime prevention strategies in countries like the USA and the UK have been targeted primarily at predatory street crimes rather than the full gamut of crimes and social harms in society.

What is clear from all these possible forms of crime prevention is that there is a great plethora of activities and initiatives associated with the term crime prevention. It is then a chameleon concept. In a recent spot of 'surfing the Web' on my personal computer, for example, I discovered a total of 244,089 'sites' classified under the label of crime prevention on the Internet.

By the time this is read there will doubtless be many more! IT (information technology) or computer-related crime is now becoming the biggest trend in property theft since the invention of the motor car. Indeed there is now advice on the Web about computer crime prevention techniques, urging system users to become 'the eyes and ears for the system's security administrator'.

The state, the politics of law and order and crime prevention

It may be useful to ask at this point how important is crime prevention to the actual workings of criminal justice and the politics of law and order in contemporary UK society? It may be argued that much of the seemingly endless 'talk' about the centrality of crime prevention to police work in particular and the criminal justice system in general may represent hype and rhetoric rather than a genuine shift from the dominant paradigm (or organizing conceptual framework) of reactive policing and deterrent penalism in criminal justice (Jones *et al.*, 1994). Reactive policing is the policing strategy of reacting or responding to a reported or witnessed crime incident as quickly and decisively as possible, while deterrent penalism concerns the widespread use of prison to deter people, individually and collectively, from crime. Is crime prevention rather more about empty slogans and gestures, placatory political statements and such like rather than about concrete and expensive policy developments and changes in the institutional practices of criminal justice agencies and other social agencies in neo-liberal societies like the UK? Indeed it is clear that the crime prevention discourse is not all-powerful in the workings of criminal justice in contemporary UK and other late modern societies. Instead it coexists alongside what has been termed a 'culture of severity' (Rutherford, 1993) and a 'recurring recourse to punitive display' (Garland, 1996) in crime control debates in late modern societies at the turn of the twentieth century.

It is argued in this book that changing trends in crime prevention should not be understood as separate from other developments in social control such as the current resurgence in mass incarceration in the USA and the UK in particular (but see van Swaaningen, 1997, on similar trends across Western Europe). This is not to deny the tensions between popular penalism and preventive strategies. Currently there is evidence of a growing distance and hostility between both criminologists and practitioners, and politicians, compared to earlier decades of the twentieth century. In particular, we may note that politicians from both the major political parties in the UK are increasingly seeking popularity through both the oratorical device and institutionalized practice of a resurgent penal populism. This resurgent penal populism follows US trends and lives off the oxygen of mass-media publicity and apparent popular, common sense fears and insecurities among the populace in late modern societies. At the time of writing it has been noted that the US model of criminal justice has resulted in more than 1.5 million people in jail or eight times as many people imprisoned per head of the population when compared to the European average (Currie, 1996). Critical commentators on the US scene such as Nils Christie (1993) have analysed the massive growth industry in crime control and concluded that there is now a new 'penal gulag' in the USA. This new 'penal gulag' is so named by Christie after Stalin's system of penal colonies in the Soviet Union for a massive range of dissidents and deviants during the 1940s and 1950s. Such developments are arguably being copied in the contemporary UK with, for example, a rise in the prison population from 45,000 in 1991 to 65,000 in 1997 and with an estimated rise of 1000 per month according to current trends. This development has been justified by leading Conservative politicians such as the last Conservative Home Secretary (Michael Howard) in the UK during the latter half of the 1990s in terms of the credo that 'prisons work' as a deterrent and that other 'soft' options such as non-custodial interventions to prevent reoffending do not. Most criminological researchers and criminal justice practitioners question the validity and veracity of the claim that incarceration is the best crime prevention measure. As long ago as 1971 the respected criminologists Leon Radzinowicz and Marvin Wolfgang, stated what has since become a criminological truism:

> Paradoxically, the more widespread crime becomes, the more essential it is to use criminal procedures and penal sanctions sparingly. A society with only a few criminals can perhaps afford to prosecute them all, to send them all to prison; a society with as many criminals as ours must increasingly use such measures only in the last resort.
>
> (1971: 3)

The criminological critique of the 'short-termism' of politicians is thus not new. The criminologists Glueck and Glueck (1936), for example, wrote of the analogy between dominant methods of crime control (namely reactive policing and incarceration) as being akin to a policy of controlling fires by putting out flames: short-sighted and wasteful when policy should address the means of preventing fires in the first place. The control of crime and delinquency may perhaps still be at the metaphorical stage of putting out flames (with gasoline!).

Crime prevention: a new paradigm of crime control?

Despite the growing rift between the positions held by politicians and criminologists respectively on questions of crime control, there is no consensus among criminologists that punitive measures for controlling crime will remain dominant. Even critics of contemporary crime prevention strategies in the UK acknowledge that the discourse of crime prevention is now the dominant 'expert' paradigm for understanding how best to reduce crime rates (Jones *et al.*, 1994). According to the new paradigm, practical methods of reducing crime that are completely unconnected with punishment or even law enforcement must be found. The growth of interest in crime prevention thus 'arises from a paradigm shift that allows us to see the reduction of crime as a separate objective from the punishment of offenders' (Jones *et al.*, 1994: 302). Furthermore, Jones *et al.* have argued that 'crime prevention policy has largely been the product of a specialised political and administrative elite' (p. 106) and so may be viewed as a professional rather than popular discourse. In a less guarded manner, crime prevention has been hailed recently by two leading 'establishment' criminologists, Tonry and Farrington (1995: vii) as 'an important subject of contemporary policy relevance'. Much emphasis in texts such as that of Tonry and Farrington is given to the failures of traditional law enforcement approaches such as incapacitation and deterrent penalties to reduce crime rates or reoffending. They suggest that the crime rate, apart from the occasional dip, remains high across Western societies and more importantly remains a source of major public anxiety which is unlikely to wane. In turn, traditional criminal sanctions such as jail or corporal punishment, according to criminological experts, have only modest effects on the rates and patterns of criminality. Recently in the UK this questioning of the value of custodial sentencing and traditional criminal justice responses as ways of dealing 'efficiently, effectively and economically' with youth crime received public endorsement from the 'independent' monitoring agency, the Audit Commission, in its report on the criminal justice system's response to youth offending, *Misspent Youth* (Audit Commission, 1996; see also Muncie, 1998). Elements of this report were also supported by the two main opposition parties in the UK prior to the 1997 general election.

Writing in the mid-1990s, the Australian criminologist Adam Sutton (1994) notes that the major promise of crime prevention for criminologists is that it offers 'renewed relevance' versus the 'nothing works' pessimism of the period during the decline of the rehabilitative ideal in the 1960s and 1970s (see Chapter 3). Sutton goes on to suggest that crime prevention initiatives may also offer the promise of a move away from punitive, divisive and 'exclusionary' models of social control to more 'inclusionary' and integrative ones (p. 6). Tony Bottoms, writing from a UK perspective, has also commented on the increasing importance of crime prevention: 'During the 1980s, crime prevention began to occupy a much more prominent place in public policy and in public consciousness than it did in earlier decades' (Bottoms, 1990: 3). Indeed there would appear to have been some important landmarks in the central state's interest in crime prevention in the UK during the decade of the 1980s. Bottoms points to the setting-up of a crime prevention unit in the Home Office in 1983, and the 1984 landmark of a Home Office and other government departments' publication of an inter-departmental circular on crime prevention, to be closely followed by a similar circular from the Scottish Office. These circulars, stressing multi-agency cooperation between the police and other agencies, became 'the cornerstone of most subsequent official policies on crime prevention in the two countries' (Bottoms, 1990: 3). Further initiatives followed such as the 'Five Towns Initiative' in 1986 and the more ambitious 'Safer Cities Programme' in 1988. Such demonstration programmes gave concrete expression to the multi-agency model of crime prevention espoused in the earlier circulars (see Chapter 5). What social science still lacks is an empirical study of the emergence and establishment of a dominant crime prevention discourse in the Home Office during the 1980s. Such a study may help answer the question why the discourse of prevention became more popular in some circles (such as academics and civil servants) than others in branches of the state such as the Home Office. It must also be remembered that there is a perennial danger in plotting the growth of interest in crime prevention among branches of the state of assuming both the popularity and strategic importance of crime prevention in the routine work of such agencies as the police. Weatheritt (1986) in particular has alerted us to the rhetoric rather than the reality of the police's institutional commitment to crime prevention. She has pointed out that very little in the way of resourcing is spent in police budgets on crime prevention when compared to other forms of police work such as investigation and detection. The current estimate is that spending on crime prevention makes up 2 per cent of all criminal justice expenditure. Crime prevention according to Weatheritt remained a marginal specialism in the police in the 1980s with designated crime prevention officers' work organized in terms of being 'primarily physical security experts' rather than community-based coordinators (p. 51). However, even when community based, critics have pointed out that such police work is 'principally public relations with no clearly articulated connection between a good press and crime prevention effects' (Harvey et al., 1989: 90). In contrast, Reiner has claimed that by the late 1980s crime prevention had become increasingly central to the government's law and order policy. Crime prevention departments in the police had become 'belles of the ball' rather than their previous status as 'Cinderellas of the service, low status, low budget and low key' (Reiner, 1992: 99). There is then a lack of consensus among academic commentators and practitioners as to the importance of crime prevention in policing policy and practice.

Unpacking the concept of crime prevention

Crime prevention is a difficult area to pin down both conceptually and empirically given the different meanings which are historically associated with it. To this day, it remains a profoundly 'slippery' and 'free-floating' signifier in the competing discourses on law and order. To this end, it is important to unpack very carefully the models of crime prevention, from the deterrence model to the currently popular versions based on what are generally termed 'situational' and 'social' approaches to the prevention of criminality. In pursuing this goal, it is vital to look at crime prevention both historically and comparatively.

Let's begin with a seemingly straightforward question: what is crime prevention? Unless one answers with the tautology (that is, the use of words that merely repeat elements already conveyed) that the aims of crime prevention are the prevention of criminal acts (!), it will soon become evident that there is no one simple answer to the question. Accordingly, for example, crime prevention may be aimed at 'reforming' or 'deterring' the offender or 'protecting' the individual victim or the community. Furthermore, crime prevention strategies may be geared towards addressing quite distinct dimensions to the phenomenon of crime whether it be the context of the crime act, the criminal motive, problems in the environment or the unprotected, 'at risk' victim. Indeed, all correctional ideologies can be legitimized by the rhetoric of prevention, ranging from ideologies of incapacitation, deterrence and retribution to those of restitution, reparation and rehabilitation right through to those of diversion, decriminalization and finally abolition! There is no simple answer then to the question 'what is crime prevention?' Instead we encounter a large body of both contested scholarly writing and policy-oriented research and evaluations over the course of this idea's history (as the chapters which follow will chart and explain in some depth).

Classifying types of crime prevention

This section introduces some of the most influential attempts in criminology to define and classify the concept and meaning of crime prevention, although there is no clear consensus among criminologists with regard to how best to define it. Instead, there are competing models and typologies, often of a limited theoretical nature, and seemingly driven by rather narrow technical concerns about the measurement and evaluation of 'success' or 'failure'. I look critically at the body of work which has sought to 'capture' the meaning of crime prevention as itself something worthy of scrutiny. This may result in the reader possibly feeling that she or he is wading through very muddy 'technical' waters: this reflects much of the tradition of 'administrative', evaluative criminological work in the field of crime prevention. However, this discussion of the largely technical attempts at the classification of crime prevention will be useful in setting up the subsequent exploration of the relationship of discourses of crime prevention and control to the historical trends in modernity and late modernity.

According to Walklate, most understandings of prevention entail the possibility of both predicting an outcome and intervening in that process to change this predicted outcome (Walklate, 1996: 297). It is further argued by Walklate that this basic starting point implies two distinct processes if the aim of preventive policy is to make some difference to human behaviour. First, in the case of crime prevention, it assumes we can agree and identify the causes of crime. Second, it presumes we know and agree on the policy responses which will prevent crime. However, such a consensus on causation and appropriate preventive policy responses is far from clear-cut. One of the leading experts on the evaluation of crime prevention initiatives, Ken Pease, has recommended caution towards any attempt to look for universality in the techniques of prevention since, when we consider the prevention of crime, we are in fact looking at a set of events joined only in their proscription by statute (Pease, 1994: 659). In a similar fashion, we may note that crime prevention itself is made up of a diffuse set of theories and practices. Caution over the existence of a single unproblematic definition of crime prevention may therefore be wise.

One of the most popular working definitions has been articulated in terms of 'the total of all private initiatives and state policies, other than the enforcement of criminal law, aimed at the reduction of damage caused by acts defined as criminal by the state' (Van Dijk and De Waard, 1991). We may ask ourselves 'how satisfactory is this working definition?' This definition clearly excludes the enforcement of criminal law (and thus legal punishment) from its conceptualization of the meaning of crime prevention. Yet it is the case that enforcement has played historically an important part in crime prevention and remains of major importance for contemporary strategies of crime control. As Garland (1990: 18) makes clear, legal punishment arising out of legal enforcement has been justified in preventive or reductive terms:

> Although legal punishment is understood to have a variety of aims, its primary purpose is usually represented as being the instrumental one of reducing or containing rates of criminal behaviour. It is thus possible to conceive of punishment as being simply a means to a given end – to think of it as a legally approved method designed to facilitate the task of crime control.

In this book, crime prevention through legal enforcement will be discussed in the context of the classicist and neo-classicist discourses, in Chapter 2. However, we also need to remain conscious that if crime prevention is viewed as covering every aspect of criminal justice, there is the danger of a form of crime prevention 'imperialism', colonizing all aspects of the criminal justice system and also becoming what Stan Cohen has referred to as a 'mickey mouse concept', like social control, which ranges from infant socialization to the death penalty (Cohen, 1985). As Lowman et al. (1987: 4) also note with regard to the concept of social control, it has become 'a skeleton key opening so many doors that its analytical power has been drained'.

There are therefore limitations as well as merits in moving beyond the restricted definition of crime prevention as employed by Van Dijk and De Waard (1991).

The most popular means of defining crime prevention in policy debates in the late twentieth century has been in terms of the distinction between situational and social strategies of prevention (to complicate matters further, the social strategies are often termed 'community' crime prevention). It has been noted that the terms situational and social prevention are fairly new, although the ideas they promote are not (Gabor, 1990: 2). Situational crime prevention chiefly concerns opportunity reduction, such as the installation of surveillance technology in public spaces, like car parks and shopping areas, to reduce the opportunities for the theft of vehicles or crimes against victims. Social crime prevention, on the other hand, is focused chiefly on changing social environments and the motivations of offenders. Social crime prevention measures thus tend to focus on the development of schemes, such as youth clubs and activity-based projects, to deter potential or actual offenders from future offending. According to Jon Bright, one of social crime prevention's major supporters in the UK, it 'aims to strengthen socialization agencies and community institutions in order to influence those groups that are most at risk of offending' (Bright, 1991: 64). Both situational and social crime prevention approaches tend to be what is termed inter- or multi-agency in orientation, rather than being driven by one agency alone, such as the police. Jock Young, the leading left realist criminologist (see Chapter 6), has defined multi-agency crime prevention as follows: 'Multi-agency intervention is the planned, co-ordinated response of the major social agencies to problems of crime and incivilities' (Young, 1991: 155). Common to both elements of this distinction between situational and social (community) crime prevention is their claim to be less damaging than traditional (retributive) justice approaches. Also common to both situational and social prevention is a narrow focus on 'street crime' and specific categories of offender (young, working-class males) rather than other social harms and offenders.

The dominant approach to classifying types of crime prevention in North American criminology, and in contrast to the twofold definition just outlined, is that there are three major models of crime prevention, borrowed from theorizing in medical epidemiology (Weiss, 1987). First, there is 'primary' crime prevention involving the reduction of criminal opportunities without reference to criminals. In primary crime prevention attention is turned to the crime event rather than the motivated offender. This approach is also linked to the lifestyle theory of Hindelang *et al.* (1978) in which attention is paid to issues of personal victimization and the routine activities of potential and actual victims of predatory crime. In the second type of crime prevention, termed 'secondary', the focus is on changing people *before* they do something criminal. Here attention is on the prevention of criminality.

Finally, 'tertiary' crime prevention focuses on the truncation of the criminal career, or reduction of the seriousness of offending, for example through the treatment of known offenders. Both secondary and tertiary crime prevention are focused on criminality.

Another attempt to provide a comprehensive typology of crime prevention strategies is found in Tonry and Farrington (1995). These authors distinguish four major strategies of crime prevention (law enforcement, developmental, communal and situational). However, tellingly in Tonry and Farrington's volume of essays the contributors effectively focus on three strategies only, excluding law enforcement, as did Van Dijk and De Waard (1991). This exclusion of law enforcement from detailed consideration may be for reasons which sociologists term 'professional closure' in the sense of leaving law enforcement to other sub-specialisms in criminology, such as police studies. In turn, the narrowing-down of the specialist field of crime prevention studies may make it easier to 'colonize' a new field of exclusive expertise, potentially the new discipline of crime prevention (see also Ekblom, 1996). The exclusion of law enforcement from the field of crime prevention does not seem to have been done for coherent theoretical or intellectual reasons but nonetheless it has of late become something of an academic orthodoxy in criminology. Let's briefly examine what the law enforcement strategy of crime prevention implies. Law enforcement is viewed by Tonry and Farrington (1995) as the traditional approach to crime prevention in the criminal justice system and is intellectually associated most famously with the philosophical work of H. L. A. Hart (1968) although its roots lie more generally in 'classicism' (see Chapter 2). According to this law enforcement strategy, criminal laws exist and are enacted so that fewer of the proscribed acts take place, and general prevention in turn is the primary justification for maintaining a system of criminal punishment (Tonry and Farrington, 1995: 3). This traditional law enforcement approach to both crime prevention and punishment operates chiefly through deterrence, incapacitation and rehabilitation.

To return to Tonry and Farrington's typology, they define the three key contemporary crime prevention strategies as follows:

> By developmental prevention, we mean interventions designed to prevent the development of criminal potential in individuals, especially targeting risk and protective factors discovered in studies of human development. By community prevention, we mean interventions designed to change the social conditions that influence offending in residential communities. By situational prevention, we mean interventions designed to prevent the occurrence of crimes, especially by reducing opportunities and increasing risks.
>
> (1995: 2–3)

The stated aim of Tonry and Farrington in designating these three types of prevention strategy is to offer a broader conceptualization of the ambit of crime prevention than is common in much of the previous literature. However, there are some limitations even to this supposedly broad typology. Where, for example, is the broader notion of social crime prevention or more recently of 'community safety' which is not restricted to the measures implied in the definition of community crime prevention above. What, for example, of the role of policies concerned with income redistribution and poverty reduction, full employment or job-sharing, skills retraining, adequate social housing in ameliorating the crime problem and, as importantly, generating social justice and empowerment in deprived and marginalized communities? It is also arguable whether developmental prevention merits the distinction of being either a new strategy or a strategy outside the broader notion of social crime prevention. In the course of the discussion of community crime prevention by Hope (1995) in the Tonry and Farrington volume, there is a confusing slippage between what others would term social versus situational crime prevention. Such confusion may have less to do with the weaknesses in this typology of prevention and instead reflect the lack of clear-cut divisions in practice between social and situational crime strategies when limited forms of community mobilization (social) and target hardening (situational) are often employed together in practice (see Chapter 5).

The final attempt at a typology of crime prevention which I examine is that of Bottoms and Wiles (1996). Bottoms and Wiles' typology is not meant to be exhaustive and it is explicitly restricted to the contemporary situation of late modernity. As a result of their typology, the same authors suggest that there is clear evidence that crime prevention is no longer solely the province of the state. Bottoms and Wiles (pp. 7–10) distinguish four major types of contemporary crime prevention activity, namely:

1 defensive strategies (such as car steering locks, rape alarms, private policing of private property, neighbourhood watch);
2 guardianship and monitoring (such as the targeted policing of likely victims or offenders, information monitoring (CCTV), responsiveness to customer needs);
3 the creation of new forms of social order (such as multi-agency forms of order, public and private partnerships, exclusions of potentially troublesome individuals, public safety initiatives);
4 criminality prevention (such as pre-school enhancement programmes, diversion schemes for young offenders and pre-emptive targeting of youth at risk of offending).

The purpose of this typology appears to be that of alerting us to the extent and variety of crime prevention in recent decades and to show how taken for granted they have become in our everyday lives.

It will be evident from the above discussion that there are many different buzzwords in contemporary academic, practitioner and political 'talk' about crime prevention. Specific contemporary contenders in the battle to find out what may work include those of 'crime reduction', 'community safety', 'situational' and 'social' prevention, 'community crime prevention' and 'multi-agency crime prevention'. All these terms are intermeshed into the same seamless, yet ever-changing and also bounded 'kaleidoscope' which constitutes the dominant discourse on crime prevention (Muncie *et al.*, 1994). I use the word 'bounded' deliberately since it is evident that this dominant discourse across academics, practitioners, media pundits and politicians is one characterized by some crucial points of consensus (for example, about what constitutes 'crime') as well as some 'absences' or omissions. As Muncie *et al.* (1994) point out in the context of 'youth' crime prevention, this is a predominantly negative discourse of 'prevention', 'reduction', 'control', 'fear' etc. trapped in a criminalizing, law and order agenda rather than a positive agenda articulating a social politics of 'social justice', 'empowerment', 'inclusion' and 'investment' based on a progressive social policy agenda (see Chapter 6). To paraphrase the famous crooner Bing Crosby, it may be necessary for criminology to pay more attention to 'accentuating the positive' and 'eliminating the negative' in its conceptualization of the *prevention* of social harms and the *promotion* of social goods. Furthermore, the focus on 'crime' as that which is sanctioned by criminal law may result in the failure to recognize other more serious harms and distract attention, in the case of the discourse of youth crime prevention, from the widespread occurrence of youth victimization.

Contexts and discourses of crime prevention

The discussion so far has illustrated the vague boundaries and ambiguities of the concept of crime prevention. We have entered the messy world of current academic and others' debate on crime prevention. It is important to recognize that while this lack of certainty over 'what's it all about' may be frustrating, the discussion so far should prove to be a valuable basis for the later and much fuller discussion of crime prevention as a changing political and ideological 'construct' as well as a set of contemporary policy 'techniques'. Thus far, it is clear that there are many different and competing notions of crime prevention and, in turn, divergent practices and policies associated with the notion. The concern of this book is not to offer the final definition of crime prevention – which is not just a Herculean test but also a hopeless quest. Instead the aim is rather to place the changing forms and meanings of crime prevention in their broader social, political and intellectual contexts. Accordingly, in the following chapters, the changing fashions in crime prevention discourses will be outlined and analysed as objects of sociological investigation in their own right. I am thus primarily interested in the ideological and historical roots of the current discourses on crime prevention and the manner in which such discourses become realized in institutional practices. In so doing it is important to both 'deconstruct' and 'contextualize' what is meant by the notoriously woolly notion of crime prevention together with the analysis of the ways that this 'signifier' is variously used as a powerful rhetorical political device, as well as being a set of institutional practices by the major agencies and actors.

Summary

This chapter has introduced the elusive concept of crime prevention. In turn an attempt has been made to move the study of crime prevention away from the dominant technical and practical orientation of much previous work on the subject matter and towards a sociological understanding of the changing discourses – and the 'absences' in these discourses – of crime prevention. It was argued that the concept of crime prevention has complex and changing meanings depending on the perspective applied to it. In particular, it is vital to be wary of assuming that somehow 'everyone knows' what crime prevention is. It is evident already from this discussion that there are many different contemporary methods and policies directed at the control of crime. At the same time, it was argued that there are some recurrent assumptions in the discourses on prevention, such as a consensus on what constitutes 'crime' and a negative criminalizing vocabulary of 'control' and suchlike. In the following chapters it will be evident that there are major problems of classification and generalization, particularly when these issues are considered in a comparative and historical manner. It is thus argued that the nearest we can get to a definition of crime prevention is to conceptualize it as *the specific and changing institutional practices and ideological components of changing discourses of crime control structured around the symbolic and politically useful notion of prevention*. Like all social phenomena, crime prevention is subject to different social constructions (and thus reconstructions). What is also evident from the brief overview of social scientific thinking on crime prevention is that the subject has to date received only limited attention from critical social theory. The chapters that follow will attempt to fill this void and thereby bring the study of crime prevention into the deeper waters of modern social theory.

Further reading

Pease, K. (1997) 'Crime Prevention', in M. Maguire, R. Morgan and R. Reiner (eds), *Oxford Handbook of Criminology* (2nd edn). Oxford: Clarendon Press.
Tonry, M. and Farrington, D. (eds) (1995) *Building a Safer Society: Strategic Approaches to Crime*. Chicago: University of Chicago Press.

chapter two

Classicism and the deterrent presences of the modern state

Introduction

In this chapter I introduce what is generally viewed as the first explicit school of criminology, namely classicism. In the examination of this 'criminological formation', I will first outline the historical context in which the classical school of criminology needs to be located, including an excursus on the pre-modern modes of social control, together with an overview of classicism's basic philosophical tenets. I then focus on the theory of crime prevention which the school articulated in the eighteenth and nineteenth centuries. Next I examine how the theory was institutionalized (and thereby adapted) in the concrete institutional contexts of modern state power in the nineteenth century. Finally, a critical appraisal of the lasting significance of this modernist discourse on crime prevention is provided.

The first school of criminology?

There is a broad consensus among academic commentators that the first recognized school of criminology was that of the classical school of the eighteenth century, most associated with the work of the Italian legal theorist, Cesaré Beccaria (Morrison, 1995; Muncie *et al.*, 1996). In truth the school was more concerned with developing rational, systematic and efficient means of delivering justice rather than understanding the nature of 'the criminal' as the object of criminological inquiry. This lack of interest in the search for the differentiated criminal type has led David Garland (1994), the foremost contemporary historian of British criminology, to argue that the classicist school is not really 'criminology'. Garland argues that criminology is a specific genre of discourse and inquiry about crime which developed in the modern era. According to Garland, criminology is an empirically grounded, scientific undertaking which is thereby set apart from legal and moral discourses. Most importantly for our purposes here, Garland contends that modern criminology emerged out of the convergence of two separate enterprises which he terms 'the governmental project' and 'the Lombrosian project'. A project here refers to an emergent tradition of inquiry sharing a cluster of aims and objectives. The 'governmental project' concerns those inquiries which direct their attention to the problems of governing – in terms of managing and/or regulating – crime and criminals. The 'Lombrosian project' refers to the tradition of inquiry begun by the positivist criminologist, Lombroso, which seeks to differentiate the criminal from the non-criminal, focusing on the 'essential' characteristics of the latter (Garland, 1994: 17–18; see also Chapter 3). Because classicism had no interest in the 'Lombrosian project' and because of its apparent lack of empirical, scientific inquiry, Garland suggests that the classical school (in his view better understood as 'criminal law reformers') is 'pre-criminological' in the modern sense. To quote Garland:

> it actually makes little sense to claim that these eighteenth-century thinkers possessed a 'criminology', given that they made no general distinction between the characteristics of criminals and non-criminals, and had no conception of research on crime and criminals as a distinctive form of inquiry.
>
> (1994: 22)

Despite these misgivings from Garland, I would argue that classicism does merit the dubious honour of being the first clearly identifiable school of criminology in retrospect. Unlike previous religious and superstitious explanations of crime as 'sin' and 'wickedness', classicism attempts to understand crime as a product of a rational free will. A criminal act is thus assumed to be something chosen as a result of the calculation of the likely pain and pleasure involved. The classical school does then have an aetiology of crime in terms of the rational calculation of 'benefit' and 'cost'. Furthermore, classicism broke with traditional retributivist notions of crime control by asserting that the control and prevention of crime lay in more rational, just and efficient means of punishment and forms of preventive deterrence. This is surely a 'governmental' project in the sense used by Garland. Finally, although not obviously an empirical 'science' in the manner of the later positivists, the analysis of Beccaria and later utilitarians such as Jeremy Bentham may be viewed as being involved in a self-consciously analytical and detached 'investigation' of crime and justice. We shall see in Chapter 4 that the traces of this first criminological formation continue to resurface on the terrain of contemporary criminological thinking and practices on crime prevention and criminal justice. On this reckoning I would suggest that classicism stands as a vital modern discourse on crime and its control and prevention, which is crucial to understanding the ideological underpinnings of such late modern, neo-liberal discourses as that of situational crime prevention (see Chapter 4).

Excursus on pre-modern crime control

Classicism grew out of a growing dissatisfaction among certain Enlightenment thinkers in eighteenth-century Europe with the irrationality of the old regime in general and the barbarity and inefficiency of criminal justice in particular. The pre-modern state's principal object of government was that of the self-preservation of the sovereign power. Punishment of the criminal was based on the principles of retribution and general deterrence. It was the sovereign, directly or indirectly, who demanded, decided and carried out punishments in so far as it was he or she who had been injured or threatened by the law (Foucault, 1977: 53). In other words it was profoundly non-utilitarian. The main weapon of the pre-modern system of crime control was the spectacular, public, bloody punishment of the offender which was also viewed as a deterrent to the rest of the populace by means of terror, with occasional shows of 'mercy' (Hay, 1975). In Foucault's words, 'The public execution is to be understood not only as a judicial, but also as a political ritual. It belongs, even in minor cases, to the ceremonies by which power is manifested' (Foucault, 1977: 47). Punishment – as spectacle – was thus aimed at the body rather the mind by means of a cluster of punishments ranging from whipping, branding and the stocks to public hangings. It is also important to note that this 'Bloody Code' of crime control, as criminal justice was popularly referred to in eighteenth-century England, was 'supplemented' by more traditional, communitarian survivals from the feudal era, such as custom and informal communal mechanisms of social control.

The power of custom and communitarian social control in the pre-modern era has been noted by historians of the early medieval feudal period in Europe, such as Marc Bloch (1961). According to Bloch, custom throughout most of feudal Europe acted as 'the sole living source of law'. In turn, the legal system rested on the idea that 'what has been has *ipso facto* the right to be' (Bloch, 1961: 111–13). Bloch goes to suggest that all men (*sic*) were bound up in multiple protective relationships and, for both chiefs and subjects, 'the ties of subjection tended at that time to fetter the whole man' (p. 360). On the basis of the work of historians of the pre-modern period in Europe, we see a similar emphasis to that of anthropologists on the power of custom and complex bonds based on interdependent obligations as mechanisms for social control. These stand in contrast to the formal statist mechanisms but also continue as traditions which both survive and resurface in the contemporary world (see Chapter 6).

It was, however, the brutalities and inefficiencies of the formal mechanisms of criminal justice in the eighteenth and early nineteenth centuries which gained the particular scorn of the classical reformers. Historians such as Michael Ignatieff (1978) have plotted the growth in the number of crimes in England bearing the punishment of death from 50 in 1688 to 225 by the second decade of the nineteenth century. Ignatieff also notes that the criminal law was increasingly viewed as not just brutal but also rigid, inflexible and inefficient by reformers (pp. 17–18). Foucault argues that the main criticism from reformers was not directed so much at the weakness or cruelty of those in authority, as 'at a bad economy of power' (1977: 79).

In place of the old retributivist, 'irrational' appeal to vengeance and occasional acts of mercy, the reformers across Europe offered a new appeal to rationality, formalism and legality. Beccaria built on these foundations in his influential 1764 treatise *On Crimes and Punishment*. The lasting philosophical influence of classicist views on crime and its prevention are to be found in utilitarianism and what has been termed social contract theory. This philosophical framework has certain implications for the study of human behaviour. Utilitarianism claims that people are primarily motivated by the desire to maximize their own happiness and in turn minimize pain. It also suggests that the duty of government is to promote the maximum happiness in society. According to this viewpoint, punishment of the criminal is only justifiable in terms of its contribution to the prevention of future infringements on the happiness and well-being of others (on the relationship between classicism and utilitarianism, see Roshier, 1989: 8–10). Social contract theory is a close intellectual associate of utilitarianism. It is based on the idea that the power and authority of government are derived from an unwritten but nonetheless binding contract entered into by members of a society, whereby they surrender some freedoms in order to secure freedom against the predatory acts of others.

The classical theory of crime prevention

According to the classical school, punishment was not to be viewed as a moral imperative or an absolute duty of the state but rather as *an instrument of social control to achieve certain desired ends.* The desired ends in turn would be achieved by less emotional and more rational ways than was the case in the *ancien régimes.* Punishment involves pain and is therefore an evil. As a consequence, it is argued that it can only be justified if it accomplishes the exclusion of some greater evil. To do this, punishment as a deterrent and preventive measure must be warranted, effective and 'profitable'. According to the classical school, crime is rational behaviour and so the criminal is a calculator of risk. In particular, the criminal, like all of us, is guided by the pain and pleasure principle as a result of which she or he calculates the risks and rewards for his or her actions. Lilly *et al.* (1995: 16–17) have usefully suggested that there are 11 key elements to Beccaria's influential thesis on punishment and the prevention of crime:

1 to escape from chaos and war, individuals give up some of their liberty and establish a contractual society, governed by the sovereign nation (state);
2 criminal laws place restrictions on individual freedoms, therefore they in turn must be restricted in scope;
3 the law presumes the innocence of the putative offender;
4 there needs to be a complete written criminal law code;
5 punishment is based on retributive reasoning;
6 the severity of punishment is limited to what is necessary for crime prevention and deterrence;
7 punishment should fit the crime not the criminal;
8 punishment needs to be certain and quick;
9 punishment is not to be exemplary nor reformative;
10 the offender is viewed as independent and reasoned;
11 and crucially for our purposes, the aim of every good system of legislation is seen to be the prevention of crime.

In what was, historically, a radical discourse, classicism emphasized that it is better to prevent than to punish. We also find a rather uncomplicated view of the criminal as rational, calculating 'man'. Beccaria's contribution also teaches us that the late twentieth-century concern with 'calculating' and 'managing risk' is not a new preoccupation of social theorists of crime and prevention. It is also emphasized that crime prevention and thus social control are achieved through the knowledge that punishment will follow crime in same way as night follows day. The best way to prevent crime is therefore by deterring the individual from committing crimes. Furthermore, if punishment is sufficiently unpleasant, the offender will not repeat the crime. However, we have seen that classicism also stresses that it is more important to deter others. We also need to keep in mind that deterrence, unlike retribution, is future- rather than past-oriented. Here we may note the crossover between the discourse on crime prevention and that of penality (Hudson, 1996).

Underpinning Beccaria's work was the doctrine of free will or the capacity of each individual to control her or his life by means of rational thought and action. Alongside this doctrine was the corresponding obligation to bear responsibility for the consequences of exercising control, including full criminal liability for illegal acts. In line with such views of human nature, punishment must be 'essentially public, prompt, necessary, the least possible in the given circumstances, proportionate to the crimes, dictated by the laws' (Beccaria, 1764: 13). Arising from these premises came the notion of 'psychological hedonism' whereby humans calculate pleasures and pains in advance of action and regulate their conduct by the results of their calculations. As a consequence, the classicists were able to construct a penal and preventive philosophy and strategy based on the precise calculations of rational actors.

Deterrence as crime prevention is about affording rational, self-interestedly calculating individuals reasons and opportunities not to commit crimes. This assumption provides the crucial connection between this discourse of prevention and the contemporary thinking of situational crime prevention. Furthermore, since punishment must be something that can be calculated, it must be the same for all individuals, regardless of age, status, gender etc. As such it is a theory premised on equality of treatment for all. It is the act which is judged not the individual.

Let me briefly repeat the key features of this theory of deterrent punishment. As noted earlier, Beccaria and the classical school saw prevention as being more significant than punishment. 'It is better to prevent crimes than to punish them. This is the ultimate end of every good legislation' (Beccaria, 1764: 93). Beccaria argued that prevention requires that the law be simple, clear and universally supported. In turn the body of laws should be restricted to decrease the possibility of these being infringed. They should also be made clear so that interpretation is unnecessary. In addition, the classical school argued that education is necessary to allow people to understand the importance of preserving the social contract. In Beccaria's words, 'See to it that enlightenment accompanies liberty' (p. 95). The classical school was thus proposing that deterrence and prevention were more appropriate to the emergent secular and rational modern state than the traditional *ancien régime*'s arbitrary whims and obsession with the retributive punishing of wrongdoing.

In Britain, Jeremy Bentham was the most influential 'apostle' of this utilitarian discourse on prevention and deterrence. According to Bentham, punishment was in the best interests of the offender and utilitarianism cast it as an impartial act of social necessity. He rejected retributive theory and instead sought to take the anger out of punishment. It was no longer to be an 'act of wrath or vengeance' but rather an 'act of calculation, disciplined by considerations of the social good and the offenders' needs' (quoted in Ignatieff, 1978: 75). Ignatieff describes this new way of thinking about punishment and prevention as follows:

Punishment should not be scattered by the monarch's wrathful hand, but apportioned to each crime as precisely as the market allocated prices to commodities. Ideally, machines could be used to inflict the exact price of crime. Punishment would then become a science, an objective use of pain by the state for the regulation of the egoistic calculus of individuals.

(1978: 76)

In contrast to the unfair, irrational and inefficient old order, utilitarians such as Bentham in nineteenth-century Britain thus argued for a new rational and efficient preventive system. Such thinkers questioned whether crime could be viewed in the old way as a simple function of individual depravity. As Gattrell (1996) notes, the rise of materialist psychology led Bentham and others to argue that criminals were not driven by original sin but by their ignorance of how best to calculate the costs of their wrongdoing. It was argued that an efficient, economical means of preventing crime could only be produced by adhering to an abstract criterion of strict justice and a predetermined system of penalties premised on rationalization, formalization and equalization.

A new governance of crime

Jenkins has noted that the writings of utilitarians and members of the classical school had quite an impact on the reformation of parts of the criminal justice system across Europe and the USA in the latter half of the eighteenth century and the first half of the nineteenth century (Jenkins, 1984). The modern codification and rationalization of the criminal law may be traced to Beccaria's ideas. However, most legislators chose to modify the classical model in practice. In particular the principle of strict proportionality was difficult to sustain. It was generally agreed in the nineteenth century, for example, that children and 'lunatics' should be excluded from the full rigours of the law (given their inability to calculate pleasure and pain rationally). As a result, 'neo-classicism' became the dominant legal discourse which informed the practices of most criminal justice systems. According to neo-classicism, the core doctrine of free will and calculative rationality is retained but it also acknowledged that certain wills were freer than others and so proportionality needed to be adjusted accordingly. This qualification in practice to the pure expression of classical notions about culpability opened up the way for subsequent positivist notions that some human actions, including criminal acts, are determined and that offenders in turn might be essentially different from non-offenders (see Chapter 3).

Overall, classicism represented the effort to establish what Garland (1996) terms 'sovereign crime control'; in other words that the state is there to provide security, law and order and crime control within its territorial boundaries. It has also been argued by Morrison that classical criminology gives us 'the route of a state-led criminology'. The approach did so by pointing towards a science of government in which the state lays rules in which state agencies sanction patterns and specify certain forms of formal social control. It offers the prospect of a 'knowledge at the service of the bureaucratic specialists' (Morrison, 1995: 212). This governmental project was enhanced during the nineteenth century in countries like Britain with the establishment of a public police force with a professional monopoly over the function of crime control (or more accurately, public order). Let's now examine how classicist ideas became institutionalized in the discourses of crime control in the nineteenth-century state.

Deterrent presences of the nineteenth-century state

By the late eighteenth century and early nineteenth century, societies like Britain were caught up in the changes wreaked by the processes of modernization. Key institutional changes were taking place alongside the new intellectual currents associated with classicism and liberalism. Thus this era witnessed the emergence of both the centralized nation state and the national economy, as distinct objects of both inquiry and governance. A legal system together with new institutions of regulation such as the police, asylum, prison and workhouse gave concrete expression to the emergent 'modernist discourse on crime' (Garland, 1994: 32). Throughout the nineteenth century the state took on increasing control of the criminal justice system and as it did so the police were placed, in Gatrell's phrase, 'in the vanguard of the disciplinary enterprise' (Gattrell, 1996: 384). Law was mobilized as the means of reinforcing social discipline in an increasingly complex and changing society; order was the primary objective of this enterprise and the state was its necessary agent.

In contrast to this use of law enforcement as both deterrent against disorder and discipliner of social relations, the law in eighteenth-century society had been an expensive discipline of last resort (Gattrell, 1996). The institutionalization of deterrent crime prevention may thus be dated in Britain from the birth of the modern police force and the modern prison in the early nineteenth century. Think for a moment about the icon of the uniformed police officer who, together with the less frequently seen figure of the armed soldier (unless you live in Northern Ireland), remains a powerful metaphor to this day for state power in the UK. The establishment of the Metropolitan Police Force in London in 1829 ushered in a new representation of deterrence, first onto the streets of London and by 1857 into most towns in Britain in the shape of the 'bobby' on the beat in militaristic uniform, tall helmet and truncheon where previously there had not been much of a presence, other than the isolated, part-time traditional constable. From the start, the brief of the new police officer was to balance prevention and enforcement. Historians now argue that the 'need' for the police in the early nineteenth century arose out of fears over maintaining public order. However, Sir Robert Peel, the then Home Secretary, chose to argue the need for a police force not on the basis of the issue of public order maintenance but because of the problem of increasing crime (Elmsley, 1994: 160). From their beginning in 1829, the constables of the new Metropolitan Police were informed that their first duty was the prevention of crime. Thus Peel in his capacity as Home Secretary famously claimed:

> It should be understood at the onset, that the principal objective to be attained is the 'Prevention of Crime'. To this end every effort of the Police is to be directed. The Security of person and property, the preservation of the public tranquillity, and all the other objectives of a Police establishment, will thus be better effected than by the detection and punishment of the offender after he has succeeded in committing the crime. The absence of crime will be considered the best proof of the complete efficiency of the Police.
>
> (quoted in Johnson, 1987: 27)

That the police may never have realized this classicist ambition matters little for our purposes for this is not a book about evaluating 'success' in some technical manner. My concerns lie with explaining how theories and practices of crime prevention change, develop and are constituted over time and space. What is therefore crucial in Peel's 'mission statement' for his times is the ambitious scope envisaged for the police as the deterrent preventive presence of the administrative state. The visible presence of the police on the street was viewed as being the key to crime prevention during this era. This assumption may have been perfectly reasonable at a time when working-class people, the historical object of modern policing, lived most of their lives 'on the street'. In reality, then, such preventive strategies led to the targeting of 'criminal areas' and of particular individuals and social groups. Elmsley has noted that the first commissioners of the Metropolitan Police spoke of protecting the wealthy district of St James by watching the slum or 'rookery' of St Giles (Elmsley, 1994: 27). Such preventive policing in terms of selective targeting of areas and categories remains a feature of contemporary policing in the late twentieth century. Bottoms and Wiles (1996), for example, have noted that the establishment of public policing in the nineteenth century meant that this public police would remain the dominant form of crime prevention for about 120 years and would exercise an ideological hegemony over how crime prevention was to be 'provided' in modern Britain. The authors go on to argue that:

> until the middle of the twentieth century crime prevention, both in fact and in public policy debates, was necessarily tied to the existence of the

new public police. In the public domain public policing was accepted as having a monopoly; whilst in the private domain crime prevention either did not involve the use of manpower or, where it did, this was of a primitive form (i.e. night-watchman), and a very junior partner to public policing.

(1996: 2)

This interpretation appears correct when we restrict the discourse of crime prevention to (neo-)classicist deterrent notions. It is far less convincing when positivist notions of crime prevention via rehabilitation enter into the frame (see Chapter 3).

The emergence of the modern prison in mid-nineteenth century may also be seen as an institutional embodiment of the new faith in the classicist philosophy of 'a just measure of (preventive) pain' for offenders (Ignatieff, 1978). For Beccaria, in order for preventive deterrence to work, a variety of public punishments would have been necessary which clearly matched specific crimes and which sent out clear threats and messages to the public as onlookers. Foucault (1977) has noted, however, that the relatively closed and private world of the prison became, somewhat ironically, the key site of such utilitarian practices. We may note again the difficulty of separating the debate on penality from that of prevention. That said, the prison in the mid-nineteenth century appeared to be the most effective and just reformative penalty for its reforming proponents (Foucault, 1977: 232). The state thus constructed an orderly and rational institution – the penitentiary – so that individual offenders would be given the space and time to reform themselves on the basis of their free will. Preventive deterrence would thus result, for both the individual imprisoned offender and the wider public. In this 'constructive prison' (Melossi and Pavarini, 1981) a place was created where the offender would undergo remorse and repentance and be 're-formed' into a law-abiding and useful person. A clear instance of the prison as crime prevention regime *par excellence*.

Foucault has argued that Bentham's architectural design of the 'panopticon' or 'inspection-house' most powerfully expressed the new thinking and re-figuring of power relations for those needing control and surveillance (beyond as well as behind that of the prison walls). 'The panopticon is a machine for dissociating the see/being seen dyad: in the peripheric ring, one is totally seen, without ever seeing; in the central tower, one sees everything without ever being seen' (Foucault, 1977: 202). Put simply the 'panopticon' was based on a central 'observation tower' surrounded by a ringed building with individual 'cells'. In the central tower, each cell could be seen but the latter could not 'see' the surveillance being undertaken in the central tower. Foucault goes on to suggest that 'this cruel, ingenious cage' proved to be extremely influential across the continuum of social control: 'it serves to reform prisoners, but also to treat patients, to instruct schoolchildren, to confine the insane, to supervise workers, to put beggars and idlers to work' (p. 205). It is not fanciful to see the continuing influence of this move from a mode of control based on punishment as 'public spectacle' and that of 'surveillance' in the current crime prevention technique of CCTV (see Chapters 4 and 5).

This discussion of the emergent institution building of deterrent crime prevention in the nineteenth century across modern Western states has illustrated the important political and institutional consequences of the classical school's 'governmental project'. The resurfacing of classical theories of crime prevention in more recent times will be addressed in Chapter 4 with regard to rational choice theory. However, it is important to note that the legacy of classicism remains vital to the broader understanding of the modern criminal justice system. Classicism produced a rethinking of the legal rights of the state over the confined and criminal and produced, in Ignatieff's words, 'the reformative and utilitarian justifications that order our thinking to this day. Out of their attack on the abuses of the old institutions came the ambiguous legacy of the modern penitentiary' (Ignatieff, 1978: xii). In the work of contemporary conservative and neo-liberal thinkers such as Wilson (1975) and von Hirsch (1976), the influence of Beccaria's concern about the virtues of just deserts, certainty and economy remain to the fore. At the same time, this school also left the embattled legacy of 'legal guaranteeism' and the importance of the independence of the rule of law which resurfaces in contemporary radical debates around human rights (see van Swaaningen, 1997, and the Postscript).

Critical appraisal of classicist crime prevention

There are some quite specific criticisms of the classicist theory of crime prevention which I discuss in the next chapter on positivism. It is important to note that to a large extent the positivist discourse on crime and its prevention developed in reaction to the rationalist model of the offender in classicism. Not surprisingly, therefore, critics have pointed out that there are limits to the power of rational calculation in human behaviour and thinking. It may also be noted that classicism has a very uncomplicated psychology of human motivation which modern social scientists have sought to challenge (see the critique of contemporary 'rational choice theory' in Chapter 4).

At a more general level of critique, we have also seen that Garland (1990) has contended that classicism is not really criminology in the modern sense because of its lack of interest in the criminal type or what positivism would term 'the criminal man' (*Homo criminalis*). I would question Garland's notion that criminology is a discipline united by the 'governmental' and 'Lombrosian' projects. This view does not capture the complexity and fragmented nature of formations of 'criminology', past and present, on crime and crime control. Furthermore, Garland's claim that criminology is an empirically grounded, scientific undertaking which is thereby set apart from legal and moral discourses seems to show an unwillingness to understand the differences between British and Continental 'criminologies' on this issue (van Swaaningen, 1997). Classicism certainly offered a governmental project for criminology. Furthermore, its rejection of a separate 'species' of humans called criminal is not without its contemporary appeal in the recent radical criminologies (see Roshier, 1989) and in the 'pragmatic' approach of situational crime prevention discussed in Chapter 4. However, and perhaps more importantly for our purposes here, what cannot be denied is the lasting influence of the classical school's thinking on crime prevention through deterrent legal enforcement on modern systems of criminal justice throughout the world and legal discourse. Morrison (1995: 78) has argued that we have never moved on from the dilemmas which classicism contains. The rise to prominence of the 'just deserts' movement (von Hirsch, 1976) and the return to legalism in the late decades of this century bear testimony to this argument (although this move has also been heavily influenced by Kantian retributivism in which the 'moral imperative' argument is to the fore, namely that we punish because it is right not because it deters). The fact that classicist thinking is back in favour again also confirms that the history of thinking about crime and its control is not a linear process.

Summary

This chapter has presented the key intellectual tenets of the classical school of criminology and its theory of prevention. It has also contextualized this body of work in its socio-historical place and time and in particular its status as a product of a particular type of modernity. This chapter has also illustrated how the ideas of writers like Beccaria, particularly deterrence and reform as prevention, came to surface in the institutional practices of the modern state in the nineteenth century. Finally, the chapter addressed the key conceptual flaws in this discourse. I noted in Chapter 1 that there are several definitions and sub-types of crime prevention within contemporary criminology. Arguably the earliest legalistic expression is found in the idea of crime prevention as law enforcement. Classicism most clearly articulated this paradigm of crime prevention. Let's now look at its major modernist rival, positivism.

Further reading

Ignatieff, M. (1978) *A Just Measure of Pain*. London: Macmillan.
Roshier, B. (1989) *Controlling Crime*. Milton Keynes: Open University Press.

chapter three

Positivism and the cure of 'criminal man'

Introduction

In this chapter I examine the most influential paradigm in criminology which also spawned a discourse of crime prevention institutionalized by the modern state. 'Big' claims have been made for the centrality of the positivist paradigm to the whole criminological project in both academe and institutions of the social control complex (see Garland, 1994). It is difficult to deny this contention. It would seem that criminology during the last 100 years became inextricably associated with the new positivist science of crime causation and prevention, based on the search for, and cure of, 'criminal man'. In turn, this positivist project has been carried out within an empiricist framework in which 'theory-neutral' observation is used as a basis for inductive propositions, stressing measurement and observation. The hegemony of the 'aetiological' science of positivist criminologies can be plotted from the last decades of the nineteenth century through to the first two-thirds of the twentieth century. It is crucial to bear in mind Garland's important comment on the rise and consolidation of the modern, positivist 'science' of criminology: 'Criminology in its modern form and in its historical development, is oriented towards a scientific goal but also towards an institutional field, towards a theoretical project but also towards an administrative task' (Garland, 1994: 27).

The analysis of the complex and rich history of the discourse of positivist crime prevention in the late nineteenth and early twentieth centuries merits a volume to itself. The modest aim of this lengthy chapter, therefore, is to provide a broad yet critical introduction to the key themes and developments in these, until of late, hegemonic strategies of crime prevention. This chapter also addresses the question of why positivism in its various 'traces' will not go away from debates on crime control. The chapter is thus organized around the following sections:

- a brief outline of the basic tenets of positivism as a paradigm in modern criminology;
- in line with the book's concern to link the production of different knowledges to their social contexts, the rise of positivist criminologies as a modernist project is next examined;
- in the next section the full 'flowering' and statist institutionalization of positivist crime prevention in the twentieth century is plotted through the examination of the individual (psychological) and social (sociological) variants of positivism;
- I then examine the seeming demise of what has been termed the 'rehabilitative ideal' of individual positivism's crime prevention discourse;
- the next section plots the recent 're-birth' of positivist crime prevention in contemporary multi-factor biological and social-psychological approaches to offending;
- and finally I discuss some of the major points of critical appraisal of the positivist discourse on crime prevention.

The positivist paradigm in criminology

Positivism is a paradigm in the social sciences which is organized around the domain assumption that social behaviour can be studied by using the same scientific methods as the scientific study of natural phenomena. According to positivist thinking, people's behaviour is determined by external circumstances or conditions or internal predispositions and conditions, whether 'deviant' or criminal or 'normal' and law-abiding. It thus claims that human behaviour has causes which can be discovered by scientific observation and experimentation, that such investigation can lead to predictive laws and that, on occasion, diagnosis and cure of people's problems is possible. Knowledge of the antecedents of human behaviour thus makes possible, in principle, the scientific control of human behaviour. Treatment replaces punishment as the aim of the criminal justice system. The new science would be able to develop treatment programmes which, by addressing specific needs and problems, would prevent people from reoffending. Those who could not be reformed or prevented from reoffending should be segregated.

As is true of most paradigms in the social sciences, positivism is a fairly broad church, taking in and ranging from biological, psychological and sociological approaches. However, to continue with the religious metaphor, it is the case that some 'sects' have been more powerful and influential than others in positivist study, particularly in the realm of research and theorizing on crime. Among the different forms of positivist theorizing on crime prevention, the (bio-)psychological approach has probably been the dominant component but there has also been an influential social orientation too, from the work of Durkheim (1893) to that of the Chicago School of Sociology in the United States.

The Lombrosian project

An early exponent, and arguably the founder, of positivist criminology was the Italian writer Cesaré Lombroso. Lombroso was in fact more interested in distinguishing the characteristics of the 'born criminal' than the prevention of crime since if there are innate and pre-given characteristics of individuals then this places limits to prevention other than by means of carceral confinement or elimination. However, in his classification of criminal types, Lombroso did admit there was a distinction between the 'born criminal' as against the 'occasional juvenile criminal'. For the latter, Lombroso argued that it is no longer enough to repress crime; it is important to try to prevent it (Lombroso, 1968).

Lombroso's ultimate objective, and that of the intellectual tradition he set in motion, was that of building a science of the causes of crime (and a science of corrections and preventive measures) which has driven much criminological work throughout the decades of the twentieth century. At the heart of this positivist criminology was the radical proposition that crime was not a simple matter of individual choice, unlike that of classicism, but instead needed to be understood as a non-rational and determinate product of certain causes. In turn, these causes were there to be studied and isolated by means of clinical or statistical methods. The key heritage left by Lombroso was the promotion of a self-consciously 'radical scientism' (Garland and Young, 1983). Lombroso's true significance lies in establishing the possibility of a positive knowledge of human subjects (positivist criminology) which claimed to be superior to other rival discourses. The *scuola positiva* (positivist school) boldly claimed that criminality is the result of a pathology within the individual. Nor was this new knowledge of purely academic interest. It also appeared to offer the potential for clinical correction as chillingly captured in the following statement from another supporter of positivist criminology, De Fleury, at the turn of the century: 'the soul is there, under our scalpel' (quoted in Garland, 1985: 92).

The 'Lombrosian' project has not remained set in aspic since Lombroso's initial interventions. By the turn of the century, positivist criminology increasingly took on board an eclectic, multi-factorial approach to the 'scientific' solution and prevention of the social problem of crime. In passing we may note that this multi-factorial perspective clearly characterizes the currently influential work of researchers like Farrington (1994) on 'developmental prevention' and the isolation of 'risk factors' regarding youth crime. Already we can see that Lombroso appears to be less of an antiquated monstrosity and rather more of a precursor of contemporary positivist criminology.

Positivist crime prevention and the modernist project

It is a central claim of this book that it is important to understand competing discourses on crime and crime prevention in terms of their socio-historical contexts. Particular attention has already been paid to the crucial importance for the changing discourses of crime prevention of the social transformations associated with the processes of modernity and late modernity. Criminological positivism, in the shape of Lombroso's Italian school represented an ambitious and self-conscious challenge to classicism. It was intellectually armed with its rationale of experimental scientific investigation to discover new systems of prevention (and treatment) to protect society and 'mankind'. A number of other commentators have noted that positivism in general must be seen as an intellectual child of the historical period which sociologists term 'modernity', the broad meaning of which I examined in the Introduction. According to Giddens (1991: 115), positivistic thought represented a 'guiding thread of modernity's reflexivity', while for Beck (1992) theories of 'simple' modernization shared a sort of utopian evolutionism, which involved great faith in linear progress resulting in the 'good society'. Central to the modernist project was the notion that evil threat could be forestalled by human insight and intellect. Modernity was thus a constructivist project with modern life viewed as a rationalized existence based on planning and control (Morrison, 1995). Modernity was also associated with popular trust in what Giddens refers to as 'expert systems'. Such expert systems refer to the technical accomplishments or professional expertise that organize large areas of material and social environments (Giddens, 1990: 27). In turn, modernity is often contrasted with 'post-modernity', or as I prefer 'late modernity', in which the belief in the ability of science and rationality to achieve progress and to provide solutions either no longer holds (post-modernity) or is in decline and under challenge (late modernity).

We have seen that the positivist discourse in criminology since the late nineteenth century has been described by Garland as the 'Lombrosian' project. Its objective is different from the other major project in criminology, termed the 'governmental' by Garland, which is concerned to enhance efficient and equitable administration of justice through charting crime patterns, monitoring the practices of criminal justice agencies etc. (Garland, 1994; see also Coleman and Moynihan, 1996). The objective of the 'Lombrosian' project is chiefly that of building a science of causes as a result of which criminals can be clearly differentiated from non-criminals. Thus the search for, and birth of, what may be termed *'Homo criminalis'*. Again, this project was not just about 'theory'; it was closely bound up with a programme of practical action. Positivistic thought gave an impetus to a scientifically-informed regime for the prevention, treatment and elimination of criminality, untrammelled by classical concerns with formal egalitarianism. Positivism thus sought to expunge moral judgements and aesthetic criteria from the transformative processes it helped to set in motion and of which it also provided interpretation and analysis (Giddens, 1991: 155). Morrison (1995: 121) has noted that:

> In ideal form positivism side-steps the issue of criminal justice . . . it substitutes concerns for social justice . . . social protection and social management. It does not need a crime for its power to operate since crime is only a symptom, an outward sign of a *pathology*. You do not need a trial and representation by lawyers, due process is not involved: instead you require a hearing by a committee of social scientific experts.

Such utopian aspirations for the role of the criminologist as expert preventative practitioner had the advantage of meshing with emergent developments in politics, policy making and institutional practices during the late nineteenth century, particularly around the role of the expert and scientist in the governance of social problems. As Garland (1994: 40–1) notes, this criminological programme offered certain regulatory and legitimatory possibilities which made it attractive to late nineteenth-century governments and administrators.

Garland's analysis owes a clear debt to the insights of the maverick French historian of ideas, Michel Foucault. Foucault (1977) has located the discourse of criminology in the complex interweaving of knowledge and power that developed with the modern state and the emergence of the social sciences in the nineteenth century. He conceptualizes the modernist expert discourses in terms of them being guided by questions of control and discipline, whether in the realm of governing whole populations or in the treatment and classification of offenders. In turn, this historical project establishes academic 'disciplines' in the modern sense of the word, such as criminology, psychology and sociology. Foucault saw therefore a constitutive role assigned to science and knowledge in the regulation of human populations during modernity. As a result of the positivist discourse which emerged in the late nineteenth and early twentieth centuries, a new disciplinary power was articulated and realized which worked through and upon the individual offender or potential offender. 'Normalization' is the term used by Foucault to describe how the aberrant or deviant individual was to be corrected. Accordingly, the technique of normalization followed the delinquent's life course back not only to the circumstances of his or her 'crime' but also to the causes of the crime. This new preventive discourse which emerged in the latter nineteenth century logically led to proactive intervention in the lives of 'problem populations' in order to normalize them (Foucault, 1977; see also O'Malley, 1992: 251–2). As tangible evidence of this new reforming zeal, we may note the massive investment in institutional edifices from the mid- to late nineteenth century up to the mid-twentieth century in societies like the UK, the USA and France. Such institutions as the juvenile reformatory and the penitentiary were arguably created to give institutional realization to the new discourse. By such preventive interventions, positivist criminology appeared to offer a more extensive, more effective and more humane form of regulation and prevention than either classicist deterrent law enforcement or conservative retributive punishment.

With the birth of *Homo criminalis* as the object of 'penality' (Hudson, 1996) and crime prevention, there is a substitution of the professional gaze for the public spectacle (of, for example, the scaffold). The offender was now understood as a sub-species whose aberrant characteristics or predispositions required specific preventive treatment regimes. During the second half of the nineteenth century in Britain the number of first offenders was declining and there was a levelling-out of crime statistics, both of which suggested that the Victorian 'war against crime' was a success. However, the number of recidivists committed to prison was increasing. As Elmsley notes, the recidivists were regarded as evidence of the prison's overall failure to deter or reform criminals. 'The problem became linked to the changing perception of professional criminals less as a "class" and more as a hard core bolstered by a much larger group of social inadequates who constituted that part of the population least able to cope with the pressures of modern life, especially modern urban life' (Elmsley, 1994: 175). This changing perception fed into policy-making in general. Increasingly, the treatment of offenders was focused on what was viewed as the needs of particular individuals. Accordingly, probation was introduced for first-time offenders in 1887 and Borstals were set up in 1908 for young offenders which were encouraged to employ the scientific systems of 'therapeutics' (Wiener, 1990; Elmsley, 1994). As Hudson (1996: 124) notes, Foucault puts such developments into a 'wider political economy of power, enabling us to see them as part of the modernist project of "normalization" '. The preventive focus was to be on actors versus actions with the goal that of moulding the normal, socialized subject. Foucault and his followers like Rose (1989) may be guilty of exaggerating the all-powerful nature of this discourse. In particular, it is important to remember that the modernist positivist discourse was always tempered, and contested, by other strategic devices (such as legalistic (neo-) classicism, retributive conservatism and administrative pragmatism in the criminal justice system).

Psychological and sociological positivisms in the twentieth century

Rehabilitation as 'prevention'

The 'scientific' positivist criminology which developed in the UK and other Western states between the end of the nineteenth century and the Second World War was dominated by a medico-psychological approach. This approach focused on the individual offender or delinquent and was closely tied in to what Garland (1994: 53) terms 'a correctionalist penal-welfare policy'. This penal-welfare model of crime control was based both on ideas of determinism and pathology but also on individualistic assumptions. It also assumed a central role for a powerful yet benevolently paternalistic state empowered to intervene in an ever-increasing number of areas of social life. It is then in the late nineteenth century and early twentieth century in the UK, as in other modern states, that we find the origins of that archetypal positivist philosophy and practice of crime prevention, namely rehabilitation. The criminal, like other deviants such as disabled people (Hughes, 1998a), had thus truly become 'a suitable case for treatment'. Garland (1985) has argued that the period between the Gladstone Committee of 1895 on prison reform and the First World War represented a significant transition from the Victorian uniform system of crime control to new, more individualized techniques of control and prevention. The effect of this shift of strategy was not restricted to events inside the prison but reverberated throughout the merging correctional and preventive regimes in the social control system in subsequent decades.

It is this changing context that helps us explain the rise of medico-welfare professions as preventive agencies together with the 'scientific' identification of the 'problem family' as a major cause of crime and delinquency in the twentieth century. It appeared that the state increasingly had the requisite knowledge to undertake responsibility for organizing treatment programmes that would facilitate rehabilitation, and thus the prevention of criminality, through individualized, psychological treatment and training. A more sophisticated system of classification for the offender population emerged. Again, according to Garland (1985), there were three different sectors which he terms 'the normalization sector', 'the correctional sector' and 'the segregative sector'. The normalization sector dealt with less serious cases and was intended to straighten out characters and reform their personality in accordance with the requirements of 'good citizenship'. Rehabilitation thus played an increasingly key role in all sections of judicial proceedings. As a result of the rise of this normalization sector, a series of competing yet allied types of professional expertise increasingly had a voice in court proceedings (for example, psychiatry, social work etc.). The correctional sector consisted of a new series of institutions designed to deal with those offenders which the normalization sector had failed to reform. Such institutions, like the Borstal for young offenders, provided a regime of corrective training and education and operationalized notions of treatment and cure. Finally the segregative sector – that is, the prisons – was preserved for those who had refused or were unable to acquiesce to the discipline of the dominant order. The role of the prison thus shifted from correction to segregation (Garland, 1985: 238–44).

By the 1930s in the UK, the individualizing discourse about the criminal was given further impetus by the growing influence of psychological and psychiatric theories of both crime causation and prevention. As a result of the work of psychologists such as Cyril Burt (1925) it was claimed increasingly that such 'measurable' factors as defective family relationships and particular types of personality and temperament significantly correlated with delinquency. This served to reduce the emphasis on structural factors such as poverty. The implication for the control of crime was that each young offender would need to be diagnosed in psychological clinics and individualized treatment programmes developed to fit the specificities of each case. Such rehabilitative thinking was always contested in criminal justice (classicist notions and religious/moral appeals never disappeared here) but it would seem that positivist notions of rehabilitation had an increasing influence on the state's social control strategy particularly towards youth in this period (Muncie, 1998). We can see the institutional expression of positivism's influence in the 1933 Children and Young Persons Act which collapsed the categories 'neglected' and 'delinquent'. The discourse of the positivist 'psycho-sciences' during this period were thus mobilized and employed to both control and prevent crime through rehabilitation.

Such trends continued apace into the post-war period. Morrison has described the development of psychological positivism as involving the 'positivization of the soul': 'Once it was common to talk of humans possessing a soul; the positive approach reduced this to a matter of mental hygiene' (Morrison, 1995: 139). In the influential work of psychologists such as Bowlby and Eysenck in the UK during the post-war period, the assumption was made that law-abiding behaviour was normal while to breach the law was abnormal, resulting from certain pathological constitutional factors. In turn, clinics blossomed as the institutional manifestation of the positivist knowledge which claimed to explain the psychological functioning of troublesome people. As Morrison contends, the aim of such knowledge was to visualize in terms of eugenics the 'healthy' and get rid of 'pathological' aspects in humans (Morrison, 1995: 163).

Community development as 'prevention': the Chicagoan project

Alongside the continuing growth of the 'psycho-sciences', the positivistic ideal of curing the pathology of crime received further affirmation from sociological positivism in both the USA and Western Europe. This variant of positivism focused on the social or group pathology behind crime, in particular the role of 'social disorganization' in causing crime and disorder. In turn, sociological positivism suggested that community development, and the opening-up of opportunities for disadvantaged and disorganized groups which ensued, would be the best cure or method of prevention against the social pathology of crime.

From the 1920s onwards, the Chicago School of Sociology represented the most famous and influential body of work within twentieth-century sociological positivism (Shaw and McKay, 1969). Members of this school attempted to evolve a scientific approach to the problems of order and disequilibrium in the modern city. They drew inspiration from work by bio-ecologists in their construction of what is generally known as the 'social ecological' approach. The ecological approach in the science of biology highlighted a process whereby animal and vegetable life adapts to the wider environment by distribution over an area in an orderly pattern. The Chicago School sociologists saw a similar process at work in the city in which sections of the population were viewed as competing and struggling for spatial positions that would provide them with the necessary terrain to perform their different functions in the division of labour (see Morrison, 1995: 243–9). According to the Chicago School, data on where delinquents lived in the metropolises of the United States showed a concentration in city areas characterized by low rents and physical deterioration; that is, the inner cities. In these areas – termed 'zones of transition' – there was also a rapid turnover of the population which led to chronic or pathological 'social disorganization'. As a result of this social pathology, children were ineffectually socialized and controlled. In turn, delinquent traditions could become established and passed on. Within this perspective of sociological positivism, effective crime prevention had to be targeted on the pathological *social* conditions that determined the criminogenic tendencies of the inhabitants of the inner city. This discourse represented the blossoming of the social disease model of crime causation and the social health promotion model of crime prevention. Accordingly, the preventive objective behind the Chicago School's research and policy initiatives was to 'treat' and 're-form' communities, not individuals.

Tim Hope (1995) has argued that the Chicago School's enduring legacy for community crime prevention on both sides of the Atlantic is the rationale of 'community action' or development. Key members of the School such as Shaw and McKay (1969) were at pains to develop practical ways of modifying those aspects of socially disorganized community life which promoted and sanctioned delinquency careers among its members. The crime prevention strategy which emerged was one which targeted specific 'problem' areas and attempted to compensate poor communities for their lack of a 'normal' institutional infrastructure by initiating programmes of community building. Hope (1995: 27) has noted that the Chicago Area Project, initiated in 1932, has remained the source model for community action or development to this day. In this project, recreational programmes for children, campaigns to improve conditions in the neighbourhood and outreach work with delinquents and gang members were developed although the main aim was to develop opportunities for socializing young people into appropriate norms by the participating, 'role model' community adults. If successful, such projects would build community institutions that would regenerate themselves without subsequent external intervention and despite change in membership. This was the Chicago School's own 'test' of success. As Hope (1995: 29) notes the Chicago Area Project did not pass its own test but it nevertheless continued to influence subsequent urban, 'community' crime prevention initiatives in countries like the UK, particularly in the 1960s and 1970s (see Hope and Shaw, 1988).

The post-war 'triumph' of social democratic positivism in the UK

Looking back, the mid-twentieth-century regimes of prevention via treatment and rehabilitation and community development now appear as part of an age of criminological optimism. By the post-Second World War period and the rise of the social democratic welfare state in the UK (Hughes, 1998b), positivist thinking, both psychological and sociological, on crime and its prevention was an integral part of the institutions of government and of the welfare state's programme of social democratic reconstruction. There was a widespread belief that the political will and scientific means now existed to remould and improve virtually all aspects of UK society. The new professionals and bureaucrats of the social democratic welfare state were given the responsibility to intervene proactively in society's whole range of social ills, not least in treating crime. Positivist crime prevention strategies, particularly those targeted at juvenile delinquency and the 'problem family', were thus a small but important element in the post-war welfare settlement in the UK and across much of Western Europe (McLaughlin, 1998).

This era of the welfare state is sometimes described as the 'epidemiological age' because of the widely-shared commitment to intervene proactively on certain sections of the population with regard to society's ills, as in mass health promotion initiatives. Thus criminogenic families (examples of the 'problem family') became the targets for positivist-inspired reform. By the 1960s in the UK, with a well-established welfare state and full (male) employment, it was argued that deprivation or lack of opportunity could no longer be considered to be at the heart of the social problem of delinquency. Instead the source of the problem was viewed as residing within the pathological characteristics and dynamics of certain 'problem families' and in the transmission of 'inadequacies' from one generation to the next. Delinquency was thus seen as a temporary problem residing in certain working-class families left behind in the post-war social democratic prosperity. In turn, the new quasi-professions of the welfare state, such as health visiting and social work, were seen as being crucial in tackling this problem. It was their task to educate families in child-rearing and to rehabilitate the residue of young people that came under the jurisdiction of the criminal justice system. The family therefore had to be reformed if delinquency was to be tackled. During the 1960s in particular in the UK, there was a powerful movement to decriminalize delinquency and to transform juvenile courts effectively into family therapy clinics. As a result, the traditional neo-classical concepts of crime control policy – criminal, responsibility, guilt, innocence, punishment, criminal offence – were being questioned by a discourse organized and mobilized around notions like welfare, treatment, disease susceptibility and of course rehabilitation. In England and Wales, the 1969 Children and Young Persons Act embodied many of these principles (see Pitts, 1996). Accordingly, 10–13-year-old offenders were to be dealt with by 'care' rather than criminal proceedings. Attendance centres and Borstals were to be abolished and replaced by 'intermediate treatment' centres. Within these institutions it was psychologists who were the chief carriers of the rehabilitative ideal.

Lilly *et al.* (1995) have pointed out that we should not ignore the contribution made by some positivist interventions in the field of crime prevention. For example, the rehabilitative model emphasized that the causes of crime and delinquency were changeable and so ameliorative action was recommended. In particular, it was suggested that it was possible to rectify psychologically and socially the troubles of criminals through counselling or fixing social environments rather than merely punish on the grounds of retribution.

The 'demise' and 're-birth' of the rehabilitative ideal

The rehabilitative venture was never without its critics throughout the decades of its dominance. By the 1970s its success had turned increasingly

sour. There was a growing dissatisfaction with both its claims and consequences, voiced by critics of both the left and right. There were, for example,
criticisms of its theoretical faults and sociologists drew attention to the unintended consequences of greater levels of social control under the guise of
treatment (Cohen, 1974). However, the most cruel blow came from positivist evaluations which suggested that different types of preventive treatment regimes made little or no difference to the subsequent reconviction
rates of offenders. Martinson's 1974 study of 231 treatment programmes in
the USA has become the most famous critique of crime prevention through
rehabilitation. The central claim of Martinson's study, that 'nothing works',
was taken up as the major indictment of the rehabilitative edifice by subsequent critics. In the wake of such criticisms and the apparent bankruptcy of
the rehabilitative ideal, the major development to take place was a revival in
the debate on punishment and neo-classical notions of 'just deserts'. Criminologists such as James Q. Wilson (1975) in the United States were at the
forefront of this revivalist debate on punishment. Bolstered by such an intellectual backlash, a neo-conservative politics of law and order came to the
fore in both the UK and the USA in the 1980s. In place of prevention
through treatment and rehabilitation, the right demanded (and realized in
part through government policy) deterrence through selective targeting and
incapacitation. You will remember that we discussed the continuing importance of 'penal populism' in the politics of law and order in Chapter 1.

Looking back at the fate of the rehabilitative ideal, Bottoms (1980: 9–10)
felt confident in asserting that:

> No one now seriously pretends (as once they used to) that 'rehabili-
> tation' has any utilitarian value in the general reduction of crime rates,
> or in the prevention of the recruitment of recidivists. Important ethical
> and other questions remain about the residual role of 'treatment'; but
> for our purposes of the general planning of the penal system, it would
> seem that the rehabilitative ideal cannot be effectively revived.

However, from the vantage point of the late 1990s, such a dismissal of
treatment and rehabilitative strategies of crime control appears rash. There
is some evidence of the continuing appeal of positivism in the late twentieth-
century discourses on crime prevention. Of late there has been a resurgence
of interest in the medicalization of crime and deviance. Furthermore, biological and social-psychological determinism has come to the fore in much
current work on youth crime and delinquency. For example, we have the
increasingly popular concept of 'pre-delinquency'. 'Pre-delinquency' represents 'the idea that before any violation of legal norms has occurred, the
presence of certain symptoms indicates that a given youngster will move
inexorably towards delinquency and possibly crime' (Johnson, 1987: 2).
Following on from this 'scientific' discovery, positivist theorists claim to
identify and predict and, if possible, control the psychological and social

correlates of future criminality or what are often termed 'risk' and 'protective factors' (Farrington, 1994).

Let's now focus on two interrelated strands to what may be termed 'born again' positivism in the era of late modernity: first the genetics of offending, and second the social-psychological profiling of actual or potential offending associated with 'developmental crime prevention'. Psychological profiling is used in the broad sense of the term here. It is not to be equated with the often spectacularly crude and self-publicizing work carried out by 'forensic' psychologists with regard to serial killers (see, for example, Holmes and Holmes, 1996) and which has also become the fantastical stuff of the British TV drama, *Cracker*. Psychological profiling here relates chiefly to the early interventionist and multi-factorial explanations of children and youth at risk of offending.

The new genetics of criminality

The leading exponent in contemporary criminology of biological and genetic explanations of criminality has been Sarnoff Mednick (Mednick *et al.*, 1987). In particular, Mednick and his colleagues claim to have discovered what they term the inherited 'autonomic nervous system' (ANS) among offenders, and that such ANS people are less sensitive to environmental stimuli. This slow arousal would make them less likely to develop the responses necessary to inhibit antisocial behaviour. The policy implications of such a deterministic explanation are clear: if the effects of ANS are non-irradicable then segregative containment – rather than rehabilitation – would appear to be the only prevention strategy for persistent and serious offenders. This appears to be a message that underpins the mass incarceration programme in the USA at the time of writing.

The resurgence of biological, neo-Darwinian thinking about crime and its prevention in recent years reached its apogee in the decision of the US National Research Council to sponsor a 15-year study effort on the possible existence of 100,000 genes. According to this research agenda, early detection and intervention will succeed in preventing criminal outcomes (Lilly *et al.*, 1995: 208–9). Further populist support for 'neuro-scientific' studies of crime and violence has come from the American essayist, Tom Wolfe. Wolfe (1997: 7) outlines the breakthrough by researchers at the US National Institute of Mental Health's Violence Initiative as follows:

> This was an experimental program whose hypothesis was that, as among monkeys in the jungle . . . much of the criminal mayhem in the United States was caused by a relatively few young males who were genetically predisposed to it; who were hardwired for crime, in short. Out in the jungle, among mankind's closest animal relatives, the chimpanzees, it seemed that a handful of genetically twisted young males

were the ones who committed practically all of the wanton murders of other males and the physical abuse of females. What if the same were true among human beings? What if, in a given community, it turned out to be a handful of young males with toxic DNA who were pushing statistics for violent crime up to such high levels? The Violence Initiative envisioned identifying these individuals in childhood, somehow, some way, some day, and treating them therapeutically with drugs.

The metaphor of the jungle (a characteristic of nineteenth-century racist analyses of crime and disorder) in describing crime-ridden America has thus come back with (apparent scientific) vengeance.

At this point we may note the parallels between the new genetics of crime control and prevention and the seemingly fantastical, futuristic worlds of science fiction. To give just one example from fictional writing, Philip Kerr in the novel *A Philosophical Investigation* presents a compelling narrative in which a genetic breakthrough occurs in the twenty-first century 'science' of crime prevention with regard to serial sex killers. The scientific programme in this novel is known by the aphorism LOMBROSO or 'Localization of Medullar Brain Resonations Obliging Social Orthopraxy'. In Kerr's tale a machine has been developed in the first decade of the twenty-first century which is able to 'determine those males whose brains lack a Ventro Medial Nucleus (VMN) which acts as an inhibitor to the Sexually Dimorphic Nucleus (SDN), a preoptic area of the male human brain which is the repository of male aggressive response' (Kerr, 1992: 42). In turn, Kerr plots the fictitious decline of social and economic explanations of crime and offers a view of the future in which genetic determinism gains ascendancy in crime prevention specifically and social control more generally. With the establishment of ID cards which include DNA-profiling for all citizens, Kerr depicts a brave new world scenario where the machinery is in place to enable governments to 'track' the individual before 'he' offended at all.

The idea of discovering a genetic basis for criminality is of course neither new nor merely the stuff of science fiction. Instead it is part of a long (and tarnished) tradition of claiming to 'cure' or prevent crime and deviance through the medical discovery of a pathological deficiency, and the supposed science of 'eugenics' in the early twentieth century (Hughes, 1998a: 68–74). Eugenics laid claim to being the science and study of the methods of improving the quality of the human 'race', especially by means of selective breeding to produce a 'strong race' and thereby avoid the 'contamination' of the 'racial stock' brought by immigrants and criminals (with the latter two often seen as synonymous). According to this body of work, certain 'populations' (e.g. 'the poor', other 'alien races', 'the feeble-minded', criminally-inclined 'moral imbeciles' etc.) were seen as having genetic defects which could not be changed. In turn, such 'defective' and 'dangerous' people were likely to threaten moral values and social order and in particular they were likely to

reproduce more defective and dangerous people. Eugenics was, and is, arguably less focused on the individual as a subject to be 're-formed' when compared with other medical and 'scientific' interventions. Instead, eugenics was
concerned with whole populations which were there to be reorganized and
reconstituted. This approach reached its lowest point in Nazi Germany
where 400,000 people had been subjected to compulsory sterilization by
1939 and, after 1939, as a result of the euthanasia programme, about
200,000 disabled people died. This programme also developed the technology for the mass genocidal murders of the Jewish and other holocausts
by the Nazi state (see Proctor, 1988; Morris, 1991). The appeal of eugenics,
particularly the notion that the 'mentally deficient' were an inferior and
dangerous form of human life, was not reserved for the exceptional example
of Nazi Germany. Ideas associated with eugenics continue to resurface in
contemporary debates on genetic testing and what has been termed the 'new
eugenics' in the late twentieth century. The 'new genetics', discussed above,
appears to institute genes as the first cause of various human experiences and
behaviour and tends to assume that human social action is caused by genetic
endowment. The term commonly used by social scientists to describe this
process is that of 'biological determinism'.

This discussion of eugenics should have alerted you to the important links
between the medical and 'scientific' classification of 'defective' categories of
human minds and bodies and the wider processes of social control of problem populations. The medical discourse has played a significant role in wider
ideological debates about the fears of class unrest, 'racial contamination'
and the control of unproductive and 'dangerous' deviants throughout the
twentieth century. Furthermore, in the light of our brief discussion of the
resurgence of the 'new genetics' in the late twentieth century you should also
be aware that the issues raised by eugenic theories are not of mere antique
curiosity value but have resurfaced in contemporary debates on the supposed 'underclass'.

Developmental crime prevention

Let's now examine the rise of developmental crime prevention, work most
associated with the social-psychological positivist research of David Farrington (1992, 1994). Farrington's starting point is the thesis that offending
is part of a larger syndrome (a medical term for a set of symptoms indicat-
ing the existence of a condition or problem) of antisocial behaviour that
emerges in childhood and tends to persist into adulthood (1994: 510).
Furthermore, he argues that an early onset of offending 'predicts' a long and
serious criminal career, because of what Farrington terms 'an underlying
criminal potential' (1994: 566). In the tradition of positivist criminology,
Farrington suggests that an 'anti-social personality syndrome' may exist
among persistent or criminal career offenders and that more research is

needed into the methods of preventing and treating it. Working to the same research agenda, Trembliss and Craig (1995) suggest there are three main delinquency risk factors, namely socially disruptive behaviour, cognitive deficits and poor parenting. From the small-scale experiments with juvenile delinquents to date, Trembliss and Craig claimed that there are positive results in terms of successful intervention when the work is aimed at more than one risk factor and when the project lasts a long period of time, particularly when implemented before adolescence. Furthermore, and crucially in an era of cost-cutting and the cult of budget, Trembliss and Craig argue that such experiments suggest that these rehabilitative interventions will save money later with regard to remedial and correctional services (p. 225).

This body of developmental crime prevention research is in turn critical of the short term, narrowly policy-oriented preventive research sponsored by the Home Office in the UK during the decades of the 1980s and 1990s (see Chapter 4) and instead aims to pursue the longitudinal investigation of potential offenders. Furthermore, the goal of offender reduction is tentatively linked by Farrington to the reduction of other 'ills' such as alcohol and drug abuse, sexual promiscuity, family violence, truancy and school failure, unemployment and marital disharmony (1994: 569). Once again, just as in the nineteenth-century panic over the 'residuum', or the dangerous class, we see the project of crime prevention in the late twentieth century hitched up to the wider 'bandwagon' of the fight against the current malaise of social disorder.

It has already been noted that developmental crime prevention based on social-psychological positivism is seen by one of the leading commentators on crime prevention in the UK, Tony Bottoms, as a third possible style of crime prevention for the future, alongside situational crime prevention and social/'community' crime prevention. As Bottoms (1990: 15) notes,

> if this small number of persistent offenders could be identified at an early age, then one form of crime prevention worth attempting would be to work with them in a range of voluntary preventive programmes; the indications are that early identification, on the basis of troublesome behaviour and other data available at age 10, is possible although difficult.

This body of preventive research and interventionist practices by social workers and psychological therapists is structured around the problem of both reducing risk factors and increasing protection factors. According to Tonry and Farrington (1995: 10), 'The central insight is Shakespeare's, that the child is father to the man'. We may note that there is a degree of self-publicity at work from proponents of developmental prevention. For example, Tonry and Farrington (1995: 10–11) claim that 'Developmental prevention is the new frontier of crime prevention efforts' and 'Theorists will probably have to pay more attention to individual differences between offenders'. The credo of this resurgent branch of positivist criminology is eminently practical: 'Crime prevention strategies should be based on wide-ranging theories about the development of criminal potential in individuals and about the interaction between potential offenders and potential victims in situations that provide opportunities for crime' (Tonry and Farrington, 1995: 11).

There is further support for this explanation of offending and technique of prevention from the positivistic 'control theory' of Hirshi (1969; see also Gottfredson and Hirshi, 1990). In the work of Hirshi, the traditional questions asked about crime are reversed. The problem for Hirshi was not why people commit crime but rather why they do not do so on the whole. In turn, Hirshi sees delinquency as resulting from the weakening of the individual's bond to society with the bond constituted by four components: attachment, commitment, involvement and belief. As a consequence of this viewpoint, crime prevention is necessarily committed to the re-establishment of the elements of this bond when weakened. Control theory researchers have pointed to the causes of crime as lying in the loss of self-control of certain individuals and in the loss of the social control function on the part of institutions, particularly since the 'permissive' 1960s. Gottfredson and Hirshi have emphasized the crucial importance of the self-control achieved as a result of the quality of parenting in a child's early years. However, if children have neglectful and ineffective parents during child-rearing, they 'tend to be impulsive, insensitive, physical (as opposed to mental), risk-taking, short-sighted, and non-verbal, and they will therefore tend to engage in criminal and analogous acts' (Gottfredson and Hirshi, 1990: 90). In terms of the imperative of successful crime prevention, families are viewed by such control theorists as the key site for intervention since in metaphorical terms, 'families are incubators for or prophylactics against crime involvement' (Lilly et al., 1995: 105).

The policy implications of control theory are not a million miles removed from the interventionist project associated with the social-psychological 'turn' in positivism during the early decades of the twentieth century (despite control theory's apparent disdain for the fixation with causation). What we can learn from this is that theorizing in criminology and crime prevention has what O'Malley (1997: 256) terms 'histories in which the "death and resurrection" of strategies is the norm rather than the exception'.

The work of cognitive and behaviourist psychologists and clinicians in the UK during the mid-1990s has led to a much publicized call from the Audit Commission in its 1996 report on youth crime (*Misspent Youth*) for a 'radical' rethink from the criminal justice system about the way it deals with the prevention of crime among young offenders. According to the Audit Commission, both research studies and early interventionist treatment programmes developed by psychologists appear to offer the way out of the expensive and failing traditional approaches to dealing with offenders in the courts and via occasional custody. In particular, the Audit Commission heaps praise on the work of researchers-qua-therapists drawn together in the volume edited by John McGuire (1995), himself a 'forensic clinical psychologist'. In this volume of case-studies, it is argued that preventive intervention does work well overall compared with either no intervention or punishment. The authors claim to have scientific support for this argument in favour of rehabilitative treatment from the popular technique in psychology of 'meta-analysis' – an approach used for reviewing large bodies of research through statistical techniques. In the views of its supporters meta-analysis appears to have shown 'unequivocal evidence . . . that rehabilitative programmes did work' (Hollin in McGuire, 1995: ix). We see, then, a bold reassertion that certain types of preventive work do work positively in reducing recidivism. Particular projects are cited as exemplars of good practice in this preventive work, such as 'contingent reinforcement', 'reinforcement and family contracting' and 'behaviour modification employing family teaching programmes to reduce stealing and aggression'. In conclusion it is asserted that 'It may not be reflected in current penological practice, but on scientific grounds at least we are in a position to say we have witnessed nothing less than the "death of deterrence"' (McGuire, 1995: 25).

From the discussion to date it is evident that positivist criminologies, whether biological, (social-)psychological or sociological in focus, remain influential (see Cullen and Gilbert, 1982). They retain this influence because in the words of Muncie *et al.* (1996: xviii) 'they prolong the modernist concern to account for crime with reference to some quantifiable and objective criteria. They also hold on to the hope that because some people are propelled into crime through a range of determining factors, then it will always remain possible to treat or neutralize the underlying causes'.

Critical appraisal of the positivist crime prevention discourse

It is not possible to appraise the range of positivist approaches to crime prevention as if they all share the same agenda. There are instead important points of difference as well as areas of consensus across the different theories and approaches within positivist criminology. In this brief critical appraisal I first discuss some specific questions with regard to the major 'sub-species' of positivist crime prevention. The chapter ends by evaluating some of the common, underpinning assumptions of the paradigm.

The biological-cum-genetic turn taken of late by some positivist work on crime prevention has some potentially worrying and sinister ethical undertones with historical parallels with eugenic solutions pioneered in the early twentieth century towards 'inadequates' and 'defectives' (Hughes, 1998a). According to Pease, for example, it is arguable that the so-called 'incurably' or 'genetically criminal' will be offered very severe containment sentences acting as 'a kind of quarantine for the criminally contagious' (Pease, 1994:

668). On a less profound and chilling note, the tradition of biological positivism is able to ignore the problem of 'hidden crime'. It similarly ignores the problems inherent in any absolutist definition of what crime is, given the powerful claim from radical sociologists of the labelling perspective (Becker, 1963) that offending must be viewed as a context-specific form of rule violation and that crime itself is a socially constructed category.

When we examine the 'developmental' psychological approach to the prevention of criminality we may also ask ourselves, how new is this strategy? There appear to be clear parallels with, and echoes of, social democratic policies pursued towards the poor earlier in the twentieth century. In such social democratic policies there was a combination of social insurance, welfare and correctional policies aimed at creating 'new types of civilized and self-directing citizens' (Stenson, 1991: 27). When we consider the current vogue for early childhood and family intervention, are we seeing a re-birth of the 'child-savers' programme of the nineteenth century? Instead of 'helping' young people and families in need, preventive interventions and monitoring may possibly result in greater stigma and criminalization due to the early 'infection' of these parties by the criminal justice system. A crucial flaw in the cognitive and behaviourist psychological work of commentators such as Farrington, Hirshi and Gottfredson, and McGuire appears to be what Currie (1985) has described as 'the fallacy of autonomy'. According to this fallacy, what goes on in the family can be separated from the forces that affect it from outside. The search for both the causes of crime and the means of preventing crime in terms of family dynamics would seem to down-play the potentially decisive effects of wider social forces. Can we, for example, ignore the consequences of the social fabric of whole communities being shredded? I would argue that these processes in turn have placed youth collectively in these areas at risk, as a consequence of economic and social policies of marketization and mass unemployment in recent decades in countries like the USA and the UK.

Sociological positivism in the guise of the Chicago School is less guilty of ignoring these broader trends than is individual, psychological positivism. However, it still relies, when using such notions as 'social pathology' and 'social disorganization', on a disease model of crime and its prevention which is a recurrent and general flaw in positivism. This body of work also pathologizes certain communities as 'disorganized' and fosters an image of high-crime neighbourhoods as being an atomized collection of households which recent ethnographic research problematizes (Hope, 1995: 69). Finally, the success story of community mobilization on both sides of the Atlantic is far from clear. Again I return in greater depth to the politics of 'community' crime prevention in Chapters 5 and 6.

Let's now look critically at some of the common assumptions of the positivist paradigm on crime prevention. Writing in 1977, the positivist criminologist Gold argued that 'The prevention and treatment of delinquency is still in its pre-scientific phase. That is, it is guided by beliefs that are more nearly articles of faith than cogent theories, and observations on its effects more by wish and by fact' (Gold, 1977: 218). Here we see a clear example of the persistent faith in the researcher/intellectual as modernist 'legislator' (i.e. bearer of unsullied, uncontestable truths) as against the growing recognition that the best intellectuals may hope for in the complex and ambivalent late modern world is that of being interpreters of contestable knowledge (Bauman, 1993). It is important, therefore, to remember that the human sciences are themselves human cultural enterprises attempting to understand other human cultural enterprises. As such, the human sciences cannot produce certainty since this would require some place outside what is termed the 'hermeneutical circle' from which to judge pure truth (Morrison, 1995: 6).

The 'Lombrosian' or aetiological project of positivism, as has already been noted, is guided by the scientific objective of differentiating the criminal individual from the non-criminal. Out of this search arise certain preventive strategies which may be genetically-, psychologically-, or socially-oriented, or a mixture of these. The domain assumption is that there is a clear, scientifically-identifiable gulf between the criminal offender and the rest of the population. This begs many awkward questions. Crime is a phenomenon whose definition varies according to the historical and cultural contexts in which it is embedded. 'Criminality' is thus a *social* category rather than an unchanging 'natural' essence. Positivist crime prevention, targeted only on regulating and re-forming the pathological dispositions of identified offenders, may therefore be based on a false premise about the nature of crime. The image of the criminal in the Lombrosian tradition is arguably that of a fundamentally constrained subject, deterministically propelled into criminality by a range of factors over which the person has little control. Enter the expert in the prevention or correction of such tendencies. More recent sociologies of crime and deviance would question both the existence of such an over-determined 'hypostatized subject' (the criminal 'other') and the scientific solution proffered. As well as the lack of acknowledgement of human creativity in crime, positivism is also largely silent about the process of criminalization in terms of specific and discriminatory patterns of labelling for certain categories of the population.

Pearson suggests that the origins of the modern system of social control – and thus criminology itself – lie in the nineteenth-century dominant class response to the problem of creating a stable pool of factory labour in an unequal capitalist society (Pearson, 1975: 125). Pearson's Marxist analysis is somewhat crude in drawing a direct causal link between the 'needs' of capital and the rise of particular intellectual discourses such as criminology. However, he is probably correct in emphasizing the role of non-academic determinants of intellectual developments. For example, Pearson shows that the Lombrosian theory of the constitutional nature of criminality expressed already-popular notions of criminality and further consolidated and developed such notions (p. 151). Indeed, both Pearson and Bottomley (1979) support Chevalier's (1973) thesis that the birth of (positivist) criminology coincided with the broader fears of mob rule in the nineteenth century; 'it is there that the scientific curiosity in the reified misfit is born' (Pearson, 1975: 205). This period also saw the consolidation of a racialized discourse of colonialism. In this discourse we witness attempts to classify 'races' hierarchically, both externally and internally to the 'nation'. Recent 'scientific' breakthroughs in terms of the genetically-programmed offender and the under-socialized and psychologically-damaged delinquent discussed above may therefore be seen as part of a more recent retelling of the old fears about 'the underclass' and how best to scientifically 'treat' its pathologies. Matza has noted that positivist criminology attempted what he terms the almost impossible; that is to separate the study of crime and its control from the contemplation of the state. By doing so positivist criminologists, in Matza's eyes, have acted as the technicians of the state (Matza, 1964).

Summary

This chapter has plotted the main features of the positivist discourse on crime prevention. In particular, it focused on its central intellectual premises and how these ideas became embedded in institutional practices of the modern state during the late nineteenth and twentieth centuries. Particular attention was paid to both the psychological and sociological variants of positivism which blossomed during the twentieth century. The chapter then examined the demise and recent resurfacing of rehabilitation and treatment models of preventive intervention. The chapter ended by highlighting some of the limitations to this discourse of crime prevention.

It would be a serious error to exaggerate the dominance of positivist thinking in the development of both criminology as a practical science in modern societies generally and in the routine operation and philosophy of the criminal justice system more specifically. Positivist treatment methods and prevention regimes have always been contested by the rival claims of classicism around free will and legality, and the pragmatic rather than scientific concerns of administrators in the agencies of criminal justice. Indeed, the next chapter will examine the latest challenger to the 'throne'; namely situational crime prevention.

Further reading

Foucault, M. (1977) *Discipline and Punish*. Harmondsworth: Penguin.
Garland, D. (1994) 'Of Crimes and Criminals: The Development of Criminology in Britain', in M. Maguire, R. Morgan and R. Reiner (eds) *Oxford Handbook of Criminology* (1st edn). Oxford: Clarendon Press.

chapter four

Situational crime prevention:
the pragmatics of crime control

Introduction
A Home Office 'administrative criminology'?
  Clarke's definition of situational crime prevention
Lessons from the USA
Rational choice theory
'Some things work': the pragmatics of crime prevention
Critical appraisal
  Explaining the hegemony of the situational crime prevention discourse
Summary
Further reading

Introduction

The next three chapters focus on three key, closely interrelated contemporary developments in both the thinking on and the practice of crime prevention in late modern societies. These are the situational, multi-agency and 'community' strategies of crime prevention. In this chapter I specifically examine the rise to prominence of situational crime prevention. In Chapter 5 the focus turns to multi-agency initiatives which combine both situational and social crime prevention measures. Chapter 6 then looks at appeals to community in crime prevention debates in the late twentieth century, focusing on both 'conservative' and 'radical' variants of the communitarian discourse on crime and social justice. I will examine each of these developments separately. However, it is vital to note that these divisions and separate headings are for the most part a heuristic device to help us think about these often closely interdependent strategies of crime prevention. A heuristic device is any procedure which involves the use of an artificial construct or model to assist in the exploration of social phenomena.

This chapter is organized as follows. First, the historical roots of situational crime prevention in Home Office thinking in the 1970s in Britain and in the theory of natural surveillance in the USA are briefly traced. Second, I discuss the key features to rational choice theory as the theoretical underpinning to this preventive discourse. Third, the policy consequences of the approach are examined. Fourth and finally, a critical appraisal of the situational crime prevention approach is provided, focusing in particular on its 'elective affinity' with neo-liberalism.

A Home Office 'administrative criminology'?

It is generally agreed that the situational theory of crime prevention was most fully developed by 'administrative criminologists' working at the Home Office Research Unit in the late 1970s in Britain. Jock Young (1994) first coined the term 'administrative criminology' to describe the dominant 'establishment' approaches to understanding both crime and its control in Britain at this time. The term 'administrative' is used to capture the politically pragmatic and seemingly atheoretical perspective of such criminologists when compared with the previously dominant 'aetiological' perspective of mainstream criminology. The latter was, according to its Home Office critics, obsessed with the search for the causes of criminality (often termed the 'aetiology of crime'). In contrast, administrative criminology argues that the search for causes is futile, but the opportunities to commit crime can be controlled.

The historical context behind the emergence of this new approach in the UK may be summarized as follows. Between the 1940s and the 1970s in the UK as elsewhere, both criminologists and policy-makers tended to concentrate on 'dispositional' rather than 'situational' variables in their explanations of crime and in their strategies of prevention and control. This focus led to an emphasis on treating individual dispositions to crime rather than altering the situations in which crime might be committed. 'Dispositional' variables are those features associated with the character, intelligence, values etc. of offenders which disposed them towards committing crimes. However, by the 1970s there was arguably a major problem, if not crisis, facing both policy makers and 'their' Home Office criminologists in Britain. This crisis revolved around the rising crime rate throughout a period of affluence and of the welfare state, and the collapse of faith in the rehabilitative ideal (see Chapter 3, and on the broader 'crisis' of the welfare state, see Hughes and Lewis, 1998). In response to these problems Home Office criminologists and officials appeared to broadly agree that:

- there was no evidence to show that deterrence through punishment would have any significant effect on the rising crime rate;
- improvements in policing or increases in police resources would have no significant effect on the rate of crime;
- crime prevention through social reform might be desirable *per se* but it was not a realistic possibility and there was no evidence that it had any measurable effect on reducing crime;
- treatment programmes geared to changing the criminal disposition of offenders were unproductive.

Instead, Home Office researchers looked to other more pragmatic pieces of research for a possible answer to the problem of what was to be done to reduce or prevent crime. In particular, they found some inspiration in:

- 'defensible space' theory from the USA which claimed that improved architectural design could engender a stronger sense of proprietorial territoriality among residents and increase opportunities for 'natural' surveillance by them;
- theories of 'natural' victims which suggested that victimization rates were a function of risk factors and which focused on the situational interaction of potential targets/victims and motivated offenders;
- ecological studies which focused on the places where crimes take place;
- crime analysis research which analysed the temporal and spatial distribution of different types of offences;
- the revisiting of 'soft' psychological research on motivation.

As a result of this emergent research and policy-oriented agenda, attention shifted away from dealing with offenders and towards the immediate circumstances surrounding the commission of criminal acts.

Clarke's definition of situational crime prevention

The following definition of situational crime prevention has been provided by Ron Clarke (1992: 4), its leading proponent within the Home Office in the early 1980s:

> Situational crime prevention . . . refers to a pre-emptive approach that relies, not on improving society or its institutions, but simply on reducing the opportunities for crime . . . Situational crime prevention comprises opportunity-reducing measures that are, (1) directed at highly specific forms of crime (2) that involve the management, design or manipulation of the immediate environment in as specific and permanent a way as possible (3) so as to increase the effort and risks of crime and reduce the rewards as perceived by a wide range of offenders.

In stark contrast to positivism's obsession with aetiology, primary emphasis is placed on the immediate features of the environment (or situation) in which an act might be committed. There is also a direct, if unacknowledged, debt to the classicist school of criminology (see Chapter 2). In common with classicism, this approach views crime as the actions of rational, reasoning people making psychological judgements or calculations in response to specific situations or circumstances. This view of the criminal as rational calculator also corresponds to how many people, not least the police and policy makers, view the world and plan for action (Rock, 1989: 5). Given the privileged institutional location of this theory in the Home Office, it was ideally placed to propagate its claims through a lengthy, well-funded and well-publicized programme of research (Clarke, 1995) which in turn was tied in to government policy developments around crime prevention in the UK.

The two guiding 'techniques' to this self-consciously pragmatic thinking are *target hardening* and *surveillance*. Target hardening is intended to make the commission of crime more difficult, often by very practical 'nuts and bolts' measures such as strengthening and making more secure the technology of everyday devices like doors or telephone coin-boxes. Surveillance on the other hand refers to the controls, formal and informal, exerted by people in everyday life. Attention, for example, is given to the design of the built environment and how this might either hinder or be redesigned to help people control their own environment. This concern with surveillance draws on the early work of Jacobs (1962) and Newman (1972) in the USA and was epitomized in the UK by Alice Coleman's work on redesigning the architecture of housing estates (Coleman, 1985).

Jock Young has argued that situational crime prevention in the context of the UK in the 1980s needs to be understood as the major component of the new 'administrative criminology'. According to Young (1994: 91) the main thrust of the situational paradigm has been to sidestep the problem of aetiology by suggesting that the causes of crime are either relatively unimportant or politically impossible to tackle (see the similar argument from the right by Wilson, 1975: 233). It should also be noted that this paradigm conveniently sidesteps the vexed questions of criminal *justice* itself.

Lessons from the USA

It would be misleading to try and explain the rise to international hegemony of the situational crime prevention discourse simply in terms of UK developments, however influential internationally the Home Office-based criminology has been. In fact, many situational crime prevention techniques have been developed first by the private sector rather than the state, particularly in the USA. Furthermore, the USA since the late 1960s has seen a growing, increasingly vociferous and influential conservative and neo-liberal critique of positivist explanations of crime causation and strategies of crime prevention (see Wilson, 1975; von Hirsch, 1976; Murray, 1990). In particular, critics pointed to the ever-increasing rate of crime during a post-war period of affluence and of the welfare state. There was also the accumulating research audit which seemed to show that 'nothing works' in terms of the rehabilitation of offenders (see Chapter 3).

Out of this growing dissatisfaction with the social reformist and positivist agenda on crime prevention, a new technicist focus emerged in the USA. Of particular influence were theories which emphasized 'planning out' crime. The last two decades in the USA have witnessed the rise of 'crime prevention through environmental design' (CPTED) supported by such concepts as that of 'defensible space' (Newman, 1972) and 'neighbourhood surveillance' (Jacobs, 1962), as well as what has been termed 'environmental criminology', focusing on spatial research (Brantingham and Brantingham, 1991). In particular, it was emphasized by such writers as Newman and Jacobs that territoriality had been ignored in public housing and that there was much potential in the use of planning and design to develop a sense of proprietorship.

According to Hope (1995: 41), this body of work has resulted in a new paradigm based on the idea of 'residential defence' involving the two strategies of the intentional organizing of community surveillance and environmental modification to encourage more surveillance. Such environmental strategies view both human behaviour in general and criminal behaviour in particular as a product of the opportunities and constraints presented by physical structures. In this paradigm neither the causes nor the behaviour of residential defence were viewed as problematic by Newman (1972). Defensiveness was assumed to arise out of the latent but deep-lying territorial tendencies common to all human groups. However, it was accepted by Hope that the design of some built environments (particularly mass public housing projects) prevented 'natural' surveillance and defensiveness from expressing itself (Hope, 1995: 52). Jacobs (1962) also argues that urban planning in the modern era had often undermined residents' ability to control their own environment. This worrying trend in the cities of the USA was related to the differentiation and segregation of residential environments from other land uses (e.g. for commercial or transport uses). The 'solution' proposed by Jacobs was a form of communitarian control (see Chapter 6) by which residents would regain informal control over behaviour in public places, especially on the streets. According to Jacobs, public peace is 'kept primarily by the intricate, almost unconscious, network of voluntary controls and standards among the people themselves' (p. 41). As Hope (1995: 43) notes, Jacobs aimed to strengthen the community's informal defences against predation which the urban environment was impeding. This is the meaning of 'neighbourhood surveillance' which would influence the strategy of 'neighbourhood watch' initiated by the US police in Seattle first in 1974 and which spread across the USA and the UK in the next two decades (Bennett, 1990). There have been important developments in the USA therefore which are crucial in helping explain the success of situational crime prevention across late modern societies.

The Australian criminologist Pat O'Malley has correctly observed that situational crime prevention is one of the fastest-growing techniques of crime control in the world (O'Malley, 1992: 253). Prior to the emergence of this approach in the 1970s, most criminological work on crime prevention had focused on the *offender*. In contrast situational crime prevention's particular concern is with the spatial and temporal aspects of crime. It focuses on the opportunities to commit crime, and is thus *offence-based*. Looking at developments in the public sphere (such as the ever-increasing use of CCTV in town and city centres and in the private sphere such as the new icon to consumerism, the shopping mall) throughout the industrialized world, it would be difficult to disagree with O'Malley. Perhaps one might go further and contend that situational crime prevention is arguably now the most powerful and hegemonic discourse of crime prevention in the late twentieth century (if we exclude mass incarceration through imprisonment from our calculation), perhaps because it criss-crosses the public/private divide. O'Malley captures the essence of this discourse in seeing situational crime prevention as a form of 'risk management' (p. 262). I examine these comparative trends in social control in greater depth in Chapter 7.

Rational choice theory

Coleman and Moynihan (1996) have noted that a 'pure' situational analysis of crime is only concerned with offences and the situations in which they occur. Because a pure situational perspective is not concerned with offenders, it alone could not say how offenders would behave when confronted with preventive measures. According to Coleman and Moynihan, 'Rational choice theories fill this gap by looking at the way in which offenders make decisions about offending in particular situations, and in relation to particular types of crime. They therefore mark a return to collecting data about and from *offenders*, as well as offences' (p. 139). Since the 1970s, situational crime prevention has thus became associated with a body of theorizing which is now widely known either as rational choice theory or control theory. For the sake of clarity here I will refer to rational choice theory when also discussing ideas which may be associated with writers who describe themselves as control theorists.

According to the sociologist Barbara Misztal (1996: 77), rational choice theory is striking for the 'elegance and simplicity of its model of motivation': namely the rational choices made by individual actors. Rational choice theory is best understood as a reaction to a priori macro-structural and functionalist arguments which characterized much previous sociologically-informed criminological thinking on both crime causation and prevention.

Rational choice theory also came into vogue in policy and political circles as an economical answer to an array of questions emerging in the mid- to late-1970s in countries like the USA and the UK. It sets out to answer very practical questions. As Rock (1989: 4) notes:

> It resonates with common sense, being most in accord with everyday explanations of crime and misbehaviour. It lends itself to neat, effective and attractive action. It cuts through all the complexities and qualifications of sociological theorizing and substitutes simple principles in their place.

As I have already noted, this body of work grew out of a dissatisfaction with what were considered to be unprofitable speculations about criminal motivation and disposition. According to this theory, it is not necessary to consider causes and antecedents; all that matters is the choice of actions facing a person in a given immediate situation. Moreover, it is suggested that displacement to other times, places, targets and type of crime is unlikely to occur. Rational choice theorists such as Clarke and Cornish (1983) thus argue that the idea of 'displacement' (that is the problem of what happens to the potential criminal act or behaviour which has been prevented) harks back to incorrect dispositional theories which posit that crime is the result of a drive within the individual, so that if criminals are prevented from committing a crime in one place or at one time, they will move on. However, according to rational choice theory, most crime is committed on the spur of the moment. Consequently there is no reason to assume that targeted situational crime prevention measures will not work in genuinely reducing the occurrence of criminal acts.

Arguably, rational choice theory exists as the most general and elaborated individualistic theory of human behaviour in the contemporary social sciences. When we look back to Chapter 2, the close links to classicism will be clearly evident. According to both rational choice theory and classicism, rationality is understood in utilitarian terms as a matter of satisfying the individual's calculated preference. Thus rationality consists in choosing action that is most likely to produce the highest utility for the actor. People, to use Shapland's phrase (in Tonry and Farrington, 1995) are conceived as being 'amoral calculators of profit and loss'. By means of this emphasis on rational choice and calculation, O'Malley has contended that the situational crime prevention discourse destroys the biographical individual as the central category of criminological knowledge. The biographical criminal (or positivism's *Homo criminalis*) is replaced by an abstract individual: the rational choice actor or *Homo economicus* (O'Malley, 1992: 264).

The discourse of situational crime prevention does not, however, make claims to intellectual purity. During the period of its growing influence since the 1970s, it has been happy to take on board compatible theoretical 'fellow-travellers'. Accordingly, Pease (1994) has argued that situational crime prevention thinking in fact increasingly tends to employ three major, closely-linked theoretical approaches rather than only rational choice theory. These three approaches are:

1 the previously mentioned rational choice theory associated with British Home Office criminologists (Clarke and Mayhew, 1980);
2 the control theory of Hirshi (1969) in the USA;
3 a combination of Hindelang's lifestyle theory (Hindelang *et al.*, 1978) and Felson's routine activities theory (Felson, 1986), forged together as 'life-style routines' theory (see Pease, 1994: 664).

Crucial and common to all three approaches is a concern to explain the distribution of crime events. The prospect of effective, scientific 'tracking' of crimes, victims and criminals by place, time of day and season appears to beckon.

'Some things work': the pragmatics of crime prevention

The significance of the situational crime prevention approach for policy makers and implementors, politicians and practitioners does not, however, derive primarily from its theoretical sophistication and purity. Indeed much of its appeal rests on the avowed shift of criminological direction from theory to that of the 'technical fix'. The 'success' of the approach is also linked to the important ideological and organizational work which it does for the state and other corporate interests. It offers the prospect of believing that what 'we' can do can make a difference and thus moves on from criminology's pessimism of the 1970s. We may ask what could be simpler and more commonsensical than to suggest that most people choose rationally to do what they do, be it the act of shopping or stealing. As a consequence, the most sensible approach to preventing crime is first to modify the environment, and second to increase the risks of detection. In a classic formulation of the discourse, Clarke and Mayhew (1980: 1) have defined situational crime measures as follows:

> (1) measures directed at specific forms of crime; (2) which involve the measurement, design or manipulation of the immediate environment in which these crimes occur; (3) in as systematic and permanent a way as possible; (4) so as to reduce the opportunities for these crimes.

Clarke (1995: 109) has also provided a list of the 12 techniques of situational crime prevention so far developed and which 'work'. Clarke groups the techniques into three clusters, namely those which increase the effort of crime prevention, those which increase the risks of offending being detected and those which reduce the reward for offending. Let us briefly look at the 12 techniques, with illustrative examples of specific measures. Under the cluster of those techniques involved in 'increasing the effort', Clarke lists:

1 target hardening (e.g. steering locks in cars, bandit screens in banks);
2 access control (e.g. fenced yards, ID badges);
3 deflecting offenders (e.g. pub or bar location, street closures);
4 controlling facilitators (e.g. gun controls, credit card photos).

Under the cluster of techniques involved in 'increasing the risks' of detection, Clarke then lists the following:

5 entry/exit screening (e.g. baggage screening in airports, automatic ticket gates);
6 formal surveillance (e.g. security guards, speed cameras on some highways);
7 surveillance by employees (e.g. park attendants, CCTV systems);
8 natural surveillance (e.g. street lighting, neighbourhood watch schemes).

Finally, under 'reducing the reward' we have:

9 target removal (e.g. removable car hi-fis, phonecards);
10 identifying property (e.g. property marking, vehicle licensing);
11 removing inducements (e.g. graffiti cleaning, 'bum-proof' benches);
12 rule setting (e.g. customs declaration, income tax returns).

There is clear evidence that such primary or situational techniques have resulted in tangible crime reduction successes (see, for example, Pease, 1994, 1997; Graham and Bennett, 1995). Pease, for example, has noted that the attention given to the immediate context of a crime, such as what shapes immediate behaviour, has proved to be 'remarkably fruitful in generating crime prevention ideas' (Pease, 1994: 664). Furthermore relatively simple albeit well-considered opportunity-reduction measures (such as those noted above by Clarke) are now available in handbooks of techniques and widely used by agencies, both public and private. In Pease's words, 'primary prevention is often possible and sometimes easy' (Pease, 1997: 987).

The other big attraction of situational measures to policy makers and implementors is that you can evaluate them and find out if they 'work'. Clarke (1995) has argued that evaluation of situational measures began in earnest in the late 1970s. One particularly striking early example of 'success' was the installation of CCTV cameras in some of the most victimized stations on the London Underground. Of 19 stations, 4 were fitted with cameras in 1975. In the evaluation a comparison was made between crimes committed before and after in the 4 stations and the change was also contrasted with that in the 15 stations which were not equipped. The results showed a reduction of 27 per cent for thefts compared to the 12 months before. The other stations also had a reduction in theft (although less striking), perhaps due to the deterrent 'halo effect' of the existence of CCTV in the targeted stations. We may note in passing that the CCTV 'eye' – the late modern version of Bentham's 'panopticon'? – is now a taken for granted feature of the contemporary, urban landscape: on some counts then, a clear 'success story'.

Situational crime prevention and its allied theoretical approaches see a key role for the public in both surveillance and target-hardening. Public-police cooperation, for example, is viewed as being crucial to improving police clear-up rates on crime. Informal, 'natural' surveillance methods are also prioritized at times over formal policing, as, for example, with the police-driven neighbourhood watch schemes which may be defined as 'the informal organizations of residents who agree to watch over each other's property and report suspicious activities to the police' (Hope, 1995: 44). In terms of the sheer numbers of schemes, now estimated at around 150,000 in the UK, neighbourhood watch may be judged a success. However, questions remain as to the effectiveness of such schemes in preventing or observing crimes (Bennett, 1990). According to the situational discourse, the public themselves can prevent crime more directly through taking individual responsibility for target-hardening their homes and premises. Furthermore, situational crime prevention theorists and practitioners believe that it is possible to do something about the fear of crime which, they contend, could be as damaging as crime itself. Apart from the obvious emphasis on technical target-hardening, this discourse also supports the popular political notion that 'the community' can actually do something about crime and should not be totally dependent on the state. To some extent this last point further confirms the artificiality of analysing separately situational, multi-agency and 'community' strategies of crime prevention in late modern societies.

Critical appraisal

Young (1994) has argued that the emergence of administrative criminology in general and situational prevention as a crime-fighting technique in particular resulted from the failure of orthodox, positivist criminology both to explain the growth of crime in the affluent post-war period and to counter this growth with effective preventive measures. Young acknowledges that, whatever its theoretical flaws, situational crime prevention coupled with rational choice theory is 'an innovative paradigm of great importance'. Furthermore, 'it has hammered home the earthy facts of space and actual experienced choice at a particular time to a criminology all too content to live in abstractions' (p. 91). This noted, the body of work has not been without its critics. Rock, for example, has acknowledged that rational choice/control theory deals efficiently and provocatively with the commission of crimes in specific contexts. However, it is limited in what it covers, with no interest in questions of history, context, motive and interpretation.

Not least it disembodies rationality from the social context (Rock, 1989: 6). Young has noted that the discourse of situational crime prevention, with its emphasis on target-hardening, has encouraged government policy which ignores the conditions which give rise to crime and thus an imbalance in intervention has resulted. In particular, situational crime prevention ignores the strategy of social crime prevention in the sense of changing social conditions which might generate crime, such as unemployment and poor housing (Young, 1994: 95). This is a key point to which I return in depth later in this book.

It may also be noted that there are some quite specific missing 'targets' from the situational agenda, such as domestic violence, child abuse, crimes of the state and corporate crime. Situational crime prevention has been characterized by an extremely limited focus on street crime. In particular, the criminologist Betsy Stanko (1990) has noted there has been a serious neglect of the crimes between intimates and thus the hidden victimization of women and children due to the focus in situational thinking on crime prevention measures targeted on crimes in the streets and public places rather than crimes in the home. Crimes and criminals are gendered. The dangers and violence that exist within the private sphere pose just as great, if not a greater, threat to women as crimes in the public sphere. Stanko (1990: 4–7) argues:

> Crime prevention advice, including much of the advice about avoiding sexual assault, focuses on the public domain. It is easier to give advice about checking the back seat of your car for intruders, or advising against standing in dimly lit bus stops, than finding ways of advising women not to trust so-called 'trustworthy' men . . . The place where people are supposed to find solace from the perils of the outside world should not be presumed to provide a respite from inter-personal violence. For too many, menace lurks there as well. The prevalence of battering among women's experiences of intimate relationships with men, the growing awareness among adult women of potential and actual sexual danger from male intimates, acquaintances and friends, and the memories of adults of physical and sexual abuse during their childhoods shatter the illusion of the safe home.

Corporate crimes have also been absent from the situational crime prevention agenda (Box, 1983). We may ask why has situational crime prevention ignored the crimes committed by corporate and business people against rivals, stockholders, employees, consumers and the general public? There has been a similar silence with regard to crimes committed by governments, such as crimes against human rights and the exploitation of 'Third World' countries (see Cohen, 1993; McLaughlin, 1996). More mundanely, little attention has been paid by the discourse to the routine crimes of state agencies, such as police corruption. Situational crime prevention's myopia about these crimes of the powerful is surely tied to the fact that its agenda has been largely set by the demands of its patron, either the state or the private corporation. There is the danger of research into situational crime prevention becoming a fertile ground for the blossoming of market-driven projects in which sponsors set the terms of the research agenda and may 'own' the results (Hughes, 1996c). However, this is not to argue that the techniques of situational crime prevention might not be developed to address the crimes of such powerful players as private corporations (see Braithwaite, 1996).

More generally situational crime prevention has been accused of 'victim-blaming' (Walklate, 1996) in that the key to an understanding of criminal victimization, according to rational choice theory, seems to lie in large measure in the 'precipitative' behaviour of the victimized individual, community or environment, such as walking on one's own at night on the largely deserted streets. The term used to describe this explanation is 'victim precipitation'.

Furthermore, it has been argued that the emphasis of the situational agenda on the environment-centred techniques of 'target-hardening' and 'designing-out crime' may accelerate wider trends of community segregation, attacks on civil liberties and social exclusion and further privatize previously public environments, encouraging a 'fortress mentality' towards our routine lives. Norris and Armstrong's (1997) pioneering research into the social construction of suspicion and intervention in CCTV systems lends empirical evidence to such fears of social exclusion resulting from these supposedly purely technical 'fixes' to reduce crimes, victimization and incivilities. In contrast to most 'evaluative' research on the situational technique of CCTV, Norris and Armstrong focus less on crime reduction outcomes and more on the processes involved in selecting and constructing 'suspicious' categories of people by the CCTV operators. In other words, Norris and Armstrong address the questions of who and what is watched and warrants intervention. Their work effectively shows that CCTV is not just a neutral technology merely recording what comes into view but instead involves a process of selective and discriminatory decision making from CCTV operators. One consequence of CCTV in city centres may thus be the amplification of differential and discriminatory policing rather than a contribution to social justice through the reduction of victimization. I return in greater depth to this crucial theme of the wider consequences of such strategies in Chapter 7.

The situational and rational choice perspective is of importance in taking seriously the need to understand some aspects of crime prevention from the viewpoint of the victim or criminal as actor. However, it ignores the wider contexts behind such decision-making processes, perhaps because of the technicist fixation with coming up with pragmatic and immediate situational policy measures. Furthermore, I would endorse Coleman and Moynihan's call for a broader picture to be drawn about crime prevention in terms of the creation of a 'political economy' of crime. For example, in the UK in the 1990s, we need to examine and understand the impact of years of policies establishing the primacy of free markets and the selective rolling back of the (welfare) state. It is also important to grasp the potential significance of very high rates of unemployment in certain areas and the increasingly unequal distribution of income, wealth and life-chances (Coleman and Moynihan, 1996: 139–41). Not least, we should not underestimate the dangers of the promise of a 'crime-free' urban space (Sutton, 1994: 11) in terms of the likely cost to civil liberties, the public sharing of spaces and tolerance of diversity of technically 'effective' crime prevention.

Explaining the hegemony of the situational crime prevention discourse

Marx (1995), Garland (1996) and O'Malley (1992, 1994) have offered some compelling sociological reasons for the hegemony of the neo-liberal situational crime prevention discourse in late modern societies. In particular, these sociological commentators locate the success of situational crime prevention in terms of wider cultural and political processes at work in contemporary society.

Gary Marx has argued that we are witnessing the emergence of what he terms an 'engineered society' as a result of the new technological revolutions, of which situational crime prevention techniques are a specific manifestation (Marx, 1995). According to him, 'Developments in electronics, computerization, artificial intelligence, biochemistry, architecture, materials science, and many related fields have led to a thriving and technically based social-control and crime prevention industry' (p. 226). The goal of this industry is to eliminate or limit violations by controlling the physical environment. Marx (p. 228–35) notes six ideal types of social engineering strategies:

1 target removal (e.g. the notion of the cashless society or large pepper grinder in restaurants to prevent easy theft!);
2 target devaluation (reduce/eliminate value to anyone but authorized users, for example self-destruct radios);
3 target insulation (e.g. sky-walks which shield the consuming pedestrian from the 'dangerous' streets below: Calgary, for example, has six miles of skywalks for shoppers connecting 110 buildings);
4 offender incapacitation (e.g. through the use of immobilizers such as gas bombs);
5 offender exclusion (e.g. via electronic location);
6 offence, offender and target identification.

For Marx, such techniques have great popular and policy appeal in that they appear to offer the equivalent of the 'silver bullet' solution to crime of the 1960s' TV cowboy hero 'The Lone Ranger'. Marx does admit that such techniques may lead at times to equitable results given technology's possible neutrality regarding class and other social categories. However they may also lead to dangerous unintended consequences. For example, the use of access codes for appliances may mean that crimes of burglary get converted into crimes of robbery or kidnapping since the offender will not be able to appropriate property without first getting the active compliance of the owner/victim in disclosing the code of the property in question (Marx, 1995: 243).

Marx goes on to contend that, according to the ethos of this new crime prevention industry, 'The criminal justice system is perceived as an anachronism whose agents serve only to shoot the wounded after the battle is over' (Marx, 1995: 227). Thus, unlike the crime prevention strategies associated with both positivism and classicism, this new industry and its discourse avoids 'messing' with the human subject. This analysis resonates, somewhat ironically, with Ron Clarke's own speculation, as situational crime prevention's most famous apostle, on the future work of 'situationist' criminologists. Clarke predicts a greater involvement of crime prevention experts with technicists from the private sector and notes the challenge this would open up: 'If they are successful in these settings, however, they may need to adopt as mentors not sociologists and academics, but problem solvers such as traffic engineers and public health professionals' (Clarke, 1995: 139). Unlike Clarke, Marx is sceptical about the potential of target-hardening techniques as a solution to the problem of crime. 'The search for the silver bullet represents a failure to look for the deeper causes of disorder' (Marx, 1995: 246).

Let's now examine the diagnosis of the 'crisis of penal modernism' offered by David Garland (1996) and its implications for our understanding of the 'success' of the situational crime prevention discourse in the current era. According to Garland, crime is now a prominent fact of modern life and is no longer seen as an aberration or abnormal event. Instead, crime is a 'routine part of modern consciousness, an everyday risk to be assessed and managed in much the same way that we deal with road traffic' (p. 446). The recognition of this routine fact of life has in turn led to a series of transformations in official perceptions, modes of governmental action about crime and the philosophy and practices of criminal justice agencies. What has emerged from this series of transformations is a new strategy, compared to that of the positivist-inspired 'penal-welfare' strategy which preceded it (see Chapter 3). This new strategy is driven by the aim to produce modest improvements at the margins, better management of risks and resources, reduction of the fear of crime, reduction of criminal justice expenditure and greater support for victims. In Garland's words, these are 'less than heroic policy objectives' (p. 447) but are developments which chime closely with the chorus of the situational crime prevention discourse. (I argue later in Chapters 6 and 7 that Garland may be neglectful of the importance of a resurgent and possibly regressive 'heroism' developed around the search for community and public safety associated with communitarianism.)

It is suggested by Garland that the discourse of situational crime prevention represents a leading component of 'the new criminologies of everyday life'. In this new official strategy, crime is seen as a risk to be managed. Garland goes on to argue that when crime is viewed from this forward-looking perspective as an aggregate risk rather than the backward-looking punishment view of offending as individual wrong-doing, significant moral consequences follow. In particular, Garland points to the development of new techniques for acting upon the problem of crime by means of programmes of practical action beyond the state apparatus and into the private institutions and lives of individuals in civil society (Garland, 1996: 451). We see then the further penetration and absorption of crime controls into the everyday routines of the 'at risk' and 'risky' citizen or what has been termed 'situational man' (Cornish and Clarke, 1986: 4).

Finally, O'Malley (1992) has asked the crucial question of why situational crime prevention has become *so* popular *so* rapidly in countries like the USA and the UK. His thesis is that it is not explicable in terms of its efficiency as a technique over other criminologies since its 'success' is by no means uncontested despite the claims of Clarke (1995), noted earlier. Nor, according to O'Malley, is the case against 'social' criminologies, such as the Chicago School, proven. Instead, O'Malley argues that situational crime prevention's great influence must be explained in terms of its relationship to broader political programmes and strategies. In particular, O'Malley points out its 'attractions to economic rationalist, neo-conservative and New Right programmes' (1992: 263). Thus O'Malley contends that situational crime prevention links directly to the core ideological assumptions of the New Right and the two directions of population management, namely increasing punitiveness with respect to offenders and, with respect to victims, the displacement of 'socialized risk management' with what O'Malley refers to as 'privatized prudentialism' (p. 263). Let's unpack this complex argument further. The term 'socialized risk management' refers to the shared and collective commitment to reducing the dangers, costs and risks of criminal victimization for the whole population in a given locality through support for appropriate public services such as the police and probation by means of taxation. By way of contrast, 'privatized prudentialism' refers to the strategy of each individual (if capable) of being prudent in a private way about managing the risks associated with criminal victimization through, for example, investing in security devices for the home, personal alarms and even payment for private security guards for their own housing area.

The effect of this latter process, according to O'Malley, is to separate still further, to the point of divorce, crime control policy from wider questions of social justice. Now it is assumed that individuals are free to commit or not commit crime (in contrast to positivism's claim that cause reduces responsibility) and free to protect themselves or not from criminal victimization. The elimination of cause as a criminological concern is thus promoted in this discourse. In turn, this discourse restores responsibility (instead of cause) to a central position in the politics of crime control with clear effects on punishment. The logical corollary of situational crime prevention from the New Right's ideological position is 'just desert' punitive sentencing for offenders. Accordingly, prevention is relocated as the responsibility of the victim and the costs of prevention are also shifted to the private sphere, opening the probability of a 'user pays system of policing security' (O'Malley, 1992: 266). There appears to be a close correspondence between this discourse and the ideology of the New Right. I would contend that this approach developed so much influence, so quickly, due to the primacy of New Right thought and neo-liberal governments since the 1970s in countries like the UK and the USA. However, we should not assume that this sort of crime prevention has no place in left-inspired strategies of crime control, as evidenced in the Left Realist agenda (see Chapter 6).

The sociological interpretation of the situational crime prevention discourse offered by Marx, Garland and O'Malley provides us with a vital means of explaining its current ascendancy in neo-liberal 'market societies' (see Chapter 7). Not least, we have the beginnings of an immodest sociology of crime prevention, highlighting the economic, cultural and political contexts and ideological and policy consequences of the theory and practice of crime prevention. As a consequence, and despite its tangible and measurable successes and its potential to attach itself to other politico-economic formations than that of neo-liberalism, we may wish to be sceptical about situational crime prevention's claims to offer an apolitical, technical fix to such pressing problems as crime and disorder, and criminalization and victimization. In particular, the importance of wider structural forces to criminal victimization has been absent from the situational crime prevention agenda. However, such concerns have not been ignored in all criminological investigations of crime nor in all strategies of crime prevention as Chapters 5, 6 and 7 will show.

Summary

This chapter has examined the main elements to one of the key developments in both the theory and practice of crime control in late modern societies. In particular, this chapter first explored the historical roots of this crime prevention discourse around the Home Office's 'administrative criminology' in Britain and the techniques of target-hardening and surveillance developed in the USA. Second, the key conceptual tenets of the discourse and the specific influence of rational choice theory were examined. The chapter then focused on the policy and practical consequences of this discourse, addressing the tangible 'successes' of its preventive techniques. Finally, a critical appraisal of situational crime prevention was offered which focused on the politico-ideological context in which the discourse needs to be located.

Further reading

Clarke, R. (1992) *Situational Crime Prevention: Successful Case Studies*. New York: Harrow & Heston.

Clarke, R. (1995) 'Situational Crime Prevention', in M. Tonry and D. Farrington (eds), *Building a Safer Society: Strategic Approaches to Crime*. Chicago: University of Chicago Press.

O'Malley, P. (1992) 'Risk, Power and Crime Prevention', *Economy and Society*, 21, 3: 251–68.

chapter five

Multi-agency partnerships: managing corporate crime prevention

Introduction

This chapter examines the main features of multi-agency crime prevention strategies. Such initiatives will be viewed as, for the most part, elements of a 'top-down', managerialist project emanating from the central state during the 1980s and 1990s in the UK. However, this project has also involved the 'local delivery' of crime prevention by means of 'multi-agency' partnerships between statutory agencies (such as the police and local authority agencies), private business and, at times, public initiatives such as 'the community' in various 'watch' schemes. In both the academic literature and policy circles, the terms 'multi-agency' and 'community' crime prevention have often been used interchangeably. This is understandable on a number of counts. First, the term 'community' retains its feelgood factor and is thus a useful legiti-mating, rhetorical device in crime prevention discourses. Second, and less cynically, some multi-agency prevention initiatives have sought to adopt a *social* crime prevention approach and thus in a sense involve members of local communities in their work. However, I will argue that this slippage between the terms 'multi-agency' and 'community' is somewhat problem-atic. It glosses over the key feature of multi-agency crime prevention which is that it is chiefly a 'top-down', neo-corporatist strategy from both central and local state regimes. In this strategy situational crime prevention tech-niques predominate and there is minimal 'bottom-up' communal partici-pation and minimal popular democratic 'ownership'. Accordingly, I wish to separate out the detailed examination of multi-agency crime prevention and 'community' crime prevention into two distinct chapters. The claims of 'community' crime prevention, and in particular contemporary, seemingly anti-statist communitarian 'solutions' will therefore be chiefly discussed in Chapter 6. Again this is not to deny the vital interconnections between situ-ational, multi-agency and 'community' crime prevention discourses as part of the contemporary debate around crime and insecurity across late modern societies.

The discussion in this chapter will be structured in terms of the following sections. I first examine how multi-agency crime prevention may be defined and distinguished from other forms of prevention. Second, an overview of the central government policy on strategies of multi-agency crime preven-tion in the UK during the decades of the 1980s and 1990s is presented. An outline of the major elements of the academic critique of multi-agency crime prevention follows, and finally the research carried out in the 1990s in the UK on the potentialities and complex character of local crime prevention and community safety strategies is critically examined.

What is multi-agency crime prevention?

> In as much as crime within local communities is likely to be sustained by a range of factors – in housing, education, recreation etc. – the agen-cies and organisations who are responsible for, or capable of, affecting those factors, ought to join in common cause so that they are not work-ing at cross-purposes or sustaining crime inadvertently.
>
> (Hope and Shaw, 1988: 13)

> Multi-agency intervention is the planned, co-ordinated response of the major social agencies to problems of crime and incivilities . . . Social control in industrial societies is, by its very nature, multi-agency.
>
> (Young, 1991: 155)

The above statements from, respectively, two Home Office 'administrative criminologists' and the major 'Left Realist' criminologist confirm that multi-agency crime prevention now has the status of a taken for granted 'fact of life' in the crime control business in the UK. Indeed the great political appeal of the call for multi-agency crime prevention lies in its apparent 'obviousness' and simple 'good sense'. The movement to multi-agency rather than single-agency intervention implies that probation, education, employment, social work and other 'family' services, health, housing, and 'private' bodies such as charities and business, as well as the police, all have a role to play in an extended preventive continuum. Examples of such multi-agency interventions would include both local authority – and privately-run CCTV initiatives, play/sports schemes during school holidays, activity-based projects with (potential) young offenders, educational projects on drugs etc. However, it will become evident during this chapter that the exact contours of multi-agency crime prevention, not to mention the 'success' of such approaches, remain somewhat unclear.

The most influential, pioneering piece of research on multi-agency crime prevention in the UK during the 1980s was that conducted by a research team based at the University of Lancaster and Middlesex Polytechnic (Blagg *et al.*, 1988; Sampson *et al.*, 1988; Pearson *et al.*, 1992). These researchers began by identifying two traditional and untested ways of conceptualizing multi-agency cooperation by both supporters and critics of the approach, namely the 'benevolent' and the 'conspiratorial' readings. The benevolent view, shared by supporters of multi-agency cooperation, saw the idea of creating a consensus between different agencies (with traditionally divergent ideologies and different goals) as an unproblematic 'good thing'. On the other hand, the conspiratorial view, associated with radical critics on the left, identified these developments with an extension of both coercive and more subtle, ideological social control from the state. However, the research headed by Pearson on the actual implementation of such prevention strategies in parts of London and a northern town questioned the adequacy of either of these polarized views ('benevolent' versus 'conspiratorial'). Instead their work highlighted the centrality of power differentials between the major state agencies involved and the importance of sectional differences within existing communities 'subject' to such multi-agency cooperation.

Overall, Pearson *et al.* (1992) found multi-agency cooperation in crime prevention to be problematic on a number of crucial fronts. In particular, the police agenda on how to address the question of preventing crime seemed to be dominant over that of other agencies, such as probation. Multi-agency cooperation also appeared to seriously compromise the role of other, more welfare-oriented agencies like social work. There also appeared to be little consultation with the communities in question which raised important questions about the appropriateness of the use of the word 'community' to describe what in retrospect may be more accurately designated as 'corporate' multi-agency crime prevention, the meaning of which I explain later.

This pioneering research has left a profoundly sceptical mark on subsequent research sorties into this area of crime prevention.

Deciphering the trends in multi-agency crime prevention in the UK

At present there have been few attempts to 'map' how the fine-sounding call to multi-agency arms has impacted across the range of localities in the UK, and this chapter will begin such a comparative mapping. In some senses this task may appear quite straightforward. However, I will argue that such an evaluation necessarily enters the deep waters of social theory in that no research and evaluation can be stripped of its theoretical clothing. Furthermore, it is impossible to discuss multi-agency crime prevention, or what is increasingly termed community safety, in the UK and beyond without engaging in a debate about the changing modalities of state power in relation to civil society and 'the public'. Indeed, notions of 'local' and 'central' state are becoming increasingly problematic with the rise of the 'dispersed' state, as a result of which we are witnessing not a diminution of the state's role but rather an extension of particular forms of state power, albeit through new and unfamiliar means (Clarke, 1996a). This development is well illustrated by the example of state power being exercised through indirect rather than direct agency, as in the current fad of preventive 'partnerships against crime' in the UK.

In this new era, responsibility for setting up and running multi-agency crime prevention initiatives at the local level is increasingly put out to 'tender', inviting bids from rival competitors. In the UK, these competing bodies are often private companies or more often charities such as Crime Concern or the National Association for the Care and Rehabilitation of Offenders (NACRO), both of which are sponsored by the Home Office. However, the establishment of such partnerships made up of a mix of state agencies, 'third sector' organizations, business and members of 'the public' does not necessarily diminish the power and influence of the central state. The very reverse situation may be the case.

It would be misleading to assume that the situation in the UK is unique or peculiar. Multi-agency 'community' crime prevention would appear to be a phenomenon whose 'time has come' on the global stage. The 'global' arrival of such a crime prevention strategy is captured in the following apocalyptic statement from the leading American criminologist Dennis Rosenbaum: 'We are entering the heyday of community crime prevention. Never before have the notions of citizen involvement in crime prevention received such widespread support' (Rosenbaum, 1988: 323). Such hyperbolic statements are not rare one-offs in the current academic and policy discourses on crime prevention. The significant place now accorded to multi-agency and 'community' crime prevention in the global context of crime control (albeit possibly in terms of rhetoric versus reality) is further evidenced in the United Nations Congress on the Prevention of Crime and the Treatment of Offenders' resolution of 1990. This resolution stated its aim was to bring together 'those with responsibility for planning and development, for family and health, employment and training, housing and social services, leisure activities, schools, the police and the justice system, in order to deal with the conditions that generate crime' (United Nations, 1991). In passing we may note that this resolution combines a multi-agency collaboration strategy with the quest for 'ultimate' causes, unlike the philosophy underpinning situational crime prevention in its purest form (see Chapter 4).

In the UK since the 1980s a similar position advocating the merits of multi-agency partnerships has been adopted on regular occasions by government ministers and officials. Let's briefly examine the official central governmental 'policy' on multi-agency crime prevention in the UK during the 1980s and 1990s and then examine how this policy has impacted locally across the UK in the 1990s.

The managerialization of crime prevention

The Conservative government of 1979 in the UK was elected on an explicit law and order 'ticket'. In the words of its party manifesto, 'We will spend more on fighting crime, whilst we economize elsewhere' (Conservative Party, 1979). However, most commentators agreed that after a decade or more of this law and order commitment, it was difficult to ignore the failures of law and order not least in the escalating official crime rate and rates of re-offending (Downes and Morgan, 1994). Despite these failures, penal populism and crime control through incapacitation continue to hold sway in the debate on law and order in the UK (see Bowring, 1997, on New Labour's 'tough' enforcement agenda). Alongside this emotionally expressive populist politics, the discourse of managerialism has come to play an increasingly important part in the restructuring of criminal justice. Indeed it has come to affect the organization and operational work of the police and other agencies of criminal justice and prevention in novel and unprecedented ways. McLaughlin and Muncie have plotted the rolling programme of privatization, deregulation and contracting-out of services which were previously delivered by the Beveridgean welfare state in the UK. As a consequence, 'prevention' is a means by which the state can absolve itself from complete responsibility: the 'fault' is 'ours'. By the mid-1990s, the criminal justice system and the wider agencies of social control were thus no longer immune from the chill winds of managerialism. A new strategy was unveiled which redefined the ownership of the crime problem and promoted managerial solutions (McLaughlin and Muncie, 1994: 117).

Pollitt (1993: 1) has defined managerialism as 'a set of beliefs and practices, at the core of which burns the seldom-tested assumption that better management will prove an effective solvent for a wide range of economic and social ills'. This 'solvent' has been applied to criminal justice agencies in several important ways. For example, 'policing by objectives' became a fashionable model of policing in the UK during the 1980s and a managerialist ethos is to the fore in the current obsession with 'mission statements', 'performance indicators', measurable 'objectives', 'customer' surveys etc. in the UK's police forces.

Of particular importance to the fate of crime prevention and community safety initiatives was the decision by the UK government in the mid-1990s to establish measurable national objectives for policing. This policy decision may marginalize social crime prevention strategies still further, given the difficulty of 'measuring' their success in terms of readily quantifiable performance indicators when compared to traditional reactive policing and the more easily measurable situational preventive techniques. The future mandate of the public police may thus be much more focused on quasi-militaristic public order control and 'serious' crime investigation at the cost of any of the 'social service' and preventive dimensions to British policing.

However, at the same time as there has been pressure for the police to be more businesslike and focused in their activities, the last decade has also seen a growing concern in the Home Office for the police and other agencies of social control to work together and form crime prevention 'partnerships' with the public. In passing, it should be noted that there is a seeming contradiction between this drive towards 'community policing' and 'community safety' and the developments noted above and in Chapter 1 with regard to the cross-party policy drift to penal retribution. That said, Jones *et al.* (1994) may be partially correct in their thesis that recent years have seen the rise of a 'new paradigm' regarding crime prevention. As a result of this way of thinking, the old paradigm that the only proper response to crime is punishment is challenged if not replaced in academic and official circles by the belief that retribution and punishment will not reduce the aggregate level of crime. Consequently, the reduction of crime must be seen as a separate objective from the punishment of offenders. Out of this paradigm shift emerges the current discourse on crime prevention and community safety. Jones *et al.* go on to argue that this way of thinking has had comparatively little influence on popular culture and 'Politicians of all parties find it easy and convenient to appeal to the old way of thinking' (pp. 302–3). Thus, alongside the new discourse on crime prevention, the 'old' but resurgent approach of punitive retribution continues to be a central plank of law and order politics in the UK and elsewhere in neo-liberal societies.

To return to the discourse on 'partnership', such partnerships between the police, the public and other agencies in crime prevention and consultation may be viewed as being part of what has been termed the 'Government's accountability package' during the past two decades in the UK (Morgan,

1992). In effect, this package has bypassed any democratic structures of accountability and, instead, 'espoused a model of police accountability as stewardship with the police consulting more widely before taking decisions and providing fuller *ex post facto* explanations of events' (Morgan and Swift, 1988: 427).

The coming of the Morgan Report and the 'partnership' approach

The Conservative government's 1984 *Circular (8/84): Crime Prevention* (Home Office, 1984) may be seen as a watershed in crime prevention policy given its emphasis on the principle that crime prevention must be accepted as a significant and integral goal of public policy, both centrally and locally. In its words, 'Every individual citizen and all those agencies whose policies and practices can influence the extent of crime should make their contribution. Preventing crime is a task for the whole community' (p. 1). In this circular, particular stress is placed on the need for a coordinated approach and joint strategies involving partnerships against crime. Although more often rhetoric than reality around the country (see below), the idea of multi-agency 'partnership' in crime prevention had clearly arrived in Britain.

By the end of the decade, the Home Office circular *Tackling Crime* (Home Office, 1989) showed the further development of the partnership and community orientation to crime prevention in the Home Office. Particular attention was given in the circular to the problem of coordination, or rather the lack of it, between agencies which made up the criminal justice system. This circular in turn led the way for what was to prove the key inspiration for much of the subsequent local government, multi-agency and seemingly 'social' crime prevention schemes of the 1990s, namely the so-called Morgan Report of 1991 (Home Office, 1991).

The formal title of the Morgan Report is the Home Office's Standing Conference on Crime Prevention report *Safer Communities: The Local Delivery of Crime Prevention through the Partnership Approach*. The main thrust of the Morgan Report was that the concept of 'crime prevention' is somewhat limiting in scope and has generally been police-driven with other agencies having only a marginal stake in it. In its words:

> The term *'crime prevention'* is often narrowly interpreted and this reinforces the view that it is solely the responsibility of the police. On the other hand, the term *'community safety'*, is open to wider interpretation and could encourage greater participation from all sections of the community in the fight against crime.
>
> (Home Office, 1991: 3)

· Effectively, 'community safety' as a guiding idea was heralded as a way of moving beyond a 'situational' definition of crime prevention to a broader 'social' definition. Figures 5.1 and 5.2 are adapted from the Morgan Report and offer a good illustration of its concern to promote social measures for improved community safety. Figure 5.1 is an example of 'a balanced portfolio of community safety activities, some short-term, some long-term' (Home Office, 1991: 31). Figure 5.2 gives an example of a portfolio of activities recommended to local multi-agency partnerships on the particular issue of young people and crime. While acknowledging that the case for a multi-agency partnership approach was hardly tested, the Morgan Report noted strangely that the case for partnership was 'virtually unchallenged'. It also emphasized that crime prevention at the time of the report was seen as a peripheral issue to the major agencies and a 'truly core activity for none of them' (Home Office, 1991: 3). In order to correct this major defect in current arrangements, the Report suggested that six key elements needed to be addressed (namely: structure, leadership, information, identity, durability and resources) in order to improve the organization and delivery of multi-agency crime prevention.

The Morgan Report then went on to argue that the local authority was 'the natural focus for co-ordinating, in collaboration with the police, the broad range of activities directed at improving community safety... Any meaningful local structure for crime prevention must relate to the local democratic structure' (Home Office, 1991: 4). The Morgan Report thus supported the notion that local authorities be given the statutory duty (and therefore the resources) to coordinate crime prevention/community safety strategies for their locality. The Report also argued that sufficient resources to make this change must be forthcoming from central government. In passing, it may be noted that the recommendations regarding both local authorities' statutory role and resourcing were not taken up by the Conservative government during the 1990s, probably due to its concerns over costs and its ideological hostility to local government *per se*. By the late 1990s, the Labour administration in the UK is proposing a statutory partnership between the police and local authorities, rather than Morgan's recommendation of a leadership role for local authorities. Labour's proposals, as part of a Crime and Disorder Act for 1998, have also stated that no extra resources would be given to local authorities for their new statutory responsibilities for crime prevention. This noted, much of the Morgan Report philosophy of partnerships, multi-agency collaboration and audits is to the fore in Labour's current crime prevention policy proposals (Home Office, 1997).

Like many critical reports in the past, the Morgan Report was shelved by the Conservative government during the 1990s or, at best, used quite selectively. This is not, however, to deny its significant effect on local authorities since its publication. Most have now 'signed up' to the new rhetoric of multi-agency partnerships and community safety and increasing numbers have dedicated posts of 'community safety coordinator' (Hughes, 1997c). The Morgan Report comes across for the most part as a report written by

Tackling the causes of crime:

- family support initiatives
- youth programmes
- community development programmes and neighbourhood initiatives
- pre-school programmes
- alcohol and drug misuse prevention schemes
- education and school-based programmes
- work with offenders and their families
- employment and training programmes
- debt counselling

Reducing the opportunities for crime to be committed:

- improved security in homes, public buildings and business premises
- improved lighting in streets and public areas
- improved security and design of residential areas, city centres and car parks
- security considerations in planning and managing public transport
- safety considerations in the management of licensed premises
- good management and delivery of local services
- adequate levels of preventive patrolling

Tackling specific crime problems:

- domestic burglary
- domestic violence
- auto crime
- racially motivated crime
- crimes against children
- crimes against the elderly

Helping victims of crime and reducing the fear of crime:

- victim support schemes
- self-protection initiatives
- securing positive publicity for successful initiatives

Figure 5.1 A portfolio of community safety activities: some examples
Source: Home Office (1991).

(local authority and police) officers for officers. In particular, the discussion of how these multi-agency officer groups relate to issues of democratic accountability was cursory in nature.

The language and rhetoric of both partnership and community safety have

---

Young people and crime

- improving leisure and recreational opportunities in areas of high youth crime
- designing specific initiatives to engage 'hard to reach' young people
- reviewing the policies and operations of all organisations concerned with young people to ensure that the scope for preventive measures has been identified and acted on
- designing initiatives to promote individual and social responsibility amongst young people particularly in high crime and disadvantaged areas
- ensuring access to adequate educational, training and employment opportunities for all young people
- initiatives to tackle specific problems faced by young people e.g. homelessness, drugs misuse
- initiatives to deal with specific crimes committed by young people e.g. shoplifting, vehicle crime, vandalism

---

Figure 5.2 Portfolio of community safety activities
Source: Home Office (1991).

become very prominent across all major political parties in the UK and in the Home Office circulars and pamphlets on crime prevention. For example, the 1994 Home Office *Partners Against Crime* pamphlet seemed to be calling for what may be inelegantly termed 'the citizenization of crime control' or what Garland (1996) has termed a 'strategy of responsibilization'. In other words, citizens are being called upon to play a crucial role in crime prevention through their actions. As in other social policy areas, there is an appeal to the much vaunted but ill-defined 'active citizen' to play a key role; in this case, in both crime surveillance and 'policing'. The Home Office pamphlet confidently asserted that 'the power of partnerships in beating crime' was proved and three complementary partnerships were presented as initiatives to be launched or given further encouragement nationally in 1995: the already well-established neighbourhood watch schemes, 'Street Watch' and 'Neighbourhood Constables'. It was street watch which was the most contentious 'community partnership' in crime prevention. The catchword, according to the pamphlet, was 'vigilant' although critics feared that there was a great risk of an extra 'e' on the end of the word. The vagueness of the scheme was perhaps best captured in the 'soundbite' of the then Home Secretary (Michael Howard) that street watch for the participating citizens involved 'walking with a purpose'. Perhaps the most telling feature of this Home Office initiative was that all the schemes were voluntary and low cost. In a similar way, Loveday has noted that much of the central government proposals for 'community' crime prevention suggest that 'voluntary community action should replace collective provision', resulting in 'a voluntary surveillance society' (Loveday, 1994: 193).

The 'mixed economy' approach of central government

It would be misguided to assume that the central government initiatives on crime prevention *in toto* can be explained in terms of mass mobilization of a new volunteer citizens' army of watching and walking neighbours! In the last decades of the twentieth century in the UK there have been a number of important developments which have led to significant, selective funding of successful 'bids' for multi-agency community safety projects. A similar process of bidding and selective funding is apparent across many other 'urban renewal' and social policy programmes in the UK (Hughes and Lewis, 1998). More than any other central government initiatives, the examples of the Home Office's 'Five Towns' initiative in 1986 and, from 1988 to 1995, phase one of the 'Safer Cities' programme gave concrete expression to the central government drive to have *locally-based but centrally-driven* multi-agency (and largely mixed 'social' and 'situational') crime prevention projects. The latter programme resulted in the creation of 3600 schemes across England and Wales at a total cost of £22 million. However, even such centrally-driven initiatives may also manifest a degree of 'relative autonomy' beyond the control of the central state authority. That noted, there are now most definitely 'winners' and 'losers' in the competitive tendering process for financial support for urgent urban renewal, increasingly under the umbrella of crime prevention. The charity/business and 'quango' NACRO, for example, proudly trumpeted its success in 1995 of having 'won' direction of 14 out of the total of 30 Safer Cities initiatives (*NACRO News* no. 14, 1995).

Both the Five Towns and Safer Cities initiatives arose out of Home Office officials' and researchers' wish to promote multi-agency crime prevention. Such initiatives were to employ both situational and social approaches, within the confines laid down by the New Right credo of the government of the time on the virtues of private-sector managerialism and the distrust of local democratic government (Tilley, 1994). As a consequence, both the programmes in question gave a secondary role to local authorities and a primary role to the central department of the Home Office. As with many of central government's policy initiatives in the UK during the last decades of the twentieth century, business representatives have been accorded 'an almost oracle status' (Loveday, 1994: 185). It was certainly hoped by central government that in the long-term ongoing Safer Cities projects would be sponsored by local business. At the time of writing, a new 'phase two' of the Safer Cities programme has begun and once again local authorities have been denied any key coordinating role. Instead the responsibility for the direct running of the successful schemes has been given to two charities-cum-'quangos', namely Crime Concern and NACRO (Loveday, 1994: 198). Here is evidence once again of the broader reworking of state power across the public domain. This entails both greater centralization of financial control and object-setting and a dispersal of agency through sub-contracting delegated authority. The end result has been the creation of new disciplinary relationships between local and central agencies and the public (see Clarke *et al.*, 1998; Hughes *et al.*, 1997).

'Don't believe the hype'? The academic critique of multi-agency crime prevention

During the 1980s and early 1990s, a body of academic work built up around multi-agency crime prevention in particular and trends in social control more generally which was deeply sceptical of the 'success' and 'progressive' claims of these new strategies of crime control. There were arguably two major 'camps', 'sceptical pluralism' and 'radical totalitarianism' (Hughes, 1997a). In this section I begin with the mainstream sceptical pluralist evaluation and critique of multi-agency crime prevention. The more ambitious 'globalizing' thesis of radical totalitarianism will then be discussed.

Sceptical pluralism

Most mainstream sociological and criminological research on crime prevention is sceptical about the achievements of such policy and practice initiatives as multi-agency crime prevention. At the same time, it avoids any strict adherence to a monocausal theory, preferring the appeal of an unspoken pluralist approach for the interpretation of these trends. The body of work is largely empirically-driven and speaks with a fairly uniform voice of scepticism, if not the 'impossibilism' of more radical critics, about both UK and international trends in multi-agency crime prevention, community policing and community consultation (see, for example, Weatheritt, 1986; Bottoms, 1990; Morgan, 1992; Pease, 1994). According to this perspective, the achievements of community policing and multi-agency crime prevention have been very limited to date, with success largely rhetorical in character rather than tangible in its effects. As noted in Chapter 4, certain commentators, such as Bottoms and Wiles (1994) and Pease (1994), do highlight the tangible achievements of multi-agency *situational* prevention in particular. That said, the overall message is that crime prevention of a more ambitious 'social' and genuinely 'inter-agency' kind remains both marginal to the work of most agencies and unproven as a 'successful' approach. This conclusion may reflect two closely related problems in the sceptical pluralist canon: it assumes the distinction between rhetoric and reality is tenable and rhetoric has no useful significance.

For Ekblom and Pease (1995), multi-agency 'community' crime prevention is, in reality, generally a composite of situational and offender-oriented approaches. They note that most so-called 'community' crime prevention is 'confusing and elusive for evaluative purposes . . . The terms 'social' and 'community' are unsatisfactorily loose and difficult to pin down . . . the description of a crime prevention project as social or communal often flags a set of values as much as a set of methods and causal mechanisms' (p. 601). Many evaluations in turn have too often 'gone' for what Ekblom and Pease term 'consolation prizes' such as reductions in fear and incivilities rather than crime reduction *per se* (p. 598). It is thus argued that social and multi-agency crime prevention initiatives tend to marginalize crime itself. Pease (1994: 688) cites the example of the Safer Cities initiative in England and Wales in the 1980s and 1990s as illustrative of this tendency where two out of the three stated goals of the initiative were not about crime prevention *per se* but instead about lessening the fear of crime and creating safer cities where economic enterprise and commercial life could flourish. It should be noted, however, that the first stated goal of the Safer Cities initiative was that of crime reduction in the chosen areas. Ekblom and Pease also point to the problem of how to disentangle the effects of such multi-agency social crime prevention from those of, for example, housing schemes, environmental improvement and poverty alleviation. This may be said to be the problem of 'the company it keeps' (Ekblom and Pease, 1995: 608).

Viewing Ekblom and Pease's position more sceptically, it may be that they should recognize and accept the limits of what the pseudo-science of evaluation can achieve. Evaluation studies continue to be dominated by what may be termed the quasi-experimental model of research. In this model 'measurements' are taken before and after the implementation of the crime prevention measure (e.g. traffic calmers, CCTV, improved street lighting or whatever) and any observed difference is then usually attributed to the new crime prevention initiative. It is part of the cult of scientific measurement which persists in policy circles as well as reflecting what Mike Maguire (1994: 236) terms 'the power of numbers'.

Such sympathetic critics of crime prevention initiatives as Pease have acknowledged that there is a danger of suffocating in a climate of impossibilism and pessimism, resulting in a new 'nothing works' mentality. Apparent failures may be the result of there not always being the motive to prevent crime, such as the unwillingness of car companies in the past to make cars more difficult to steal. We may also note the low level of resourcing for crime prevention in the UK police forces in the late twentieth century despite its supposed primacy as a policing policy goal. This mismatch has led Weatheritt to write of there being two histories, one a glorious tale based on official reports and statements and the other of routine day-to-day policing in which crime prevention is 'an activity performed on the sidelines while the main action takes place elsewhere' (Weatheritt, 1986: 49). Much multi-agency crime prevention is no more than public relations.

I noted in Chapter 4 that some prevention measures do 'work'. For example, the introduction of token-operated and magnetic card-operated fuel meters in domestic premises by local authorities led to fewer domestic burglaries in parts of the UK. Pease (1994, 1997) for one rejects the extreme pessimism and points to the success of the Kirkholt Burglary Prevention Project in Rochdale (Forrester *et al.*, 1988) in which a mixed package of multi-agency situational and social preventive measures reduced both the fear and levels of crimes of burglary. Let's look in some depth at this famous model of a 'successful' multi-agency project.

The Kirkholt anti-burglary project has become almost an icon of the 'some things work' approach with 'hard facts' such as the 75 per cent reduction in the incidence of burglary on Kirkholt estate over a three year period and the substantial reduction to negligible proportions of the rate of repeat victimization. The core aims of this famous project were as follows: the reduction of burglary in the targeted area; the delivery of crime reduction mechanisms through a multi-agency approach; the eventual local 'ownership' of the project. The Kirkholt project also initiated the important and growing body of work on 'repeat victimization' (see Farrell, 1995). The researchers on this project discovered that a useful and effective strategy for reducing harm in high-crime communities was to target effort on the disproportionate number of repeat victims who lived on the estate. It is now widely accepted that repeat victimization is highest in the most crime-ridden areas (Hope, 1995: 62). A range of initiatives were targeted on these multiple victims, including the 'situational' techniques of upgrading the security of recently victimized dwellings and the removal of prepayment utilities meters as well as the 'social' strategy of group work for local offenders and a credit union for residents. Finally, the project established 'cocoon' watching groups: that is, small groups consisting only of the immediate neighbours of recently victimized households (Forrester *et al.*, 1988). It is also important to note that this was a demonstration project which was well-funded and supported by the Home Office. Looking back on this project, some social scientists have advised caution in trying to replicate or transfer the approach used in one particular site such as Kirkholt to that of very different localities with their own distinct contexts (Crawford and Jones, 1996).

Another apparent problem of multi-agency target-hardening techniques is that of displacement (namely the displacement of the offending problem or offender onto another area or group of victims). There is a fourfold classification of displacement employed by criminologists, namely:

1 'temporal' displacement in which the offence is committed at another time;

2 'spatial' displacement (to a planned type of target in another place);
3 'tactical' displacement (involving a different method for committing an offence); and
4 'functional' displacement which involves the commission of a different crime from that intended originally.

(Pease, 1997: 977)

Again Pease has contended that displacement itself may have its benefits. Using the metaphor of moving or displacing piranhas from one part of the river to another, it may be beneficial to one's safety if there are piranhas in only one part of the river. In Pease's words, 'The conventional literature is concerned with which pair of paddling legs the piranha will attack. The alternative perspective concerns itself with why there are more piranha in certain parts of the river' (Pease, 1994: 676). Displacement may thus be benign, as in the example of the well-known, zoned 'red light' district in Amsterdam and 'safe' streets elsewhere in that city. Furthermore, as a result of multi-agency crime prevention, the frustrated shoplifter may now be playing basketball instead. However, Barr and Pease (1990) also admit that the effects of displacement may on occasions be malign, as in the example of the frustrated shoplifter committing armed robbery. Displacement may be acceptable, provided that there is some kind of public regulation of the process. If this is not the case, Pease's piranha analogy may be too blasé, especially for those areas which 'receive' the displaced 'piranha' without any choice in the matter.

On a more positive note, Bottoms (1990: 9–10) has argued that the most ambitious multi-agency, social crime prevention programmes in the UK during the 1980s were associated with NACRO and established by the Home Office. NACRO set up a series of projects on community safety in housing estates with over 80 local projects being run at one time or another. The estates chosen generally suffered from multiple disadvantages and had high crime rates. The strategy adopted by NACRO was one of active consultation with the key agencies providing services in the locality, while, crucially, holding small-group meetings with random samples of residents to tease out possible solutions to the problems from their knowledge of the area in question. Here we see perhaps the beginning of a shift away from the cult of the 'before and after' evaluation of specific *outcomes* to that of prioritizing how the *process* may be best structured and organized.

Bright (1987: 49–50) has outlined the key features to the NACRO framework as involving: strategies for involving local councils; services for victims of crime; initiatives for protecting those most at risk of victimization (such as children, women and ethnic minorities); schemes for involving the police; and schemes 'tailored' to meet the needs of different residential areas. According to Walklate (1996), the 'community safety framework' associated with NACRO overcomes a number of the critical features of the multi-agency crime prevention industry described so far in this chapter. First, the community safety framework starts from the premise that tackling criminal victimization, and the associated fear of it, is the responsibility of a broad base within the community: not just formal agencies, but also informal agencies and most crucially community networks. This approach suggests that community participation is not only ensured but actively facilitated and representative. Second, the community safety framework carries a definition of the crime problem which incorporates an understanding of criminal victimization in which the structural variables of age, sex, ethnicity (and I would add the crucial variable of social class) are taken into account. Third, this framework proposes a genuinely cooperative approach to crime prevention and thus moves closer to the idea of empowerment (Walklate, 1996: 316). I return later to the possible significance of this discursive shift from crime prevention to community safety later in this chapter.

The radical totalitarian critique

Growing out of a very different notion of political and cultural 'critique' rather than the empirical and technicist 'evaluation' of sceptical pluralism, there has been a growing body of work on the political and social costs of crime prevention alluded to previously as 'radical totalitarianism'. Radical totalitarianism is a body of work associated with authors of a radical disposition, particularly influenced by both Marxism and, increasingly, Foucauldian theory (see Foucault, 1977; Cohen, 1985; and Poster, 1990 among others). What unites this body of work is a shared concern with the broad trends at work in social control whereby the late twentieth-century period is witnessing an evermore penetrative, all-seeing (often termed 'panoptical') system of social surveillance. At this point in our discussion of radical totalitarianism, a brief application of the radical 'canon' to the topic of multiagency crime prevention and diversion schemes may be helpful.

Stanley Cohen has been the most influential proponent of the thesis that diversion and other apparently deinstitutionalizing crime prevention trends in the Western democracies have actually extended the web of social control. Drawing on the 'surveillance society' thesis of some of Foucault's early work (Foucault, 1977), Cohen has famously argued that the rise of 'community control has supplemented rather than replaced traditional methods', such as incarceration (Cohen, 1985: 44). 'Net-widening' is the term used to describe this process. The process of net-widening may be most usefully defined as the process of developing elaborate procedures for working with offenders, and drawing into those procedures people who under a less elaborate system would have been either ignored or dealt with quickly and simply.

This thesis of net-widening has been followed up by writers such as John Pratt who argue that 'instead of a shift from the inhumanities and injustices of the institution, we find these features of the carceral system now being reproduced in the community – in those projects that are supposed to be alternatives to the institution' (Pratt, 1989: 252). According to this viewpoint, the supposed 'alternatives' have never displaced the formal aspects of social control but, instead, have simply become additions in an ever-expanding network of (multi-agency) social control. It is argued that multi-agency crime prevention has not reduced the trawling capacities of the social control apparatus of the state but rather increased them, thus ensnaring ever-more 'deviants' in its nets. Such claims of net-widening, according to critics, are seemingly without much empirical substantiation and instead rely largely on 'metaphors and evocative images' (McMahon, 1990).

Radical critics of multi-agency crime prevention schemes have also been associated with the 'lack of justice' thesis. This thesis is clearly linked to the above disquiet over bringing more people into the multi-agency systems of social control but there are distinct features to this critique of diversionary schemes. Pratt again has claimed that a form of 'administrative justice' came to predominate behind the closed doors of corporatist, inter-agency, diversion schemes in the 1980s. According to Pratt (1989: 245), and following the pioneering insights of Roberto Unger (1972), corporatism refers to 'the tendencies to be found in advanced welfare societies whereby the capacity for conflict and disruption is reduced by means of the centralization of policy, increased government intervention, and co-operation of various professional and interest groups into a collective whole with homogeneous aims and objectives'. In the corporatist arrangements which Pratt argues were characteristic of such bodies as the multi-agency juvenile liaison bureaux and panels in the UK in the 1980s, the key emphasis is taken to be that of policy outcomes rather that the rights of the client (Pratt, 1989: 248; but see Hughes *et al.*, 1998).

In more general ways, such notions as 'net-widening' are employed to illustrate the general process whereby the mechanisms of multi-agency crime prevention, 'community policing' and 'communal' social control have proliferated, penetrated and extended into parts of society previously untouched by formal control and preventive processes (Gordon, 1987). Accordingly, the fad during the 1990s for 'partnerships' would be viewed as but one manifestation of the immersion of civil society in the ever-expanding social control machine, thus confirming the grand thesis of the 'extension of social control' popularized by Cohen (1985).

The attractions of this grand theory are hard to resist. Glimpses of dystopia have a powerful appeal, not least to intellectuals who, doubtless, gain vicarious pleasure from being on the 'edge', compared to the supposedly slumbering masses. With the coming *fin de siècle*, the concern over an apparently growing anomie together with the onward march of impersonal control processes is not confined to radical criminology (see Reiner, 1994: 757). Indeed it would be ill-conceived to write off the analysis offered by radical totalitarianism. However, there are some difficulties with this radical approach to social control initiatives which limit its salience to the sociological study of specific examples of multi-agency crime prevention initiatives. First, there is the problem of theoretical foreclosure, associated with a particular reading of the grand theories of Marxism and Foucauldian discourse analysis, whereby the answers to questions are already known without recourse to empirical testing. For the most part, there is also little scope for the specifics of locality and difference in such broad deterministic theorizing such as that found in radical totalitarianism (but see McLaughlin, 1994). The grand design offered by the radical totalitarian thesis thus both exaggerates the dystopian tendencies at work and the power of the intrusive social control machine, while simultaneously underestimating the scope for local resistances, manoeuvring and negotiation from countervailing alliances in particular localities. Put briefly, the present and the future may be more open-ended and complex than that implied in the radical totalitarian vision of trends in social control, including that of multi-agency crime prevention. The next section will illustrate the more complex picture which prevails in local multi-agency crime prevention initiatives around the UK in the mid-1990s.

Life beyond the central state? Local community safety strategies

In this section I discuss the major current research studies and competing academic perspectives on local community safety strategies and initiatives in the UK state in the 1990s. As a result of this overview it is suggested that there is 'life after (central government) death' for the multi-agency community safety approach of the Morgan Report on the local governmental terrain. However, it is also clear that there remains much ambiguity and confusion about the exact nature of multi-agency community safety work despite the inflated claims often made on its behalf.

Nicholas Tilley (1994) has written the most interesting account to date of the brief history of the multi-agency Safer Cities programme. Tilley begins by arguing that multi-agency crime prevention and community safety have become increasingly important in the last 15 years in the UK as responses to the rising crime rate, given the related failure of more traditional responses (such as deterrent sentencing and incarceration). The Safer Cities programme is viewed by Tilley as one expression of this policy movement. As previously mentioned, the programme had three central aims: to reduce crime, to reduce the fear of crime and to create safer cities where economic enterprise and commercial life could flourish. All the initiatives were centrally administered but locally driven. Once again the term 'partnership' was at the forefront of the rhetoric and practice of such initiatives. Having outlined the programme, Tilley then attempts to explain the shape of the Safer Cities programme and it is at this point that the analysis becomes interesting, with its complex perspective on power relations at both the central and local dimensions of the programme.

Tilley argues that there is no single factor which can explain the emergence and subsequent shape of the programme. In fact Tilley contends that a key role was played by 'administrative' criminologists both within and outside the Home Office who shaped the crime prevention programme within the constraining structure offered by the particular Conservative administration of the day and its ideology (Tilley, 1994: 42). Tilley's analysis emphasizes the importance of quite specific 'policy networks' and individuals in the construction of this multi-agency crime prevention programme. At the same time Tilley is aware that the Safer Cities programme was constrained by dominant (New Right) concerns. As he puts it, 'It is only within a given political framework that there is diversity' (p. 44). And yet Tilley does not see the programme as being, in any simple sense, a puppet controlled by central and rightist strings. Rather, he says, 'catholicity is marked' across the different local projects (p. 46). Furthermore, he contends that the emphasis placed on 'enterprise and commercial life' was for cosmetic reasons. It was self-consciously used 'at a time when hitching onto the enterprise bandwagon was a *sine qua non* of eliciting government funds' (p. 46).

As befits a sceptical sociologist, Tilley places much emphasis on the unintended consequences of action, not least in the policy formulation/implementation process. As a result of such complex relations between all the participants both within and without the Home Office, Tilley argues that it is not plausible to interpret multi-agency crime prevention as simply an expression of right wing, Thatcherite policies (Tilley, 1994: 50) unlike commentators on crime prevention during the 1980s such as King (1989) have done. Having emphasized the complex 'aetiology' of the programme, Tilley then shows the factors which explain the relatively autonomous operation of the local schemes. Coordinators, for example, were recruited from heterogeneous occupations. When allied to the 'weak centre' at the Home Office, discretion in, and diversity of, local action was to be expected. In practice, the work of the Safer Cities projects combined both situational and social crime prevention approaches although the requirement of evaluation puts a premium, wrongly in Tilley's view, on easily quantified measures associated with the quasi-experimental method which is most readily and easily used with situational techniques (Tilley and Pawson, 1994: 292).

Tilley's overall assessment of the Safer Cities programme is that it is a somewhat fragile or 'contingent' phenomenon whose chances of survival are questionable. Speculating on the future of Safer Cities, Tilley (1994: 55) argues that:

> Part of the cause of its elimination will be the very success of the (Home Office) Crime Prevention Unit in promoting institutions' attention to crime at the local level, rendering Safer Cities otiose [i.e. *serving no*

useful purpose].The ubiquity of support for crime prevention makes initiatives like Safer Cities redundant.

The significance of Tilley's contribution to the study of the central/local interface in multi-agency crime prevention lies in his emphasis on the complex origins and unintended outcomes of this initiative led by the Home Office. Although it is clear that the rightist agenda on law and order was a crucial ingredient, the overall meal which resulted was not simply Thatcherite fare. The study of complex networks at local and central nodal points of policy formation and implementation is opened up by such research, not least the study of the dialectical processes between local and central actors. Accidental contingencies are placed at the fore in this sceptical pluralist position. This iconoclasm is both a strength and a weakness in Tilley's analysis. State power thus appears to be an extremely hollow shell filled by all sorts of competing interest groups. Although passing reference is made to the overall constraining 'political framework' within which diversity occurs, not enough attention is paid to that dimension of power whereby agendas are set without explicit decisions being made. The thrust of Tilley's analysis thus points to contingency and accidents. However, surely there is a need to conceptualize Safer Cities as a part of the New Right 'dispersed' state's crime prevention project, even allowing for diversity and degrees of local autonomy in practice.

Mark Liddle and Lorraine Gelsthorpe (1994a, 1994b, 1994c) focus their attention on the extent to which the multi-agency 'call to arms' from both the Home Office Circular 44/1990 (Home Office, 1990) and the Morgan Report of 1991 (Home Office, 1991) have affected the thinking, shape and direction of local crime prevention initiatives in the UK. In particular, their research addressed the six elements seen as crucial to multi-agency crime prevention by the Morgan Report, namely structure, leadership, information, identity, durability and resources. The comparative breadth of this study makes it to date a unique project in British research on crime prevention. Liddle and Gelsthorpe make it clear that they prefer the term multi-agency to inter-agency crime prevention since the former does not imply either partnership or equality between the participants.

Liddle and Gelsthorpe chronicle the varying structures (from formal to informal), modes of leadership, involvement of 'external' agencies and relationships to both local and central government across the range of local initiatives. The authors eschew any simple critique of the varying 'models' and instead prefer to offer a description of what is going on 'on the ground' or rather in the formal structures (little or no attention is given to concrete outcomes and actions which flow from these bodies). It is, however, possible to glean from their overview what Liddle and Gelsthorpe take to be areas of good and bad practice as well as issues of general concern for local multi-agency initiatives. On balance the authors support formal structures (as against informal arrangements) in which there should be 'top-tier' support from the most senior officers of the relevant agencies. Liddle and Gelsthorpe also note that very few of the initiatives under examination had any elected members sitting on the groups. Although they recognize some of the benefits which might accrue from member participation (e.g. good for sense of 'ownership' and may lead to better resourcing), the authors express clear reservations about the benefits of linking multi-agency crime prevention with the local democratic structure. (This view is probably drawn from the interviews with officers since the views of locally-elected politicians were not elicited as part of the research project!) In particular, they argue that there are dangers in politicians vetoing initiatives and seeing it as a 'political' issue. Concern is expressed over the introduction of 'this kind of volatility' (Liddle and Gelsthorpe, 1994a: 16).

Liddle and Gelsthorpe lend support to Tilley's picture of local diversity and lack of uniformity despite the possible intentions of the central state: 'In general, real progress in specific areas seems to a great extent to have been due to local historical idiosyncrasies, or to the commitment and talents of particular individuals who happen to have taken crime prevention duties upon themselves' (1994a: 27). As with Tilley, the absence of any theorization of the new 'dispersed' forms of state power may mean that unifying constraints on the local delivery of multi-agency crime prevention are missed in this largely descriptive account due to the surface-level appearance of diversity. Suffice to say without the new modes of state power in the 'post-welfare state' described earlier it is unlikely that such multi-agency 'partnerships' would exist at all.

Liddle and Gelsthorpe (1994c) make an important distinction between 'scheme-focused' and 'process-focused' crime prevention work. 'Scheme-focused' work is driven by short-term goals, often developed as a result of sudden and short-term 'pots of gold' whereas 'process-focused' work creates structures or working arrangements which can deliver over the long term, being dependent on longer-term funding from within the existing mainstream budgets of agencies. The latter appear to be the exception to the rule in the UK (but see Hughes et al., 1998). The efficacy of 'scheme-focused' crime prevention work is questioned in that it may erode local ownership and be akin to 'puffs of smoke in the wind' (Liddle and Gelsthorpe, 1994c: 9). Despite their earlier reservations about the involvement of politicians in such work, Liddle and Gelsthorpe support the 'process-focused' approach which in turn does appear to require linkage to the structures of local democracy and the vital issue of accountability, given that it is acknowledged that 'the development of process-focused work is more dependent on ownership at the political level' (1994c: 9). This seems to be a case of 'having their cake and eating it' given their earlier concern over the influence of local politicians in such initiatives. The final point of note raised by Liddle and Gelsthorpe relates to the question of resources. They point out that the general lack of resources is the most serious problem for participants. The funding landscape both nationally and even with particular local authorities has, in their words, 'a piecemeal, uneven appearance' (1994c: 14). Surely this situation is itself a political issue of central importance.

The research undertaken by Liddle and Gelsthorpe has produced some valuable material. Most previous and ongoing research in this area has been restricted to one locality or initiative or at best two areas. Such an 'audit' also has the merit of being an 'honest broker's' description of initiatives in a broad sweep of the national scene. However, the work of Liddle and Gelsthorpe does more than this. Their arguments about the merits of 'process-focused' work are of crucial significance to this field of policy. The authors' depiction of the plurality of initiatives on the ground again confirms the complex patch-work of the crime prevention 'industry' in the UK, although their theoriza-tion of the situation may be limited. More emphasis needs to be given, however, to the important debate concerning the links between crime pre-vention work and local democracy. Finally, the major limitation of this Home Office-sponsored research is its insufficient engagement with questions of political representation, empowerment, participation and democratic accountability around multi-agency crime prevention.

Daniel Gilling has noted that the logic of collaboration, implied in the multi-agency approach to crime prevention, appears to be irresistible. Yet Gilling recommends caution in that there may often be competing discourses of crime prevention when agencies meet at the collaborative table (Gilling, 1993: 146). Gilling focuses particular attention on both the police and pro-bation services as illustrative examples of the dangers of agencies jumping on the multi-agency 'bandwagon' while possessing different conceptions of crime prevention. Thus Gilling traces the historical origins of each agency (in this case the police and probation services) and shows how this ideologi-cal baggage continues to affect the agencies' respective, contemporary con-ceptual frameworks and modes of practice.

He argues that the dominant discourse on crime prevention in the police (but not in the crime prevention units) still bears the hallmark of the crimi-nological school of classicism (see Chapter 2). Here great emphasis is placed on control of crime through both proactive and reactive deterrence. By way of contrast, probation has been characterized historically by a reformist and positivist discourse. The dominant theme in the probation discourse is thus treatment and/or welfarism, taking its cues from psychological and socio-logical positivism (see Chapter 3). Gilling (1993) then argues that the police discourse tends to be dominant in part due to the wider politics of law and order but also due to their possession of information (crime statistics) that is readily knowable and which opens up opportunities for assessing what is most preventable.

Gilling develops these ideas further by arguing that 'the multi-agency approach is a bandwagon that is too hastily joined when there is as yet no evidence to suggest that it is a panacea' (Gilling, 1994: 246). He contends that agencies are drawn into the 'collaborative net' for a number of reasons. In part, this is due to the rhetorical appeal of this self-evidently 'good idea' which comes over as both a 'rallying call and a worthy pursuit' (p. 247). Collaboration is good public relations work. It may tap into resources and not least it complies with the dictates of central government. In actual collaborative situations, Gilling suggests that the situational crime prevention approach is advantaged given that its effects are more easily measured than the longer-term effects of social crime prevention. Home Office pressure for evaluation also leads to what political scientists term 'the mobilization of bias' in favour of the neo-liberal situational approach.

Gilling is generally unimpressed by the current practices of multi-agency crime prevention in the UK. His work offers a salutary corrective to the traditional technicist tradition of research which takes crime prevention as a given and then sets about evaluating its measurable outcomes. In drawing our attention to the contradictions between situational and social crime prevention, and with his call for a tighter 'problem-oriented' and holistic approach to replace the current woolliness of much social crime prevention work (Gilling, 1996), Gilling has made a key contribution to the debate on multi-agency crime prevention and community safety initiatives. The concern with conceptual clarification about the nature of multi-agency crime prevention is also the trademark of the body of work associated with Adam Crawford.

Crawford (1994, 1995, 1997; Crawford and Jones, 1995) has articulated some important concerns about the drift to an authoritarian (communitarian) agenda on law and order and the concomitant rise of neo-corporate institutional practices of multi-agency 'community' crime prevention in the UK. Throughout Crawford's work we find an emphasis first on the complex, reflexive and negotiated character of multi-agency practice, second a critical interrogation of the meanings of community in multi-agency work and, third a revisiting of Pratt's (1989) corporatism thesis with regard to these multi-agency crime prevention fora. Let us look in more detail at each theme.

The theoretical impetus for Crawford's work seems to have come out of a sympathetic yet critical appreciation of the early research on multi-agency crime prevention carried out by Pearson et al. (1992), discussed earlier. Crucial to the work of Pearson et al. was the identification of profound differences in power and of sources of conflict between the participating agencies in multi-agency crime prevention. Building on this starting point, Crawford and Jones (1995) argue that both consensus and conflict are inherent in multi-agency work. More importantly, they agree that the primacy of power relations must be acknowledged in the study of multi-agency work but they contend that Pearson et al. (1992) give a narrow, constraining picture of power and thus neglect the creative and productive nature of action among participants in such multi-agency fora (Crawford and Jones, 1995: 20; see also Hughes, 1994).

Nelken (1985), in the tradition of radical totalitarianism, has drawn our attention to some important conceptual and political questions with regard to the appeal to 'community' in crime control discourses. Crawford builds on Nelken's work in several ways for the study of multi-agency 'community' crime prevention. Accordingly, attention is drawn to the way in which the appeal to community is used to compensate for legitimation deficits in the wider body politic in the UK. He then goes on to argue that the nature of the community to which such appeals in dominant political discourses on law and order are made is itself a highly selective rhetorical device. Crawford has noted that it is assumed (wrongly) in the dominant discourse that the lack of community necessarily leads to decline and thus crime whereas 'more' community equals less crime. Furthermore, community is assumed to be a defence against 'outsiders' and that community will be characterized by homogeneity rather than diversity (Crawford, 1995: 105–7). In accord with a long tradition of sociological scepticism on the use of this slippery word community, Crawford alerts us to the exclusionary and bounded 'majoritarian' mode of legitimation which is likely to result from the particular effects of the dominant discourse on multi-agency 'community' crime prevention in contemporary UK.

Crawford plots the shift in both responsibility and blame which is associated with the rise of a multi-agency 'community' orientation in crime prevention. Some communities in the process become pathologized while any blame is taken off statutory agencies. Furthermore, 'community involvement' is seen as a means of managing and controlling expectations (Crawford, 1995: 112–13). In passing, Crawford does note that the 'offloading' by central government of crime prevention practices onto communities, however 'represented', does have its dangers for the central state not least in the creation of spaces to be filled by such 'volatile' practices as vigilantism. The rise of vigilantism is evident in the examples of 'communities' taking the law into their own hands against 'paedophiles' and 'persistent' offenders in the UK in the 1990s. Overall, Crawford paints a dystopian picture in which the new multi-agency 'partnerships against crime' go hand in hand with a broader crisis of representative democracy. He contends that appeals to community represent a 'particular form of managerialism in local conflict governance' (Crawford, 1995: 121). I return to these concerns over 'community' in greater depth in Chapter 6.

The political contextualization of multi-agency crime prevention is addressed further in Crawford (1994) where he applies Pratt's (1989) earlier insights on multi-agency fora as examples of the corporatist tendencies in the modern capitalist state discussed above. The analysis of contemporary crime prevention strategies in terms of the wider context of shifts in the nature of state power in the late twentieth century is rightly opened up. In particular, Crawford emphasizes 'the inter-connectedness of a multi-agency approach to crime prevention and control with the decline in the welfare ideal, the emergence of new administrative arrangements for local govern-ance and the complex and shifting relationships between the state and civil society' (Crawford, 1994: 497; for a more general discussion of these trends in state and civil society see Hughes, 1998b; in press).

Crawford goes on to present some of the dangers inherent in this corpo-ratist approach to crime prevention. Thus the goal of 'unity' among the par-ticipants in concert with a lack of normative regulation is viewed as presenting a threat to 'due process' and the rights of the putative offender (Crawford, 1994: 505). Crawford also regards multi-agency 'community' crime prevention as being 'vague and open-textured' with a vision 'largely pragmatic and managerial' and forms of intervention tending to be 'short-term and situational in character' (1994: 506). More tellingly, he also argues that there is the potential for multi-agency crime prevention initiatives becoming co-opted onto the broader law and order agenda. This process of co-option means that the 'social crisis' is managed in such a way that we see the criminalization of social policy as a result of which 'fundamental public issues are being marginalized except in so far as they are defined in terms of their criminogenic qualities' (Crawford, 1994: 507).

Finally, Crawford returns to the threat which such corporatist multi-agency arrangements pose for justice and democracy. In particular, it is argued that these emerging 'neo-corporate grey areas' have the potential to be highly disciplinary and authoritarian forms of administration, in which pragmatism and efficiency have replaced 'normative regulation' in the oper-ation of such initiatives (Crawford, 1994: 511).

My own research on the politics of community safety in Northampton-shire during the 1990s (Hughes, 1994, 1996b, 1997a) has qualified some of the fears expressed by commentators like Crawford and the body of work associated with radical totalitarianism. This research focused on the development of a local police authority's social democratic policy regarding the merging of a community safety strategy and police/community consul-tative initiatives under the auspices of local lines of formal democratic accountability. It is argued that this policy process reflected the conflicts and alliances at work at both the district and county-council tiers of the local state as well as complex struggles with the central state's agenda. The debate on crime prevention and community safety in the county studied was cer-tainly politicized and qualified some of the concerns over the lack of any democratic discourse, however limited, evident in much academic literature on multi-agency crime prevention. As John Clarke (1996b: 10) has noted, 'specific words in particular contexts are subjected to attempts to articulate them to divergent projects' and in the Northamptonshire situation during the 1990s the struggle to 'democratize' community safety strategies was engaged. It would again be misguided to view any community strategy, however well-conceived and implemented, as a panacea for the historical shifts associated with late modernity and the rise of a 'culture of fear' in risk society (see Introduction). However, the very looseness and emptiness of the concept of community safety – a 'free-floating signifier' in Eugene McLaughlin's (1994) view – perhaps offers the opportunity for creative ideological appropriation by local, progressive alliances and networks which could challenge regressive local and centralist tendencies on law and order. As a backlash to the numbing mundanity of managerially-driven strategies on crime management, is it fanciful to view the appeal of the idea of community safety to local actors as a means of rekindling concerns over social solidarity and collective control over the wider social environment? The situation in various localities of the UK appears fluid and although the contest between localities and the central state is profoundly uneven, the hegemonic capacity of the post-Thatcherite 'get tough' agenda on law and order should not be overestimated.

A big question facing such policy initiatives as local multi-agency community safety strategies in this era of the audit is how do you measure their success? The most obvious measure would probably be that of a reduction in crime and a concomitant increase in security and safety among people, while avoiding the rightist moralizing closure on issues of diversity and difference. This difficult issue is certainly not amenable to measurement in any short-term manner. It is vital to recognize the complex mixture of demographic, cultural and technological factors which come into play in any explanation of the shifts in the sense of security or insecurity and in the material reality of crime and disorder. As a consequence, the chances of ever 'measuring' in a quantifiable manner the impact of a community safety/ multi-agency crime prevention strategy on crime rates is difficult to envisage. However, a more reasonable 'test' for future researchers may be to ask whether the 'good intentions' associated with multi-agency-driven community safety work end up as tangible, practical anti-despotic outcomes. There is some evidence, for example, that some multi-agency crime prevention and fear reduction strategies in specific localities have been formulated with the aim of addressing the needs of women and ethnic minorities. Some local authorities have taken gender issues seriously with regard to multi-agency crime prevention in the public domain, such as the introduction of battered women's refuges, women-only taxis and late-night bus services for women (Comedia, 1991).

The emphasis to date on local state initiatives should not be read as implying that the role of national government is either dead or necessarily malevolent. In the light of this, we should note the 'success story' of the statist '*Bonnemaison*' strategy in France during the 1980s. This policy was not reliant on individual projects, unlike the UK government's policy in the 1980s, but instead sought to embed crime prevention in ongoing social institutions and processes. The strategy was implemented through a hierarchy of communities whose membership was dominated by representatives of key national and municipal authorities. It was characterized by effective liaison between the national government and a cadre of socialist mayors with the capacity both to negotiate with central authorities and coordinate the delivery of local services. As Sutton (1997: 23–4) notes, the success of the *Bonnemaison* policy was dependent on political discipline born out of a shared ideology and made possible by socialist dominance at both local and central levels of the state. It was thus beyond practical pragmatism and instead was used as a 'flag of convenience' by the socialist government in France to raise '*la prevention*' in all sorts of social issues. Throughout the strategy we find two consistent themes, namely 'solidarity and partnership' and 'integration' (unlike the central government policy in the UK with its themes of consumerism, individualism and self-reliance; see King, 1991: 90–1). The *Bonnemaison* approach thus carried social imagery of the people as one community of 'insiders' in contrast to the imagery of 'outsiders' in much UK central state-sponsored 'community' crime prevention. This example clearly illustrates that centrally-driven social crime prevention policy is still viable and that it would be mistaken to always assume a conflict between central and local strategies.

This section has attempted to offer a synthesis of the key developments in multi-agency crime prevention and community safety work in the UK, largely through a review of the diverse current research agendas on local initiatives. Clarke's notion of the 'dispersed' state, involving a 'rolling out' rather than 'rolling back' of state power, best captures the nature of central-local strategies of crime control under review (Clarke, 1996a: 15). Thus the constraining power and influence of the central state and its departmental arm of the Home Office cannot be ignored in any examination of local, corporate multi-agency strategies. Indeed, for critics like Gilling and Barton (1997), the move towards community safety and away from the 'narrow' concept of crime prevention may be best understood as part of the central state's bid for re-legitimation in the last decade due to its perceived failures around both law and order and urban regeneration. At its worst, 'Community safety thus becomes another strategy for managing the "underclass" and of maintaining social polarization rather than integration' (Gilling and Barton, 1997: 78). However, it may be argued that current community safety and multi-agency crime prevention initiatives are not reducible in terms of either their origins or outcomes to a 'New Right' law and order agenda. The influence of this latter agenda is of course evident in much of the processes and structures examined here. Who would deny that the novel forms of governance highlighted by Crawford, the strategies of urban regeneration discussed by Tilley, the collaborative partnerships depicted by Gilling, and Liddle and Gelsthorpe, all carry potential for the disempowerment of the weak and marginal, the further consolidation of existing social divisions and modes of regulation together with a numbing silence on questions of social inclusion and democratic accountability? Furthermore, there is evidence of a growing managerialization and privatization of crime prevention in which multi-agency partnerships are often collusive.

Sutton is correct in pointing out that the conceptual boundaries of multi-agency social crime prevention are particularly vague, encompassing a diversity of schemes under the label. 'Crime prevention is becoming a "catch-all" term, exploited by a range of interest groups for its emotive impact and capacity to attract funds' (Sutton, 1994: 10). In a similar fashion, Crawford notes, 'This open-textured essence allows crime prevention to be extended, in some cases to include any form of "good work" and to be seen as synonymous with any work which is perceived to have some potential beneficial impact' (Crawford, 1994: 328). However, in contrast to previous overviews on national and international trends in social control (see Cohen, 1985), I would suggest that contemporary local multi-agency crime prevention initiatives in the UK also at times draw on, and create, agendas and projects which are beyond the control of the centre. In giving contextual factors their proper place in the investigation of multi-agency crime prevention trends, this chapter has sought to highlight the importance of the specificity of local circumstances and of interpreting general trends in the context of particular localities.

The evidence discussed in this necessarily long section would appear to suggest that local multi-agency crime prevention and community safety strategies 'on the ground' in the UK offer a complex picture of both constrained compliance and negotiation and at times struggle with the penal populism of recent UK central governments' politics of enforcement. Of course we are still left with major, unresolved questions such as how might local, multi-agency community safety programmes hope to counter the real causes of crime which may lie in the alienation of major parts of a whole generation of young people, stigmatized as failures by school and denied career-oriented work in an economy which no longer has use for their skills? (Sutton, 1994). Such massive problems cannot be left to 'the local' of course and there is a crucial role for the nation state, as an accountable public power, in positive policy making in the post-liberal age. These key questions are addressed in Chapters 6 and 7.

Summary

This chapter began by introducing the concept and practice of multi-agency crime prevention as it has emerged in both policy and academic circles in the UK since the 1980s. I then focused on the relationship of multi-agency crime prevention to the central governmental agenda on 'managing' crime control during the last two decades. In the next section, the two major academic orthodoxies on multi-agency crime prevention ('sceptical pluralism' and 'radical totalitarianism') were examined. Finally the chapter gave an over-view of the complex picture of contemporary 'local' initiatives in multi-agency crime prevention emerging from recent research studies in the UK. In the next chapter, attention is turned to the possibilities and limitations to seemingly 'non-statist' communitarian agendas on crime prevention.

Further reading

Bottoms, A. (1990) 'Crime prevention facing the 1990s', *Policing and Society*, 1: 3–22.
Crawford, A. (1997) *The Local Governance of Crime*. Oxford: Clarendon Press.

chapter six

Communitarianism: bringing 'the social' back into crime prevention?

Introduction

In the previous chapter I focused on the 'growth industry' around multi-agency crime prevention. In the course of the discussion reference was also made to appeals to 'the community' but largely in terms of state-driven and state-managed strategies. In this chapter competing contemporary communitarian theories of crime prevention are explored in depth. The chapter begins with an overview of the meanings of community in popular, political

and academic discourses. In the rest of the chapter the competing and controversial claims to develop 'bottom-up', social movement-based strategies of
communal empowerment against crime are examined. In particular, I concentrate on both conservative and radical left variants of communitarianism
and their contrasting policy and moral agendas on crime prevention.

The seductions of community

The idea of community has long been an integral part of common-sense
thinking about a wide diversity of social problems and experiences. Just like
the concept of prevention, community may be seen as a 'feelgood' word,
carrying the presumption that communities are by their very nature a 'good
thing'. The popularity and attraction of the idea in both common sense and
political discourses in part derives from its apparent unobtrusive meaning-
lessness – its ability to be utilized in descriptions and analyses of important
social developments; for example, the 'loss of community' in the modern
world – without necessary recourse to clear definition and explanation.
After all, we all know what a community is, don't we? However, the idea of
community has a long and, at times, troublesome history but it also has a
powerful resonance and volatility which has surprised even some of its most
vociferous critics (Hughes and Mooney, 1998).

From the late 1970s, political debate in the UK has been increasingly
dominated by the New Right's neo-liberalism which postulates the existence
of autonomous, assertive, rational individuals who must be protected and
liberated from state power and 'public' interference (Gray, 1995). However,
such ideas have not gone unchallenged. The dominance of neo-liberalism in
both political theory and social policy has been questioned by critics who
sought to give prominence to the 'social' rather than the 'individual'. Advo-
cates of 'communitarian' ideas in particular argue that the 'community'
rather than the individual (or the state) should be at the centre of both the
analysis of the social world and the prevailing value system. The ensuing
'liberal-communitarian' debate in the 1990s (Frazer and Lacey, 1993) was
popularized by the media which saw in the renewed interest given to community the potential for new angles on stories about crime and delinquency,
and more generally about morality, the relationship between family and
state and 'the condition of the nation'.

In the late 1980s and 1990s, notions of community 'participation' and
'empowerment' became increasingly central in the language and rhetoric of
urban 'renewal' or 'regeneration' in both the UK and the USA. According to
Allan Cochrane (1986: 51), governments (and a plethora of other agencies
in the urban regeneration business) have used community 'as if it were an
aerosol can, to be sprayed on to any social programme, giving it a more
progressive and sympathetic cachet'. The key role played by 'the community' in political assertions by both the Conservative Party and the

Labour Party in the UK during the last decades of the twentieth century in a range of policy activities, from healthcare through to education and crime, may be seen as part of a deliberate strategy to de-emphasize the role of government in these matters (see Chapter 5). According to Sandra Walklate, it is important to remember that this assertion of the role of the community in crime prevention was as much 'a part of a wider political strategy permeating a whole range of policy areas in the early 1980s as it was rooted in any evidence that community-based responses to crime prevention might prove effective' (Walklate, 1996: 294–5). Viewed cynically the rhetoric might constitute a search for a politically justifiable policy while at the same time demanding and implementing cutbacks in public expenditure.

However, like Walklate (1996), this chapter takes as its starting point the idea that communities *do* have a key role to play in crime prevention. The arguments that community 'breakdown' is a key contributing factor in patterns of rising crime and delinquency and claims that some communities are being excluded from 'mainstream' social life in a period of increased social polarization and greater social inequality will form the central theme in this chapter. The chapter will also focus on what preventive measures emerge as a consequence of such analyses. Again, it is wise to be wary about the novelty of such ideas. They appear to echo, for example, the fears (male, 'racial', class, Christian and medical) of the famous Labour politician, Aneurin Bevan, about social segregation in the immediate post-war period in the UK: 'You will have castrated communities. You will have colonies of low-income people. Segregation is a wholly evil thing – a monstrous infliction upon the essential psychological and biological oneness of the community' (Bevan quoted in Hughes and Mooney, 1998).

Similarly, in Chapter 3, we saw that the Chicago School in the USA in the 1920s and 1930s claimed to have identified a crucial link between the disorganized and disadvantaged community and the growth and sustenance of criminality. In the view of this positivist school, the absence of shared norms was crucial to understanding offending, whilst in turn the fostering of social organization and cohesion and the opening up of opportunities was the key to prevention. Thus similar claims and arguments about community tend to reoccur in different historical contexts, highlighting the continuing potency of community ideas. This chapter aims to explore some of the ways that community, and the arguments of the communitarian debate, have become increasingly central to discussions about the future direction of crime *and* welfare policy in the UK and beyond in the late twentieth century.

Basic tenets of communitarianism

The intellectual pedigree of this body of ideas is one of a decidedly diverse and mixed 'parentage'. Apart from the important connections back to

Aristotelian notions of civic republicanism and Judaeo-Christian ideas of communion, the expression of communitarian aspirations is also associated with the early utopian socialists and anarchists such as Robert Owen and Peter Kropotkin. Furthermore, communitarian philosophy may also be linked to the 'conservative' sociological tradition associated with Ferdinand Tönnies and, to a lesser extent, Émile Durkheim in which a critique of Enlightenment's project may be discerned (Lasch, 1995). As a result of this heterodox pedigree, communitarianism may be said to 'break' traditional ideas of right and left. Thus, for example, within much communitarian thought, both the market and the (welfare) state are viewed as dangers to the vibrant, organic community. Liberalism's emphasis on individual rights and abstract notions of 'enlightened self-interest' is thus subject to a critique for its neglect of the inherently social nature of humans and the collective character of human existence.

Among the attempts at capturing the essence of this resurgent discourse, the following statements from Lasch, Braithwaite and Spicker convey the broad drift of the communitarian tradition:

> Communitarianism . . . found the sources of social cohesion in shared assumptions so deeply ingrained in everyday life that they do not have to be articulated: in folkways, customs, prejudices, habits of the heart.
>
> (Lasch, 1995: 92)

> In communitarian societies individuals are densely enmeshed in inter-dependencies which have special qualities of mutual help and trust. The interdependencies have symbolic significance in the culture of group loyalties which take precedence over individual interests.
>
> (Braithwaite, 1989: 100)

> Communitarianism can be taken to stand for a highly socialised view of people in which their moral position can be understood only in terms of their social relationships.
>
> (Spicker, 1994: 7)

Much of its appeal, then, is to real people in specific, morally-bounded communities rather than abstract notions of liberty and individual rights. Herein lies its strong conservative appeal. But communitarianism also conjures up a socialist society in which the collectivity and issues of social justice count for more than the individual and 'bourgeois' formal freedoms. A strong and recurrent emphasis is placed by all communitarians on moral duties and responsibilities to the wider civil society rather than freedoms and rights for the individual. Social compliance in turn derives primarily from informal cultural controls built into everyday relations.

Conservative moral communitarianism

Etzioni on morality, crime and community

The sociologist and populist 'guru', Amitai Etzioni (1994, 1995, 1997) is the most prominent proponent of the conservative communitarian project to undertake a 're-moralization' of society (in his case in the USA). In Etzioni's words, 'Communitarians call to restore civic virtues, for people to live up to their responsibilities and not to merely focus on their entitlements, and to shore up the moral foundations of society' (1995: ix). This quotation represents the kernel of Etzioni's self-consciously 'simple' message for the communal fight against crime. Furthermore, in the preface to the UK edition of *The Spirit of Community*, Etzioni points out that the expression of communitarian ideas is increasingly to be found among politicians of diverse political persuasions in the USA, the UK and Europe. Etzioni's explanation for influential politicians getting on board the communitarian platform, and thereby apparently 'breaking the mould' of traditional party and ideological positions, is quite simple: 'they are visionary people who have seen the power of a compelling set of ideas whose time has come' (1995: ix). In the UK, Etzioni's message has been taken up with particular gusto by the leader of 'New Labour', Tony Blair, and the current Home Secretary, Jack Straw, in a series of well-publicized interventions on street incivilities and the 'parenting deficit' (see below).

What then are the main themes conveyed by Etzioni in his popularization of communitarianism? The key aim of communitarianism is, in Etzioni's words, to help 'restore communities without allowing puritanism or oppression' (1994: 2). As a self-proclaimed social movement, Etzioni's communitarianism aims to support this key aim by means of the regeneration of moral obligation between citizens. More specifically, Etzioni's (1994) manifesto focuses on three interrelated areas of concern, namely:

1 the shoring-up of morality in civil institutions such as the family, school and voluntary associations;
2 addressing and reversing the problem of 'too many rights, too few obligations';
3 the assertion of the importance of the public interest as against special interests in political life.

At times Etzioni is quite explicit in harking back to a vision of a more stable, orderly and lawful past in the 1950s when 'most Americans spoke with one voice' (1994: 22). Accepting that there was discrimination against women and ethnic minorities in the past, Etzioni nevertheless expresses concern that the assumed, previous bedrock of moral consensus has not been replaced by anything of substance other than 'a strong sense of entitlement . . . and a weak sense of obligation'. This has resulted in a 'me-istic orientation' associated with the libertarian individualism of the 1980s money-/market-based society (1994: 3, 27).

Quite specific suggestions are put forward by Etzioni on crime prevention and 'public safety' which further reinforce the dominant motifs of obligation and 'the shoring up of our moral foundations' (1994:11). Apart from support for community policing and neighbourhood watch schemes in the community, Etzioni's law and order agenda appears to lend support to a more Draconian and 'public' version of Braithwaite's (1989) 'reintegrative shaming' (see below). Thus, for first-time offenders only, a strategy of public humiliation which allows reintegration is supported, as it would 'serve to underscore society's disapproval of the crime committed rather than of the people themselves . . . Temporarily marking out those convicted in open court, after due process, seems a legitimate community-building device' (Etzioni, 1994: 141). At other times, Etzioni calls for random alcohol and drug testing in the name of the public interest. For Etzioni, the greatest threat to public safety is not excessive police powers but rather the danger of the public turning to 'extremists', presumably vigilantes and separatist groups, if the authorities do not come up with adequate law and order measures. The bottom line for Etzioni, however, in his diagnosis of the problem of crime and disorder and the means of their prevention always appears to be the existence of a tight and homogeneous community. Thus he argues that the level of crime is deeply affected by the total communal fabric. He cites Utah – a rural, highly religious and culturally homogeneous state – as an exemplary oasis of order and low criminality in the USA, 'where families are strong, schools teach moral values, communities are well intact, and values command respect' (1994: 190). Echoes indeed of 'home, home on the range' and *The Little House on the Prairie* of American romantic fiction in which the real, authentic USA is based spatially and spiritually somewhere other than the coastal metropolises.

This body of work may be termed moral authoritarian or conservative communitarianism given *inter alia* its following domain assumptions:

1 an emphasis on one moral community at the expense of a recognition of the plurality and diversity of identities in late modernity;
2 a desire to return to a traditional and nostalgic past;
3 a neglect of power structures in human societies or at least a naturalization of hierarchical relations;
4 a critique of personal rights and a call for duties but a failure to critique property rights;
5 a glorification of past solidaristic communities together with a failure to conceptualize the crucial importance of struggles versus oppression in the creation of collectivist communities;
6 finally a political and moral rallying call for a return to the 'traditional' family as the means to prevent social ills, including crime.

All in all, within this popular variant of communitarianism, there is a vision of a unitary, homogeneous community sustained by strongly-held moral certainties, celebrating in turn monoculturalism and setting, albeit at times implicitly, a morally prescriptive agenda for the social exclusion of marginalized and 'deviant' categories of people (Hughes, 1997b).

As Kelly (1995: 21) notes, it is tempting to dismiss Etzioni's pronouncements as a 'folksy, peculiarly American vision, the nostalgic yearnings of a nation desperate to reclaim the certainties of its small-town past'. However, to do so would be to underestimate its influence beyond the USA. Furthermore, the work has clearly touched a concern over the effects of marketized individualism and neo-liberalism and over the notion that it is possible to base society on the consumer's right of choice in the market place. It would appear at this point that there may be a rift between Etzioni's communitarianism and the severe neo-liberal solutions of Charles Murray (1990, 1996) in the USA and the New Right in the UK. However, Murray's influence on communitarianism does reappear in the UK in the combined appropriation of Etzioni's moralizing communitarianism and Murray's attack on the liberal intellectual establishment evidenced in the work of the 'ethical socialist', Norman Dennis and others at the Institute of Economic Affairs (IEA) (Dennis, 1993, 1997a; see also Green, 1995; Himmelfarb, 1995; Phillips, 1996). 'Ethical socialism' is a tradition in the British Labour left which supports socialism on the basis of (Christian) ethical and moral grounds rather than Marxism.

Moral communitarian appeals in the UK

At the core of Dennis' recent work on families and crime (Dennis, 1993, 1997a; see also Dennis and Erdos, 1992) is the thesis that the monogamous heterosexual family is the crucial unit of social stability in all human societies and thus the vital means of controlling and preventing crime. It is further contended that the stable family has been weakened by capitalism but more especially by the permissive, 'me, me' culture promulgated by the intelligentsia since the 1960s. For Dennis, it is this libertarian culture which has created a dramatic moral weakening in the most vulnerable sections of society, namely the lower working class which, according to Dennis, has of late become a criminal 'underclass'. In contrast to the apparent libertarian obfuscation of the radical left, Dennis claims to speak to common sense in showing that illegitimate children of single parents do less well on a whole number of fronts than do the offspring of married couples. In particular, he argues that young males from lone mother households (the 'underclass') are turning to crime and disorder in increasing numbers due to the loss of a positive and disciplining male role model. Rising crime and incivilities are thus products of a lack of moral authority and good manners. The same thesis has been argued previously by Murray (1996:127) who noted that 'in communities without fathers, the kids tend to run wild'.

Dennis is careful not to blame the rising crime rate and the 'breakdown' in law and order on poverty and unemployment. Instead, the roots of rising crime are viewed as lying in the abandonment of proper moral standards regarding marriage and, in particular, the activities of conceiving and rearing children. Echoing the views of Murray again that 'young men are essentially barbarians for whom marriage . . . is an indispensable civilizing force' (Murray, 1996: 133), Dennis bemoans the fact that the whole project of creating and maintaining the skills and motivations of fatherhood is being abandoned in contemporary Britain (Dennis, 1993: 7). In accord with Etzioni, Dennis points to the dangerous loss of both social cohesion and self-control which has occurred in the past 30 years in contrast to the apparently halcyon working-class days of his home town of Sunderland in North-East England in the 1930s when 'social control was pervasive and consensual, and therefore low-key, good-natured and effective' (Dennis and Erdos, 1992: 21). The basis of social order in general and crime prevention in particular is thus taken to reside in the informal mechanisms of civil society:

> In non-authoritarian societies – 'free' in the sense that social order depends upon self-control rather than control by the agents of the State – crimes increase to the extent that the mechanisms of socialization and the mores lose their ability to reproduce and maintain a culture of decent mutual respect, trust, and restraint.
>
> (Dennis and Erdos, 1992: 85)

Moral authoritarian communitarianism is clearly alive and well in the UK not least in the right-wing 'think-tank' of the IEA.

Support for Etzioni's approach to communitarian social control is not, however, confined to the neo-conservative right in UK politics. Writing in Demos, the 'think-tank' closely associated with New Labour, Charles Leadbetter (1996: 1) has offered a similar vision of crime prevention based on 'self-policing': 'The aim of policing policy should be to create a society better able to police itself through community self-help'. Leadbetter argues that the current crime debate between 'soft' and 'hard' options is sterile. Instead, he calls for punishment in the community which is neither soft nor hard but rather transparent in its nature and operation. Meanwhile, Leadbetter recognizes that:

> Society will only become more ordered if we create common, collective institutions capable of providing that order. To expect such order to spontaneously emerge from freely cooperating individuals is naive. To hope that the cumbersome, heavy hand of the state might deliver such order is far-fetched.
>
> (1996: 11)

The programme Leadbetter puts forward is to rebuild a layer of intermediate institutions which stand between the individual and the state and are capable of commanding authority and dispensing punishment. In turn, he argues for the repopulation of public spaces by 'law abiding people and civic values' as an antidote to the epidemic of crime which 'thrives on poor public hygiene' (1996: 13, 19). Overall, Leadbetter's answer is to develop non-statist, collective institutions to police 'our own' communities and more open punishment in the community, such as degrees of public shaming.

New Labour, communitarianism and 'zero tolerance'

What was an intellectual debate in the 1980s between liberals and communitarians has now entered the practical politics of the 1990s in countries like the UK. As Jordan (1996: 21) notes, communitarian 'solutions' in terms of providing a new cement for society are not least attractive to politicians as they appear to offer low price options for softening conflicts, producing harmony, trust and obedience to rules and identification with fellow citizens. In the UK, the current Labour administration has been much taken with the moral communitarian 'manifesto' proclaimed by Etzioni and supporters in both the IEA and Demos. This is most manifest in the proposals made by the Home Secretary, Jack Straw, in 1997 to adopt a policy of 'zero-tolerance' regarding incivilities in communities and on the streets (see Dennis, 1997b). As Darren Palmer (1997) notes, 'Zero Tolerance' is a mutation of the 'Broken Windows' thesis developed in the 1980s by Wilson and Kelling (1982). The latter thesis contends that if various forms of incivilities, disturbances and petty crimes are allowed to go unchecked, over time the community becomes increasingly fearful, demoralized and fragmented. This undermining of the communitarian bonds leads to further disorder and increased criminality and a downward spiral for such blighted communities. Finally, 'communities can reach a point where they spiral downwards into the abyss of lawlessness to become criminal no-go zones' (Palmer, 1997: 234). 'Zero Tolerance' shares the concern of the 'Broken Windows' thesis with controlling minor disorder and incivilities. However, the former also places great emphasis on hard-edged policing or what its conservative communitarian proponents term 'confident policing' (Dennis and Mallon, 1997). It is argued that 'zero tolerance' policing will help 'reclaim' the streets for respectable, law-abiding people and help overcome the 'culture of fear' (Furedi, 1997) syndrome, characteristic of late modern, urban environments.

The much vaunted and ill-defined notion of 'family values' appears to be the key to the 'remaking' of the 'decent' society or cohesive community in this political agenda, while those parents who do not meet these criteria, as manifested in the delinquent and criminal tendencies of their children, are promised punishment. In turn, a policy of 'zero tolerance' is recommended for noisy and disruptive neighbours on housing estates through the proposed use of 'Community Safety Orders' which will enable senior police and/or local government officers to obtain injunctions restraining people involved in 'chronic anti-social behaviour' (Palmer, 1997: 233). Furthermore, much is made of getting the homeless, graffiti 'vandals', 'aggressive beggars' and 'squeegee merchants' off the streets together with proposals for curfews on young people (see Hughes, 1996b: 21).

It would seem that New Labour's rhetoric of community is bound up with an exclusionary targeting of the dangerous 'other' in line with the particular variant of ('moral authoritarian') communitarianism which it has espoused. The enforcement costs of such exclusionary strategies in the future may prove very high. The take-up of the moral communitarian agenda by New Labour appears to accord with what Bill Bowring has termed its 'studied indifference to relations of power and oppression in society' (Bowring, 1997: 110). Accordingly, the source of social crisis is located in parental irresponsibility (derived from Etzioni's 'parenting deficit' thesis) or in the malicious, irresponsible behaviour of some groups and individuals, namely the so-called 'underclass'. 'The logic of this position is the social censure and exclusion from society of those who will not take responsibility, or persist in deviant behaviour' (Bowring, 1997: 110).

Critiques of moral authoritarian communitarianism

The body of communitarian work discussed above has met with some harsh criticism. For some, the logic of its argument leads to the regimentation of opinion, moral closure, the repression of dissent and the institutionalization of intolerance, all in the name of morality and law and order. According to John Clarke, the word 'community' used in the context of moral authoritarian communitarianism thus sounds like a prescription for bigotry and parochialism given its attempt to resolve the complexity and antagonisms of an increasingly diverse population through the ideological device of a 'regressively imagined people' which excludes 'aliens', 'lone mothers' and 'the underclass' from its naturalized ranks (Clarke, 1996b; see also Young, 1990). The scapegoating of a welfare-dependent 'underclass' would thus appear to be to the fore in such analyses.

According to Barbara Misztal (1996: 213), in this conservative discourse slogans of community and social cohesion, which are presented as being connected with social harmony, stability, social order and the absence of crime, are used to fill the void created by neo-liberalism and individualism by playing on people's feelings of insecurity and nostalgia for the sense of belonging. The dangers of such a discourse are that community feelings formed by the sharing of impulses may have a special role of reinforcing the fear of the unknown or the unusual and may result in 'converting claustrophobia into an ethical principle' (Sennett, 1977: 217). Sectarian forms of solidarity may thus be the price paid for the mobilization of such feelings around fears about crime and incivilities.

Much of the conservative communitarian work discussed above offers a voluntaristic, 'self-help' view of community empowerment (Hope, 1995) and avoids the analysis of power relations, particularly the crucial historical role played by the state at times as a positive force in the struggles for justice in Europe. Coote (1995) has also noted that this variant of communitarianism does not tackle the uneven distribution of power around divisions of gender, class, 'race' and generation.

Campbell (1993) has offered a trenchant feminist critique of moral communitarianism. Indeed, Campbell's alternative explanation for the behaviour of unruly and criminal men in Britain's 'dangerous places' in the late twentieth century and her diagnosis of the role of women as 'community-builders' may make her a (no doubt) reluctant 'feminist communitarian'. Campbell argues that most writers ignore the significance of the gendered fissures between men and women, not least in the once 'working' (and now increasingly 'workless') class. In apparent alliance with the anti-feminist Dennis (1997), Campbell highlights the selfish and aggressive irresponsibility – expressed in a cult of machismo and brute force – of young males in many of Britain's deprived housing estates. That said, unlike Dennis, Campbell does prioritize the interplay of material factors like unemployment, poverty and political marginalization as well as internecine harassment from the police in producing these brutish 'lads':

> They could penetrate anything while they themselves remained impregnable. What they admired and serviced was the criminalized brotherhood; what they harassed and hurt was community politics. It was an entirely and explicitly *gendered* formation.
>
> (Campbell, 1993: 244)

By way of contrast, 'The redoubts of active citizenship on these estates were run by women whose improvized self-help systems denied their reputation as lairs inhabited by an inert underclass' (Campbell, 1993: 247). The possibility of 'community' and so a progressive communitarianism against crime and disorder in Britain's most deprived and criminalized estates thus rests in the hands of women:

> Solidarity and self-help are sustained by networks that are . . . open, expansive, egalitarian and incipiently democratic. Their challenge is to the systems that bear upon their local life. Crime and coercion are sustained by men. Solidarity and self-help are sustained by women. It is as stark as that.
>
> (Campbell, 1993: 319)

Campbell's contribution offers an important corrective to the masculinist romanticism of writers like Dennis and Murray. It doubtless speaks an important truth about 'lawless masculinity' but it may play down the complexity of 'divergent masculinities'.

Finally, according to Hope (1995: 74–7), 'voluntaristic' communitarianism, often rhetorically symbolized in neighbourhood watch schemes, is also unable to address the wider processes of both counter-urbanization (involving what Giddens (1990) terms the 'lifting out' of social relations from the close proximity of residential environment) and poverty concentration. Such a criticism in turn recognizes the need for the state to play a key role in the re-manufacturing of community through such initiatives as significant social investment and support for institution-building to hold communities together. Such community institutions, in turn, would be crucial in acting as the two-way conduit between the community and wider sources of wealth and power (Hope, 1995: 78). By alerting us to the moral communitarians' silence surrounding the material and political determinants of both community decline and regeneration, Hope's critique leads us to more radical analyses and visions of community.

Radical left communitarian re-imaginings of the community-crime nexus

The second half of this chapter examines how communitarian ideas of rights and obligations have been conceptualized in radical left ways by intellectuals in Europe, North America and Australasia. It will be argued that these radical re-imaginings of community offer an alternative agenda on questions of crime prevention and law and order to that of the regressive and exclusive tendencies of Etzioni and allied moral authoritarian commentators.

Social welfare, justice and the common good

Debates on crime prevention and law and order in the UK have, as yet, been relatively untouched by the body of European writing associated with such socialist thinkers as Gorz (1992), Gough (1994), Jordan (1992, 1996, Jordan and Arnold, 1995), Keane (1996) and Offe (1992). However, the debates around human needs, basic (citizens') income and the common good in which such writers are currently engaged may be of major future importance in moving analyses of crime and its 'prevention' further into the deeper waters of political and social theory. The above writers are to varying degrees 'communitarian' in that they endorse the principles of spontaneous solidarity, rules of reciprocity and small-scale communities with participatory democracy. Bill Jordan (1996: 186) captures the working definition of 'community' adopted in this body of work as follows: 'the voluntary exchanges within systems of mutual obligation that include members through reciprocity, sharing and redistribution'. As radical egalitarian communitarians, such writers 'prioritize policies to eliminate poverty, defined as a degree of deprivation that seriously impairs participation in one's society'

(Gough, 1994: 54). Unlike the conservative communitarianism of Etzioni and Dennis, material conditions are thus to the fore in this radical left agenda on community as with the recent debate on basic income in which Gorz, Jordan and Offe have participated (see Little, 1998). And yet, unlike statist Marxism, the role of communities in the production of a dynamic, pluralistic and inclusive democracy is privileged.

Jordan offers us the most significant contribution to the current debate on 'what is to be done about law and order' on the radical left edge of communitarian thinking. In particular, his insights on the exclusion of the poor and the need to allow them re-entry into what is termed the 'common good', in part through the provision of a universal basic income for all, may provide the basis for a progressive communitarian agenda on crime and injustice. According to Jordan, recent years in the UK and other neo-liberal societies have witnessed a deterioration in social relations due to the denial of access for the poor to majority goods and thus their experience of majority power as unjust. As a consequence, 'both the autonomy of poor people as citizens and the quality of life in the community were jeopardized' (Jordan, 1992: 157).

Such processes of social exclusion and polarization do not necessarily destroy communities in any simple sense but Jordan recognizes that new forms of particularistic communities do emerge in the absence of any notion of a shared, common good. What has emerged following the neo-liberal transformations of the last two decades is the formation of contrasting associative networks with very different ways of providing their characteristic collective goods. In particular, Jordan contends, following Hirst (1994), that two starkly opposing communities have emerged, namely communities of 'choice' and of 'fate'. The particularistic concerns of 'communities of choice' are the development of individual household strategies for income security and utility associated with comfortable, 'safe', convenient, healthy and status-giving private environments, exemplified by the imagery of the gated suburbia. On the other hand, 'communities of fate' are bound together into long-term interdependencies because of the lack of opportunities to move, gain access to good education or healthcare, get decently-paid formal work, or share in the cultural resources of mainstream society. The characteristic interdependencies and collective goods of such communities arise from the sharing among young males of high-risk lifestyles, such as informal economic activities, crime and drug use, and among women of long-term networks of reciprocal social care (Jordan, 1996: 187). In both types of community, exclusive loyalty rather than inclusive belonging emerges in this increasingly dualized society.

A universal, unconditional basic income for all citizens is viewed by Jordan and others as one specific means of sharing out the common good in a more equitable fashion (although on its own it is no policy panacea). The existence of a basic income for all would also open up the possibility for individuals and groups to participate in their own chosen projects and commitments. Such a scheme would also reduce the institutionalized traps and barriers to labour-market participation, particularly for members of 'communities of fate'. As well as a sharing-out of income, we would thus have a 'sharing-in' mainstream society and the benefits of social cooperation. On the basis of greater material equality, the communitarian concern with membership of, and mutual obligation to, collectivities would be realized. Jordan thus argues that we need to move beyond liberal theories of justice towards an adequate theory of distributive justice which 'must include an analysis of democracy, membership and participation, and hence a theory of social relations which takes account of the ways in which people share their lives as a community' (Jordan, 1992: 159).

In accord with the work of André Gorz (1992) and in contrast to the moral authoritarian communitarians described earlier, Jordan is keen to emphasize that individual moral autonomy is assured and realized through specific projects and commitments. The concrete expressions of such practices are not necessarily highbrow but instead reside in 'everyday and humdrum aspects of a society's civic culture, such as polite, convivial and tolerant relations between citizens in public places. In this sense, morality itself is a public good' (Jordan, 1992: 162). It is argued that marginalization, inequality and exclusion lie at the root of much crime and antisocial activities. As a consequence, the radical communitarian, positive agenda on crime prevention gives ethical priority to decisions over *redistribution* which in turn allows all members to participate both in the decisions themselves and, crucially, in the shared life of their communities. Unless such developments take place, Jordan suggests that the decay in consent and in allegiance to democracy will continue and with it the growth of more coercive and authoritarian methods of government and social control: 'the politics of enforcement' will also gather greater force (Jordan, 1992: 167).

Jordan and Arnold (1995) present some important reservations about the appeal to community and communal participation in criminal justice and crime prevention issues. In particular, the dangers of populist appeals to a 'participatory' politics of enforcement in crime control, which has been to the fore in the USA and the UK in the 1990s, are highlighted. They note the dangers of opening up criminal justice issues to democratic participation at precisely the moment when relations of trust between groups of citizens and between citizens and government have been at their weakest. In order to counteract the dangers of a reactionary and exclusionist moral majoritarian backlash against the criminalized, Jordan and Arnold argue that 'Balanced democratic governance may require the public power to repair social conflicts through actions in other spheres before attempting to open up criminal justice policy for public participation' (1995: 180). In other words, they are arguing for a key role to be played by the state in healing the wounds in the social fabric by measures of social justice. This strategy stands in stark contrast to what the Conservative governments in the UK during the 1980s and 1990s had done, which was to translate issues of social justice into issues of criminal justice. This contribution thus raises the question as to whether the state has to first 'repair' the social wounds before 'the community' can be allowed to participate in an inclusive politics of crime control and *social justice*.

The left realist programme

The school of left realism was established in the early 1980s in the UK as, in its own telling of the version of events, a reaction to both the popularization of a right-wing 'law and order' politics and to the vacuum in the radical left's thinking on crime and crime prevention. Its rallying call to left criminologists has been 'to take crime seriously' (Lea and Young, 1984). Left realism accepts that crime, particularly street crimes against person and property, is a real problem. Left realism sees street crime as an effect of structural dislocation, marginalization, relative deprivation and powerlessness but also as a phenomenon that reinforces and perpetuates such powerlessness. Furthermore, it is argued that crime has the great capacity to divide communities and so can lead to further serious social disorganization and decline. The public's fear of crime, particularly in the poorest localities, is viewed as being rational and well founded.

Street crime, and other forms of antisocial behaviour, are viewed as being caused by the experience of, and reaction to, brutalizing circumstances, but they are also a result of the weakening communal bonds of civil society, namely the degree of informal social control. Crime control policies are thus viewed as a social good. However, in accord with other radical communitarians, left realists argue that the 'social bricks and mortar of civil society' are a society's 'major bulwark against crime' (Young, 1994: 115). According to left realists like Jock Young in the UK and Elliot Currie (1997) in the USA, such bricks have been smashed and the mortar eroded in civil society – particularly in the most oppressed and marginalized communities – by the deluge of a philosophy and policy of rampant neo-liberal marketization in the last two decades on both sides of the Atlantic. However, the left realists are not 'soft' on the criminal. In pointing out that most working-class crime is intra-class, such as mugging, domestic violence and burglary, the left realists want to argue that such offences are morally wrong and thus the offender should feel morally responsible and be punished appropriately (Young, 1991). In an important intervention, Young has argued for the harnessing of the democratic process and communal participation in any multi-agency strategies of crime prevention in order to improve representation of all groups in the community (Young, 1991:157). In Chapter 5, the gap in the literature on multi-agency initiatives with regard to the relationship between agencies and the public or participatory communities was noted. This remains a crucial but still largely ignored issue in the research literature on crime prevention initiatives.

A major contribution to both the left realist programme on crime prevention and to the radical communitarian debate on crime, disorder and the decline of communities in the USA is found in the work of Elliot Currie (1985, 1993, 1996, 1997). Currie contends that the most serious problem facing contemporary America is that of its most disadvantaged communities sinking into a permanent state of terror and disintegration. In his study and diagnosis of the American drug crisis, Currie (1993) paints a chilling picture of the complex deprivations of inner-city life. At the same time Currie analyses the failure of the state's response to the drug crisis through the massive levels of incarceration of offenders and the simultaneous cut-backs in welfare provision for the racialized 'underclass' of Blacks and Hispanics. Currie argues that the lessons of past research into chronic serious drug abuse have been ignored by the dominant New Right policy makers in the USA. The social causation of drug abuse and thus crime is captured in the following extract:

> An enormous body of accumulating evidence continues to link mass drug abuse with the intertwined social defects described in the fifties and sixties: poverty amongst affluence, poor jobs and economic marginality, the disintegration of families and communities, the weakening of sustaining cultural values.
>
> (Currie, 1993: 76)

According to Currie, what increasingly characterizes the American 'underclass' is a 'surplus of vulnerability' exacerbated by the pervasive movement toward a more depriving, more stressful, more atomized and less supportive society. It has been noted by Schwendinger and Schwendinger (1993) that the decline of community and the crisis of the family is not the preserve of the Right. Many parents in the most deprived communities are thus overwhelmed by multiple disadvantages and so cannot counter effects of family crises on their children. The cultural (and communal) deficit which characterizes contemporary America is explained by Currie (1993: 142) as follows:

> The policies of the seventies and eighties, then, did more than merely strip individuals of jobs and income. They created communities that lacked not only viable economic opportunities, but also hospitals, fire stations, movie theatres, stores, and neighbourhood organizations – communities without strong ties of friendship or kinship, disproportionately populated by increasingly deprived and often disorganized people locked into the bottom of a rapidly deteriorating job market. In many cities these disruptive trends were accelerated by the physical destruction left by the ghetto riots of the 1960s or by urban renewal

projects and freeways that split or demolished older, more stable neighbourhoods and dispersed their residents.

Radical communitarian commentators like Currie are thus arguing that
behind the growth of crime is a *cultural* as well as a *structural* transformation of poor communities. In this regard, there are some common themes
to both the conservative communitarians such as Etzioni and radical left
communitarians such as Currie. The connecting points are around the concern with cultural deprivation and morality. However, there are also important breaks between the two variants of communitarianism, as exemplified
in the radical left's concern with structural inequalities, promotion of diversity and the key and positive role of the state in addressing social 'wounds'.
Crucial to this latter diagnosis of the crisis of law and order is a recognition
of the centrality of a multi-agency approach together with a strategy of
social and economic inclusion to reconstruct communities rather than the
dominant strategy of penal exclusion which has to date resulted in a prison
population of 1.5 million people in the USA. Currie's practical suggestions
for crime prevention, or what he prefers to call 'community safety', include
a call for an active national employment and training policy, supported by
four other national strategies for social reconstruction, namely those aimed
at revitalizing public healthcare, supporting families, assuring decent shelter
and rebuilding the physical infrastructure (Currie, 1993: 305). Indeed,
Currie shares the European radical communitarian vision of preventing
crime by moving *beyond* the crime prevention debate as traditionally
viewed. For example, Currie (1997) has argued for a strategy of 'workshar-
ing' and reduced work time as well as an expansion in the public and non-
profit sectors of the economy, and these ideas sit close to the proposals of the
basic income theorists in Europe discussed above. According to Currie, the
challenge is to 'build a society that is less unequal, less depriving, less inse-
cure, less disruptive of family life, less corrosive of co-operative values' and
in which we learn to 'live together in compassionate and co-operative ways'
(1985: 225). In response to the accusation that such appeals are utopian in
character, Currie retorts, 'Few ideas are more utopian than the belief that we
can stop crime by changing the way it is handled within the formal system
of criminal justice' (1985: 229).

What we see in the work of Currie and other radical social democratic
commentators in the USA, such as Galbraith (1996) and Lasch (1995), and
their British and Australian equivalents such as Hutton (1995) and Braithwaite (see below) is an appeal to the importance of vibrant, inclusive communities for social harmony supported by progressive state power.
Furthermore, in contrast to the technicist and individualistic focus of the situational crime prevention discourse, this radical communitarian crime prevention discourse looks to deep-lying structural factors as its key
explanation of the 'crime problem'. And so, according to Galbraith (1996:

25–6), 'Crime and social convulsion in our great cities are the products of poverty and a perverse class structure . . . the presently accepted solution is police action, the warehousing of the criminally inclined . . . the humane and quite possibly less expensive solution is to end the poverty that induces social disorder'.

A radical twist on responsibility?

Pat O'Malley (1994: 21) has noted that much of the rethinking in criminology of late has focused on 'the place occupied by responsibility in crime and crime prevention'. In Chapter 4, we saw that the notion of responsibility was central to the neo-liberal agenda around rational choice as well as to the moral authoritarian communitarian agendas discussed above. However, responsibility as a concept and signifier need not belong just to reactionary and regressive agendas on crime. Indeed, O'Malley argues that it is important to critical criminologists also, as with the example of police responsibility to local communities. 'Discourses of responsibility for crime and crime prevention are thus not the possessions of the political Right, and they do not imply only a punitive response to offending' (O'Malley, 1994: 22).

O'Malley's modest proposal is to take up the discourses of responsibility (so effective in the hands of the right) and 'turn them back on those that wield them'. 'The primary issue . . . is to confront them with demands, proposals, strategies which problematize the conditions under which responsibility can be exercised' (O'Malley, 1994: 22). In particular, O'Malley makes two suggestions: first that a measure of responsibility is proportional to the community's degree of self-determination, so radicals should press for the creation of conditions in which responsibility can be exercised and maximized; and second that the responsibility of the community for crime prevention could enable the call for consultation with, and participation of, communities 'while at the same time stressing that communities require resources and autonomy in order to exercise such responsibilities' (O'Malley, 1992: 268). Here we see a linking of the notion of responsibility to that of empowerment. The political use of responsibility by radicals may also help foster the recognition that what O'Malley terms 'shared risk' or 'social risk' may not be disconnected from social justice and social solidarity (p. 268).

Restorative justice and 'reintegrative shaming': excavating the future from the past?

In this section attention is turned to some examples of the contemporary 'resurfacing' of appeals to traditional non-statist communitarian modes of crime prevention. The restorative justice movement has gained most momentum in societies which have managed in part to 'rediscover', to varying degrees, the systems of justice of their indigenous peoples. The focus here is chiefly on the contribution of John Braithwaite to this radical communitarian perspective (see Braithwaite, 1989, 1993; see also Braithwaite and Pettit, 1990; Braithwaite and Daly 1994; Braithwaite and Mugford, 1994). There is of course a much wider 'abolitionist' body of literature on restorative justice (see Christie, 1977; de Haan, 1990; van Swaaningen, 1997) but none captures the communitarian tendency of its agenda as acutely as the work of Braithwaite.

Braithwaite is unusual in contemporary criminology because of, *inter alia*, his profound misgivings about 'statist' responses to the crime problem, his critique of the 'paralysis of pessimism' in most criminology, and his support for 'preventing crime through mobilizing social movements' (Braithwaite, 1992: 6). Grass-roots social movements are viewed as being the crucial means of generating a wider public and community disapproval of antisocial and oppressive behaviours, including crimes, which statist responses have largely failed to address successfully. In particular, Braithwaite (1995: 278) has celebrated 'how progressive social movements are finally mobilizing community disapproval against our protected criminal species'. Let's now examine the most 'practical' and influential communitarian strategy of crime prevention pioneered by Braithwaite and others in Australia and New Zealand, namely 'reintegrative shaming'.

Braithwaite outlined his general theory of communitarian restorative justice and crime prevention in his book *Crime, Shame and Reintegration* (1989). In it, and in line with other communitarian theorists, Braithwaite is quite explicit about the nature of a good society. It will be 'both strong on duties and strong on rights, and especially strong on duties that protect rights' (p. 158). Unlike conservative communitarians such as Etzioni (1994), it is of interest that Braithwaite chooses to emphasize the duty to protect rights. However, in accord with the general drift of communitarian thought, Braithwaite does not flinch from arguing that society's response to crime must be moralizing (but not rejecting). His broad Durkheimian thesis is that highly integrated societies have relatively low levels of crime (for example, Japan) and in turn individuals enmeshed in close interdependencies with others (for example, women in families) tend also to be less at risk of criminality than those in 'anomic' or less rule-bound and less integrated situations (for example, young unemployed men). From this starting point, Braithwaite develops his highly influential claim – particularly evident in the policies and practices on youth offending since the late 1980s in Australia and New Zealand and increasingly 'marketed' worldwide (Blagg, 1997) – that 'reintegrative shaming' represents the most successful means of crime control and prevention. Braithwaite (1993: 1) has defined reintegrative shaming as follows:

Reintegrative shaming is disapproval dispensed within an ongoing relationship with the offender based on respect, shaming which focuses on the evil of the deed rather than on the offender as an irredeemably evil person, where degradation ceremonies are followed by ceremonies to decertify deviance, where forgiveness, apology, and repentance are culturally important.

Reintegrative shaming also expresses society's disapproval of the act by bringing the wrongdoer, the victim and close associates of each party together in a group setting. It is seen by Braithwaite as standing in opposition to 'disintegrative' shaming, the norm in modern Western states, as a result of which there is labelling and stigma and the creation of a class of outcasts. It is argued that much of the preventive success of reintegrative shaming lies in its work on the offender's conscience. However such preventive processes will only work in situations where loss of respect counts heavy. Braithwaite (1993: 2) thus acknowledges that it is 'communitarianism that makes shaming possible'. Unlike modern Western systems of justice and punishment which isolate and stigmatize the guilty through exclusionary disposal (such as custody), reintegrative shaming aims to accept the guilty back into the community and so help prevent future offending through a process of active reintegration. We may note that Braithwaite (1995: 297) accepts the general criticism of the workings of criminal justice in contemporary Western societies that pride is not given enough importance as a complement to shame in the prevention of offending. In accord with this claim, Braithwaite (1995: 283) has noted the great importance of the family in preventing crime in that 'what families do is much more important to the causation and prevention of crime than what police forces do'. More generally, it is acknowledged that 'most social control is communitarian control rather than state control and that most of the day-to-day successes are achieved by dialogic regulation, with state regulation stepping in to mop up the failures' (Braithwaite, 1995: 302).

In some important ways, Braithwaite's approach is close to that of the North European abolitionists such as Christie (1977), de Haan (1990) and Hulsman (1986). Abolitionists are keen to remind us that the events and behaviours that *are* criminalized make up only a minute part of the events and behaviours that *can* be so. They suggest that crime is not the object but the product of crime control philosophies and institutions. More particularly, social problems, conflicts and troubles are an inevitable part of everyday life and therefore cannot, or rather should not, be delegated to professionals and specialists claiming to provide 'solutions'. When professionals and state agencies intervene, the essence of social problems and conflicts is 'stolen' and re-presented in forms that only perpetuate the problems and conflicts. In this 'replacement discourse' (van Swaaningen, 1997: 117) to that of traditional and dominant crime prevention discourses, the criminal justice system is seen as a major 'social problem'. It is suggested that the abolition of the 'crime control industry' (Christie, 1993) would also revitalize the social fabric by allowing other forms of conflict resolution, peacemaking and community safety to be imagined and properly resourced.

Much of Braithwaite's analysis sits easily with this destructuring impetus although he is not himself an abolitionist, arguing that it is right to shame certain kinds of conduct as 'criminal' in certain contexts. For Braithwaite, most modern statist systems of social control involve the use of social distance, as in the criminal label and exclusionary shaming. The results of such processes are seen as reducing further the bonds of the social networks in which the offender was located and which were crucial in both sheltering and constraining her or him. This loosening of communitarian bonds in turn increases the likelihood of offending in the future. The growth of formal systems of control thus reduces informal and localized control.

There are obvious risks with this strategy of shaming of which Braithwaite is well aware. As he notes, 'shaming can become the principal weapon of the tyranny of the majority' (1989: 158). This concern has led Braithwaite to argue that the securing of liberty or 'the maximization of the dominion of individual people' must lie at the centre of what he terms 'civic republican justice' (Braithwaite and Pettit, 1990: 54). Despite claims that shaming is unlikely to work in the complex, anonymous societies of the modern era, Braithwaite has made a strong argument for its continuing salience as a crime prevention approach in our current situation. As he notes, 'Today's enormous proliferation of roles in fact makes us more vulnerable to shame in a way that is peculiar to a world of such role proliferation' (1993: 14). He also argues that shaming within his communitarian project is far from being reactionary and targeted at the most vulnerable minorities. Braithwaite argues that it is a crucial communitarian resource in mobilizing against those offenders who brutalize and exploit as well as restraining those who would wish to trample on the rights of citizens who wish to be (harmlessly) deviant (1993: 16).

Braithwaite provides quite concrete examples of how this approach to both restorative justice and crime prevention may be realized in practice. In one paper (Braithwaite and Mugford, 1994), examples are offered of community conferences (or family group conferences) for young offenders in New Zealand which are 'based' on Maori traditions conducive to reintegrative shaming, involving kin and significant others of both the victim and the offender. Such conferences appear to have led to genuine diversion from the court and incarceration (Braithwaite and Mugford, 1994: 146). Furthermore, Braithwaite and Mugford praise such conferences for the creation of a new mode of knowledge, namely 'citizen knowledge'. In acting as a form of 'communion', they further contend that such conferences are 'de-professionalizing, empowering of women, oriented to flexible community problem-solving and for the most part, narrowing the nets of social control' (1994:168).

The feminist potential of communitarian crime control and prevention as part of a 'grass-roots' social movement has been articulated in Braithwaite and Daly (1994). Braithwaite and Daly begin by noting the failure of the criminal justice system's interventions in the area of male violence against women across most contemporary societies. As a response to this failure, the authors argue the case for 'community conferences' as a more viable means of addressing this 'grave problem' by confronting exploitative masculinities with pro-feminist voices and by treating the participants as citizens rather than legal subjects. Again they contend that the approach can work practically, indeed the 'genius' of the Maori approach is 'that it is a particularistic, individual-centred communitarianism that can work in an urban setting' (Braithwaite and Daly, 1994: 195). Although the authors see a constraining role for Western universalist legal principles, the future prospects which they would support in Australia are of an 'empowered legal pluralism' geared to the needs of a multicultural society. Finally, it is contended that the great appeal of such community crime prevention conferences lie in their capacity to make 'incidents of violence become occasions for community debates about brutalising masculinities and inequalities spawning violence' (Braithwaite and Daly, 1994: 208).

Great claims are clearly made by Braithwaite for community conferences as one mechanism of communitarian restorative justice and crime prevention. However, it is wise to remain circumspect about their potential for creating the concrete conditions for a radical, non-discriminatory communitarian approach to justice. Significant and worrying questions do remain with the theory and practice of reintegrative shaming as a form of simultaneous restorative justice and crime prevention. For example, it has as yet to be shown that reintegrative shaming will not be mobilized against the most vulnerable sections of the society and indeed be employed for trivial offenders without any reduction in the use of traditional custodial sentences. Ken Polk (1997: 197), commenting on the use of family conferencing in Australia, for example, has criticized the lack of any systematic attention to community reintegration directed at employment, training or schooling. It would appear that the most criminalized groups in both Australia and New Zealand (respectively Aboriginal people and Maori people) are the most common subjects of both 'reintegrative shaming' community conferences and high (and increasing) rates of incarceration. Harry Blagg has argued that the 'franchizing' of conferencing in Australia highlights the difficulties and dangers of trying to impose a mechanism associated with one culture (that is, reintegrative shaming ceremonies associated with the structured, hierarchical tribalism of Maori culture in New Zealand) onto that of different cultures (Aboriginal peoples in Australia in which there is no fixed, hierarchically-structured tribalism). He also questions the claim that shaming is a universal theme to all cultures. Blagg contends that the 'Wagga Wagga' model of conferencing in Australia has extended the powers of the police over young Aboriginal people (whereas the New Zealand reforms in the

1980s were part of a deliberate, de-colonizing strategy of Maori empower-ment). As Blagg (1997: 481) notes, 'The product being franchized in Aus-tralia (and marketed internationally) promises to intensify rather than reduce police controls over Aboriginal people'. Finally, Blagg suggests that the discourse of 'human rights' should be the crucial strategy for providing justice to oppressed indigenous peoples rather than reintegrative shaming since this discourse offers the best means of protecting them from their own governments which have been the greatest (criminal) threat to their survival (Blagg, 1997: 501).

Nor can we be sure how the 'community' comes to be represented in such settings. In contemporary America, for example, current shaming tech-niques include the forced carrying of billboards announcing 'I am a crimi-nal'. In the UK in the late 1990s, there is also a proposal from the current Home Secretary, Jack Straw, to name, and thus shame, young offenders in court. There is also a populist campaign to publish the photographs of young offenders in the press. We should note the danger of shaming in prac-tice degenerating into vindictiveness. In this context, van Swaaningen (1997: 209) rightly points out that there are powerful economic, political and sym-bolic interests behind criminalization and the 'power to punish' to which the reintegrative shaming thesis pays insufficient acknowledgement. The extent to which reintegrative shaming is employed routinely against powerful indi-viduals and agencies, not least shaming intolerable criminal justice practices, also needs much more critical attention. Furthermore, the lack of account-ability and the absence of protection for the offender in terms of appeals to legality and due process remain major areas of concern. It is wise not to see reintegrative shaming as a panacea to all the ills of crime and social harm. At the same time, it is questionable whether any of the above criticisms negate the progressive potentialities of communitarian restorative justice *per se*. Rather, such criticisms demonstrate both the pitfalls of poor implemen-tation and the subversion of restorative justice's principles in specific 'pro-jects'.

Critical appraisal of the radical left politics of community-based crime prevention

Unlike the moral authoritarianism of communitarian thinkers like Etzioni and Dennis, this body of work appears to represent both a radical reappro-priation of the appeal to community but also a recognition of the crucial role for the state and economic policy in effecting greater social justice. Nor can these radical left communitarians be accused of holding 'the belief that the solution to neighbourhood crime problems can be achieved primarily through the self-help efforts of residents' (Hope, 1995: 66). Indeed, radical communitarians would surely concur with Hope in arguing that:

'Disintegrating urban communities may need significant investment in their institutional infrastructure to offset the powerful tendencies of destabilization of poor communities within the urban free-market economy' (1995: 78).

However, the extent to which such aspirations for a radical, left social democratic political agenda can be realized in the face of both the authoritarian penal populism and the fragmentation of communities in late modernity remains open to further debate. This noted, the sense of belonging through a politics of democratization in turn appears to be an essential condition for the development of mutual trust and toleration in the struggle against social harms and injustice.

This body of radical left communitarian work is not without its limitations. It is limited as a pragmatic social science given the lack of empirical substantiation for its participatory democratic visions of civil society and vibrant, expansive communities. There also remains the not insignificant problem of how we may get from the present 'here' to the future 'there'. Oldfield (1990: 155) may be correct in noting that radical writers have tended to duck the question of how to motivate individuals to engage in the practices of citizenship and thus community-building, even if his claim that it has to be authoritatively inculcated may not sit easy with some. Significant tensions exist about what sort of institutional arrangements might enable the realization of such an inclusive and vibrant civil society. Furthermore, the big question remains as to what might create the more redistributive economic strategies upon which these radical communitarian visions of crime prevention and social reconstruction are dependent. Bottoms and Wiles (1996: 35) have noted that:

> informal group control and trust undoubtedly reduce the amount of crime, but it is not clear that these can be easily created by acts of public policy (although that does not mean that we should not examine how far available alternative policies might, or might not, undermine such control and trust).

This is an important caveat to bear in mind in weighing up the potential for a radically progressive communitarian agenda in which the role of public policies in stimulating the development of vibrant and less corrosive communities is aired.

Most contemporary sociologists and criminologists are deeply sceptical about the use of appeals to community in crime prevention 'talk' and practice (see Chapter 5). According to Garland (1996), this appeal to, and use of, community and the 'active citizen' as a new means of 'governing' crime may again be best understood as part of a wider adaptation to the realization of high crime rates as a normal 'social fact' in late modernity. More than this, the appeal to the self-help community is viewed by Garland as a deliberate project emanating from the state in tandem with the situational and multi-agency prevention discourses outlined in Chapters 4 and 5. Put crudely, communitarian crime prevention initiatives may be seen as representing forms of top-down manipulation of the population from the central political authority. They are viewed as being part of a 'responsibilization strategy' or 'governance at a distance' by means of which the state devolves responsibilities for crime prevention onto agencies, organizations, groups and individuals outside the state and persuades them to act appropriately. According to the logic of this 'responsibilization strategy', the sources of crime and also the means of its control and prevention are viewed as lying in the behaviour and attitudes of individual citizens qua consumers and their local communities. It is clear that the rhetoric of community and agency partnerships may be seen as dovetailing neatly with the notions of individual citizen responsibility and a coercive communitarianism which are at the centre of a neo-liberal vision of a reduced role for the state in free-market societies. At the same time, it is noted by Garland (1996: 452–4) that this development of 'governance at a distance' ironically leaves the centralized state machine more powerful than before with an extended capacity for action and influence.

Garland is not the first theorist to plot this top-down, and outwards dispersal movement to explain the rise of community-based crime prevention discourse in the last two decades (see McLaughlin, 1994). There is much that is compelling about this diagnosis of the changing state/public nexus on law and order issues. Indeed, for Garland the combined use of both social and situational crime prevention strategies involves a 're-ordering of the conduct of everyday life right across the social field . . . Where the state once targeted the deviant for transformative action, it now aims to bring about marginal but effective changes in the norms, the routines, and the consciousness of everyone' (Garland, 1996: 454). An ambitious social engineering programme indeed! However, this grand theoretical approach may be guilty of neglecting countervailing forces at work on the wider social fabric/body politic and of underplaying the possibility of 'unsettlements' of the state's dominant agenda on crime control. We may, for example, ask what of a political mobilization around community as symbolic of new resistances and solidarities in opposition to the central state's programme of popular penalism and 'privatized prudentialism'? (see Hughes and Mooney, 1998). I return to these questions in Chapter 7 below.

Summary

This chapter has focused on the different appropriations and uses of community in contemporary communitarian debates on crime and crime prevention. In particular, I examined the conservative communitarian discourse on community and the 're-moralization of society'. In the second half of the chapter, the radical communitarian agenda on crime prevention and social justice was critically explored. From the discussion to date, it will be apparent that there is much 'unfinished business' around appeals to the ideologically volatile vision of 'community' in contemporary debates on crime prevention and social justice.

Further reading

Hope, T. (1995) 'Community Crime Prevention', in M. Tonry and D. Farrington (eds), *Building a Safer Society: Strategic Approaches to Crime*. Chicago: University of Chicago Press.

Hughes, G. (1996a) 'Communitarianism and Law and Order', *Critical Social Policy*, 16, 4: 17–41.

chapter seven

The futures of crime control in late modernity

Introduction

This final substantive chapter looks at the influential theorizing around late modernity and risk society and explores what the implications of these diagnoses of the condition of our times (both utopian and dystopian) are for the understanding of comparative trends in crime prevention. In this chapter I begin with an overview of the sociological thesis on late modernity and risk society, focusing on the simultaneous trends towards both globalization and localization. Following this exposition, I examine how these broad trends might be connected to current, international developments in crime prevention. I then present three possible scenarios of the futures of crime prevention, associated with:

1 the model of privatism and social exclusion;
2 the model of authoritarian, statist communitarianism; and
3 the radical communitarian model of inclusive cities and local programmes of community safety.

It will be emphasized that the diagnoses on which these models are based are both analyses of current processes and 'imaginaries' of the possible futures of social control.

A word of caution is merited about the use of comparative examples in social science. There are some well-recognized problems in comparative analysis in the social sciences since such work often appears to be based on impressionistic accounts drawn from other countries with which the researcher is often only superficially knowledgeable. There is often a lurch between 'the grass is always greener on the other side' conclusion, to implicit cultural stereotyping and ethnocentrism, both of which miss the complex nuances evident in a particular cultural formation (see Fukuyama, 1996 for a recent example of such crude stereotyping). This noted, I would argue that the opportunities opened up by comparative analysis still make it a 'risk' worth taking.

Late modernity, risk society and social control

Throughout this book I have used the late modern risk society thesis as a key conceptual frame for understanding both the history and contemporary manifestations of crime prevention discourses. Let's now revisit, following the initial remarks on this thesis in the Introduction, its key tenets as a theoretical framework for understanding the forces for both change and order in contemporary societies before its specific implications for making sense of current and future trends in crime prevention are explored.

Anthony Giddens (1990, 1991) has argued that one of the key societal changes brought by late modernity is the alteration in the environments of both trust and risk and the growth of ontological insecurity. In brief, it is argued that modernity undermines the salience of kinship ties, fractures the hold of the local community, and undermines the authority of religion and appeals to tradition. Giddens claims that these effects can be attributed to 'disembedding mechanisms' which detach social relations from local contexts and restructure them across indefinite spans of space and time. In order to formulate this thesis, Giddens employs the classical sociological 'trick' of drawing up two exaggerated ideal types of the pre-modern and the (late) modern world. It is important to remember that this a heuristic device to help the sociologist present his or her central thesis more clearly. It is thus not to suggest that 'the past' and 'the present' were ever so simply characterized.

Accepting these qualifications, Giddens contends that pre-modern societies were 'environments of trust' based on kinship relations, local community as place, religion and tradition. Kinship relations acted as the organizing device for stabilizing social ties across time and space. Religious cosmologies functioned as modes of belief and ritual practice, providing a providential interpretation of human life and of nature. Tradition, as past-oriented belief and practice, acted as a means of connecting the present and the future. The local community existed as a spatially- and socially-bounded place which provided a familiar milieu for its members. In such societies, then, there is the overriding importance of localized trust in maintaining social control (Giddens, 1990: 102).

In stark contrast to this situation and environment, Giddens contends that we now inhabit the (late) modern world where trust is both embedded in personal and intimate relations and vested in disembedded abstract systems of expert knowledge. Personal relationships of friendship or sexual intimacy now act as the key means of stabilizing social ties, instead of kinship. In turn, abstract expert systems now act as the means of stabilizing relations across indefinite spans of time and space. Tradition and religious cosmologies are increasingly replaced by future-oriented, counter-factual thought as a mode of connecting the past and present. Modernity has thus encouraged trust in abstract, expert systems such as positivist science and social science as the motor of rational progress. With the development of high or late modernity, however, we have witnessed the growth of counter-factual thought and greater scepticism about expertise, be it concerned with safe food or crime control or whatever.

Giddens (1990) has described living in late modernity as being akin to 'riding a juggernaut'. Late modernity is thus somewhat like a runaway engine of enormous power which it is possible to ride to some extent but which also threatens to run out of control. Accordingly Giddens emphasizes that current and future trends are complex and uncertain with a puzzling diversity of options and possibilities opened up: 'Living in the "risk society" means living with a calculable attitude to the *open* possibilities of action, positive and negative, with which, as individuals and globally, we are confronted in a continuous way in our contemporary social existence' (1991: 28 my emphasis). Giddens certainly recognizes the importance of accelerating processes of surveillance and the attraction of 'privatism' in the era of late modernity on which most subsequent radical writers on contemporary trends in social control have focused. However, Giddens (1990: 137) also points to the possibility of 'radical engagement', that is, an attitude of practical contestation towards perceived sources of danger:

Those taking a stance of radical engagement hold that, although we are beset by major problems, we can and should mobilize either to reduce their impact or to transcend them. This is an optimistic outlook, but one bound up with contestory action rather than the faith in rational analysis and discussion. Its prime vehicle is the social movement.

Beck (1992) has written about the consequences of scientific and industrial development during the twentieth century as unleashing a set of risks ('*effets pervers*'), the likes of which humanity has never previously faced. These risks are not just the 'already destructive consequences' but also the 'potential element' of risks in the future (Beck, 1992: 33). In accord with this development, our survival is now dependent on modernization becoming reflexive (for example, being critical of scientific claims 'to know best'). In Beck's terms, 'science's monopoly on rationality is broken' (p. 29) and yet technical experts are still given the pole position to define agendas and impose bounding premises on risk discourses, in whatever field we wish to examine. Overall, Beck sees the pace of changes in the techno-economic system as being so rapid that 'Science fiction is increasingly becoming a memory of past times' (p. 185).

Beck has defined risks as being the probabilities of physical harm due to given technological or other processes. Unlike the factory-related hazards of the nineteenth century and the first half of the twentieth century, risks are no longer limited to certain groups or localities, but instead exhibit a tendency to globalization (Beck, 1992: 13). These are of course very 'big' claims and controversial in themselves. It is arguable, for example, that we are actually living in the second era of globalization (Jordan, 1996), following that of nineteenth-century imperialism. Beck seems to conveniently forget the global risks of enslavement, opium addiction and colonization associated with imperialisms in the past.

According to Beck, risk society is now dominated by the question, 'how can the risks and hazards systematically produced as part of modernization be prevented, minimized, dramatized, or channelled?' (Beck, 1992: 19). Calculable risks are viewed as being to the fore with the 'provident state', and risk-fighting is now big business. This stands in contrast to the key question of industrial or class society which, for Beck, was how socially produced wealth could be distributed in a socially unequal yet also legitimate way? In passing, I would note that there may be great exaggeration from Beck with regard to our contemporary society's departure from the previous historical era of industrial class society: such hyperbole is common for 'prophets' of social change (Kumar, 1978). Beck does in fact admit that some groups are more deleteriously affected than others by the distribution and growth of risks. In other words, there are different 'social risk positions' (Beck, 1992: 23) but Beck argues that risk positions are not synonymous with class positions. One example may be that of being an urban dweller and, in some cases, the shared risks that this involves for different income groups who participate, for example, in using the underground train service or 'the tube'. The unevenness of risk positions is most acute in the international context of 'Third World' countries as against the wealthy 'Western' societies.

Beck contends that our contemporary consciousness has become future-oriented: 'The centre of risk consciousness lies not in the present, but in the future . . . We become active today in order to prevent, alleviate or take precautions against the problems and crises of tomorrow and the day after tomorrow' (1992: 34). This new consciousness is viewed by some commentators as crucial to understanding the massive growth in concerns about, and strategies of, risk management in the field of the control of crime and disorder. Beck has also noted that the risk society is also the globalizing science, media and information society which is moving beyond being organized as nation-states. This in turn may bring about 'communities of danger' that ultimately can only be comprised in supra-national networks (Beck, 1992: 47). Again the implications of such general trends towards transnationalization are potentially immense for crime control in the future.

What then of the possible futures according to Beck's self-consciously polemical thesis? He appears to offer us both dystopian and utopian possibilities. According to his negative, dystopian reading of the possibilities, Beck sees the strong chance of a 'scapegoat society' and 'a tendency to a *legitimate totalitarianism of hazard prevention*' (Beck, 1992: 80, original emphasis). In other words, the dangers of crime, pollution, disasters and epidemics may become viewed as so great that liberties, freedoms and democratic debate may be sacrificed and replaced by an all-powerful single political authority. On a more optimistic front, Beck (1996) has argued that we are, not least, expected to live with the most diverse, contradictory global and personal risks. We all now face, as individuals, 'risky freedoms', the answer to which seems to lie in a new form of communitarianism: 'At the same time the question as to the *we*, that is able to bind and motivate the individualized individuals, becomes urgent' (Beck, 1996: 30). Hope for the future also seems to lie with risk society's tendency to be a self-critical culture.

Both Giddens' and Beck's answer to the problems of insecurity and uncertainty in late modernity appears to rest on the importance of new relations of trust embedded in reflexive knowledge. They see a re-embedding and growing importance of personalized trust, based on deliberately cultivated, face to face relationships. There is thus a renewed role for interpersonal trust together with a decline in trust in abstract expert systems. In turn, it is recognized that such developments in late modernity can lead to passivism and privatism, but they may also help generate new forms of social activism. For the sceptical critic, such a position may be seen as an example of 'wanting to have it both ways'!

Let's now examine what the implications of such abstract social scientific speculations are for our problem of the future(s) of crime prevention.

Connecting developments in crime prevention to late modernity

Risk society theorists would contend that there is a clear link between the growing concern with both individual and collective security/safety and heightened fears of risks. The claim that 'Risks experienced presume a normative horizon of lost security and broken trust' (Beck, 1992: 28) seems to ring bells with the message from communitarian analyses of both regressive and progressive variants discussed in Chapter 6. According to Beck, class societies were to be understood in terms of the normative project of the ideal of equality. However, Beck suggests that this is not so for late modern risk society. 'Its normative counter-project, which is its basis and motive force, is safety. Whereas the utopia of equality contains a wealth of substantial and *positive* goals of social change, the utopia of the risk society remains peculiarly *negative* and *defensive*' (p. 49). The driving force in late modern societies would thus seem to be not about attaining something good but rather preventing the worst: 'The driving force in the class society can be summarized in the phrase: *I am hungry!* The movement set in motion by the risk society, on the other hand, is expressed in the statement: *I am afraid!* The *commonality of anxiety* takes the place of the *commonality of need*' (p. 49). Again, much of the regressive, moral communitarian work on crime control discussed in Chapter 6 appears to reflect this fear and anxiety. Beck remains unsure whether this commonality of anxiety may work as a binding force for society at large. In particular, he raises the question of how capable this commonality of anxiety is of compromise given the dangers of 'irrationalism, extremism, or fanaticism' (p. 49).

Of late, an increasing number of social theorists have taken up the challenge of relating developments in crime prevention and risk management to the large-scale, historical shifts highlighted in this grand theorizing on late modernity. It is important at this point to note that I wish to resist the temptations of teleological argument here. A teleological argument is one where it is assumed that events or processes are heading towards one inevitable goal. In what follows, some possible, perhaps probable, futures for crime prevention and public safety are explored. I begin with the comparative overview of crime prevention trends in late modernity developed by Bottoms and Wiles (1996) before examining in depth three stark models or 'ideal types' of the possible futures of crime prevention and public safety. In particular, I address the contrasting dystopian and utopian scenarios of:

- the 'privatized fortress cities' model;
- the 'authoritarian statist-communitarian' model; and
- the 'inclusive civic, safe cities' model.

Again these models are heuristic devices and ideal types which simplify the complex nature of the 'lived realities' of crime prevention in any specific context. They are also likely to underplay the complex convergences across the separate ideal types in reality.

Bottoms and Wiles on comparative, globalizing trends

Bottoms and Wiles (1996: 10–26) have usefully distinguished six features of recent social change in late modernity which are of special significance for the understanding of comparative contemporary trends in crime prevention. These six features of late modernity are:

1 economic changes (e.g. the increasingly obvious internationalization of capital and business, changes in the production process and the decline of manufacturing, growing income polarization, the growth of the consumer economy);
2 tendencies towards globalization and localization (e.g. location for economic activity based on corporate choice rather than geographical necessity, unevenness of economic development, 'hollowing out of the state');
3 technology and its consequences (e.g. use of technology for purposes of surveillance, cultural consequences of intermediate technology);
4 changes in the sources of trust (e.g. from localized trust in tradition to open-ended trust relations embedded in disembodied systems and personally-chosen trust relationships);
5 changing forms of social differentiation (e.g. erosion of class as a signifier, growing importance of lifestyle, changing significance of gender);
6 managerialism (e.g. state agencies as integrated policy systems to be managed, strategic plans, performance indicators, active monitoring, bureaucratic-administrative law).

Bottoms and Wiles (pp. 26–35) go on to illustrate how these related changes help explain the four main types of contemporary crime prevention which they classify as 'defensive strategies', 'guardianship and monitoring', 'the creation of new forms of social order' and 'criminality prevention'.

Under the umbrella term of 'defensive strategies', Bottoms and Wiles first point out that post-war economic growth, the increased affluence of the average family and growing consumerism neither reduced relative inequalities nor the rate of crime. However, increased affluence did lead to countervailing defensive strategies against property theft. In turn, the breakdown of traditional forms of differentiation and group-based trust (particularly around class and locality) produced a new heightened social anonymity. New defensive strategies against personal crimes and in support of enhanced personal security thus emerged. The new anonymity also means that individuals increasingly turn to abstract systems in which they can place trust (for example 'reassuring' technology). Defended locales develop, often involving a series of private realms bounded by the 'dangerous' public realm outside.

The second type of contemporary crime prevention is that of 'guardianship and monitoring'. Bottoms and Wiles claim that the social changes outlined earlier produce an increased demand for guardianship beyond that provided traditionally by the public police. In the market place there are now new providers of guardianship, particularly in the guise of private security police. Technological guardianship devices also become a normal part of the urban landscape, such as CCTV. The simultaneous and contradictory consequences of globalization and localization also mean that public control agencies are forced to devise locally-targeted services as well as national and supra-national cooperation between agencies. Monitoring of information has also become a crucial feature of organizations in late modernity in the wake of the new abstract trust systems and the rise of new managerialism. This concern to manage and control the organization's activities through the monitoring of information collected is to the fore in crime prevention agencies. This development may result in the growth of 'paper success' which bears little relation to what is happening on the ground.

The third type of contemporary crime prevention is that associated with 'the creation of new forms of social order'. According to Bottoms and Wiles, an important consequence of late modernity is the decline of the nation-state as a sovereign power (sometimes called 'the hollowing out of the state' thesis). At the same time, the inefficiencies of 'the system' of criminal justice are exposed by the new 'information society'. To make matters worse, late modernity also weakens traditional sources of informal, communitarian social control. Taken together, these processes generate three related responses. First, there is the push to improve 'system efficiency' by encouraging state agencies to work together (for example, multi-agency crime prevention). Second, there is the growing recognition of the limits to state power and the need to seek 'partnerships' with other organizations to achieve crime control. Third, in the wake of the declining informal mechanisms of social control, there is an attempt to create new formal or semi-formal structures of social control (such as 'community safety' strategies). More generally, the decline of the nation-state's pre-eminence as a sovereign power has led to the emergence of an increasingly private provision of order and the emergence of multiple social orders, each resorting to the powerful social control tactic of exclusion. Finally, globalization appears to stimulate the development of perceived new harms, such as international fraud and drug trafficking, which are outside the ability of the nation-state to control. Supra-national crime prevention initiatives are the likely consequence of such developments.

The final type of contemporary crime prevention outlined is that of 'criminality prevention'. Criminality prevention or 'developmental crime prevention' (see Chapter 3) is largely focused on targeting children or young people and their families for intensive intervention. Bottoms and Wiles argue that this 'new' strategy of crime prevention needs to be explained in terms of changes taking place in the institutions of socialization, such as the family and schools, during late modernity. In particular, they note the increasing importance attached to elective, personal relationships rather than traditional or received forms of relationship as the basis of everyday trust. This change weakens greatly the social control and normalization capacities of institutions such as the family, the school and the church. The rise of 'criminality prevention' represents an attempt to develop policies which will prevent such changes or create alternative sources of moral education and control. The consequences of such targeting and the possibility of improved technical capacities, allowing the identification of current offenders and the prediction of likely future offenders, is not without its risks and costs. As Bottoms and Wiles (1996: 35) note, 'Improved technical ability to identify and act against offenders will mean that consciously developed policies of reintegration may be necessary if dangerous polarization and exclusion are not to be the unintended consequences'.

In conclusion, Bottoms and Wiles do emphasize that the effects of late modernity are very uneven on a localized basis (although their substantive analysis gives little indication of such an open-ended situation!). The overall picture painted by them is a depressing one. I would argue that they down-play the positive or progressive potential of some developments in late modernity identified by Giddens and by Beck (see Model 3 below).

Let's now focus on the three ideal typical scenarios of crime control. I begin with the model of 'fortress cities' in which privatism and social exclusion are to the fore. It is worth noting that it is this first dystopian model, epitomized by developments in North America, which has received most attention from criminologists and sociologists in their efforts to discern 'the master pattern' at work in crime and deviancy control (Cohen, 1985).

Model 1: 'fortress cities', privatism and social exclusion

Radical theorists of social control in contemporary North America have pointed to the militarization of city life and the rise of the 'fortress city' (Davis, 1990), the growth of more subtle forms of prevention and regulation through the seductions of privatized consumerism (Shearing and Stenning, 1985), and the not so subtle modes of risk management through targeted containment and exclusion of 'risky' populations (Feeley and Simon, 1992). Let's now briefly examine these three influential analyses of trends in crime prevention 'US-style'.

Davis on Los Angeles: the fortress city

In Mike Davis' book *City of Quartz* (1990) we are given some grim greetings from the metropolis of Los Angeles. Davis' depiction largely accords with Beck's fears regarding the negative and defensive 'Utopia' of the risk society (Beck, 1992: 42). The following passage captures the major elements of Davis' depiction and analysis of Los Angeles as 'the fortress city' of the future:

> The carefully manicured lawns of Los Angeles' Westside sprout forests of ominous little signs warning: 'Armed Response!' Even richer neighbourhoods in the canyons and hillsides isolate themselves behind walls guarded by gun-toting private police and state-of-the-art electronic surveillance. Downtown, a publicly-subsidized 'urban renaissance' has raised the nation's largest corporate citadel, segregated from the poor neighbourhoods around it by a monumental architectural glacis . . . In the Westlake district and the San Fernando Valley the Los Angeles Police barricade streets and seal off poor neighbourhoods as part of their 'war on drugs'. In Watts, developer Alexander Haagen demonstrates his strategy for re-colonizing inner-city retail markets: a panoptican shopping mall surrounded by staked metal fences and a substation of the LAPD [Los Angeles Police Department] in a central surveillance tower. Finally on the horizon of the next millennium, an ex-chief of police crusades for an anti-crime 'giant eye' – a geo-synchronous law enforcement satellite . . . Welcome to post-liberal Los Angeles, where the defence of luxury lifestyles is translated into a proliferation of new repressions in space and movement, undergirded by the ubiquitous 'armed response'. This obsession with physical security, and collaterally, with the architectural policing of social boundaries, has become a zeitgeist of urban restructuring, a master narrative in the emerging built environment of the 1990s.
>
> (1990: 223)

In reading this account of Los Angeles you may have been struck by its proximity to the fictional and filmic representations of inner cities 'of the future' (e.g. *Gridiron, Bladerunner, Robocop, Escape from New York* etc.). According to Davis, this is not surprising since such Hollywood movies 'only extrapolate from actually existing trends' (1990: 223). In this context we may note Beck's (1992: 185) comment on science fiction being 'the memory of things past'.

Davis sees trends in Los Angeles as a precursor of similar developments in the 'emerging built environment' elsewhere in post-liberal cities. Davis places great emphasis on the tendency to merge urban design, architecture and the police apparatus in 'a single, comprehensive security effort'. Alongside this new partnership of public and private agencies in crime prevention, a growing market in 'security' is generated: ' "Security" becomes a positional good defined by income access to private "protective services" and membership in some hardened residential enclave or restricted suburb' (1990: 224).

What of the non-affluent poor in this scenario? According to Davis, the poor and homeless of Los Angeles become perceived as 'the other', 'the underclass' who are to be contained and segregated in the new 'townships' and subjected to the militarized policing, or 'low-intensity warfare' of the LAPD. As a consequence of these trends, Davis argues that we live increasingly in 'fortress cities', brutally divided between 'fortified cells' of affluent society and 'places of terror' where the police battle the criminalized poor: 'Even as the walls have come down in Eastern Europe, they are being erected all over Los Angeles' (1990: 228). Davis' thesis thus indicates that in Los Angeles risk is class-specific and racialized, and thereby contradicts some of Beck's (1992) wilder claims about the break with the past ('industrial') society.

Perhaps the central message of Davis' portrayal of Los Angeles is the destruction of accessible public space. Space becomes either privatized for the affluent and the paranoid or is segregated into ghettos made up of ethnically strong, almost 'neo-tribal', territories. Commenting on Davis' work, Morrison notes that Los Angeles has become a post-liberal space where the overriding concern to defend luxury lifestyles creates a network of repressions in space and movement. Furthermore, the 'ideal of the control of space becomes the denial of social integration (Morrison, 1995: 267–8). As Rose (1996: 336) notes, the 'gated city' is one of the variety of new ways of 'imagining security' by which the collective logics of the community are brought into alliance with the individualized ethos of neo-liberal politics in what may be termed 'new prudential regimes' of a risk-obsessed late modernity.

In many cities of the world, then, we are witnessing the erection of real physical barriers as well as economic and social exclusions between the affluent and the poor. In the USA this process is profoundly racialized, with a Black 'criminal underclass' given the role of the 'evil other within', following the demise of communism as the 'evil other without'. If the distribution of crime prevention were to be left to the rules and vagaries of the market place, certain groups would inevitably be excluded from this market place since they could not afford to pay and thus participate. *In extremis*, this situation could lead to the creation of a dualized society of 'fortress'-like, defended locales – united by Beck's (1992: 49) 'commonality of anxiety' – and undefended 'badlands' of crime and insecurity, with membership of the 'gang' often offering some hazardous protection and belonging for those who could not compete in the market place. In Davis' chilling expression, the result of all this is 'urban apartheid' (1990: 236).

Questions remain as to the generalizibility of the 'extreme case' example of Los Angeles for other cities in the world. For example, is the USA, because of its culture and inequalities, particularly criminogenic (Currie, 1997)? However, it may also be argued that the trends discerned by Davis are not unique to the USA but are clearly discernible in such diverse countries as Brazil, South Africa, Israel, Indonesia and India (see, for example, Caldeira,

1996; Sheptycki, 1997). The earlier exposition of Bottoms and Wiles' (1996) comparative overview of crime prevention trends lends credence to this viewpoint.

Feeley and Simon on the new penology

Feeley and Simon's work (1992, 1994) specifically examines the emergence of a new strategy of corrections which they term the 'new penology'. This new strategy is characterized as follows. First, it focuses on the probabilistic calculation of risk ('actuarialism') and analysis of statistical distribution as applied to populations. 'Actuaries' are experts in insurance who calculate potential risks and determine insurance premiums accordingly. As a crime prevention approach, 'actuarial justice' is organized around the principles of social utility and efficient management rather than the principles of responsibility and culpability. Second, central to this emergent discourse is a new policy objective, namely the clear categorization of risky people in order to identify and manage them. Third, its techniques for the management of the identified risky people are by means of penal incapacitation for high-risk offenders and 'holding pens', such as the 'boot camps', for middle-range risk populations.

According to Feeley and Simon, such emergent tendencies in crime control mean that we are witnessing a shift away from the discourse of normalization of the positivist and modernist 'punitive-welfare project' (see Chapter 3). The late modernist discourse of the new penology challenges old penology's focus on the moral and pathological characteristics of the individual. Instead, its 'gaze' is on the probabilistic calculation of risk and the analyses of statistical distributions as applied to populations. The emphasis is increasingly on that of managing rather than changing people. Questions of social utility and efficient management are prioritized over questions of individual responsibility and blame. Crime and incivility are thus risks to be managed. Potentially the target becomes not the offender, nor the criminal justice system, but the community of *potential* offenders. The danger posed by this strategy is that the priorities of risk management may override justice and the disadvantaged, non-changeable and risky 'underclass' increasingly become subjected to Draconian containment or elimination.

Shearing and Stenning on corporate, non-carceral control

A less overtly chilling diagnosis of crime control in North America is offered by Clifford Shearing and Philip Stenning (1981, 1985). They highlight the emergence in the late twentieth century of a new managerialism and privatization of policing and criminal justice together with the rise of a private, non-carceral disciplinary mode of social control, particularly associated with globalizing corporations. This new mode of control is both instrumental and preventive in character, and fits easily with Beck's (1992: 34) characterization of risk consciousness as being 'future-oriented'. It is based on the profit /loss calculus of the corporation versus questions of right and wrong and involves entire non-criminalized populations being subjected to increasing surveillance and regulation (chiefly via situational techniques and information technology) and drawn into acting as control agents (due to communal/familial responsibilities).

Shearing and Stenning (1981: 228) have also argued that there is an increasing movement towards 'mass private property', defined as referring to 'control over large tracts of property (to which the public have access) by corporate interests dominated by relatively small groups of people'. In Europe, Bottoms and Wiles (1996: 3) note that this phenomenon has been termed 'intermediate spaces'; that is, private spaces accessible to the public. The legal status of such spaces would appear to be of great importance in the policing of crime prevention.

According to Shearing and Stenning, corporations concerned with the consumption of goods and services stand at the forefront of this develop-ment. In shopping malls and theme parks, we witness the clearest and most advanced expression and institutional realization of this preventive and seemingly non-coercive disciplining of subject populations. 'Disneyworld' is arguably the apogee of this trend towards pervasive, seductive control. George Ritzer in his funny and polemical work on contemporary American culture, *The MacDonaldization of Society*, confirms that social control is increasingly pervasive and all-encompassing in the new zones of socializa-tion with the following illustrative observation: 'Columnist Charles Krauthammer, following a visit to Walt Disney World with his children, describes the "false cheer" of the workers and comments that he "had the momentary feeling of having wandered into a Chinese re-education camp where everyone, guards included, was on Thorazine"' (Ritzer, 1993: 110). In van Swaaningen's words, we see social control through 'infantilization' (1997: 179).

A rampant global privatism?

The overall message from critical criminologists and sociologists from North America is that of a process of the exclusionary privatizing of safety and security (as against being a 'public good'). In turn, this exacerbates the tendency for the more affluent to retreat into enclaves from which 'trouble-some'/'dangerous' minorities – criminalized as 'flawed consumers' (Bauman, 1997: 41) – are both excluded and subjected to Draconian policing and con-tainment elsewhere.

Such developments are not the exclusive preserve of North America, even accepting the heightened expression of them there. Accordingly, O'Malley (1992) has also noted the development of 'actuarial' technologies of power (in which the calculation of risk for insurance purposes is to the fore) across late modern societies. In particular, he highlights how situational measures can, by reassigning costs of prevention to potential victims, exacerbate the segregation of urban environs into zones of high and low risk. This may produce a 'metroquilt' (Sutton, 1994: 9) of safe facilities and the less secure network of public streets. In a similar vein, Garland sees such measures in the UK as resulting in both a demise and residualization of the 'civic ideal' and an 'eclipse of the solidarity project' of the welfare state of the post-war period (1996: 463) – a project which Garland may romanticize somewhat, ignoring its exclusions and oppressions such as those around 'race', gender and disability (see Hughes and Lewis, 1998).

Cohen (1996) has offered some important comparative food for thought in his recent essay on the politics of crime control across contemporary capitalist states. He argues that political effort with regard to risk has been displaced of late from the military terrain and onto the terrain of domestic order. Writing about the capitalist states of Western Europe and the USA, Cohen suggests that 'the cult of national security represented by the Soviet threat has given way to a cult of personal security which links the hazards of predatory crime with other nameless risks (whether toxic waste, nerve gas in the subway, harmful food and obscurely motivated terrorism)' (p. 10). Cohen's essay is of particular importance because of its argument that criminologists need to understand and explore further how the mundane politics of crime control fits into this wider discourse of order, risk and security.

Bottoms has argued that the trends outlined above may be seen as the consequences of the hegemony of individualism in the late twentieth century. According to Bottoms (1990: 20) such individualism carries clear dangers:

> For if individualism really is unstoppable, the end result, or nightmare, could ultimately be a society with massive security hardware protecting individual homes, streets, and shops, while all adult citizens would carry personal alarms, and perhaps guns, for individual protection while moving from place to place.

It may be that in such neo-liberal market regimes, there are now two systems of social control, one based on seduction and the other on repression. Seduction is for the core members of society and repression is for those who are not core members of that 'consumer' society (see Bauman, 1997; Hughes, 1998c). In concluding the outline of this first model, we may ask whether we have arrived at Beck's (1992: 80) feared 'scapegoat society' in which a 'legitimate totalitarianism of hazard prevention' prevails.

Most commentators on the links between late modernity, risk society and trends in social control have taken up this dystopian side to the thesis and have, in the process, assigned communitarianism to the status of being a reactionary project (Garland, 1996). However, within the late modern risk society thesis there is also an alternative reading of possible, progressive trends which relates closely to the radical variant of communitarian thought (see Chapter 6). Remember Beck's urgent question as to 'the *we*, that is able to bind and motivate the individualized individuals' (1996: 30). If this question stands then the variants of communitarianism, both conservative and radical, are perhaps best viewed as expressions of the fissured late modern consciousness rather than merely being a nostalgic throwback to an earlier way of seeing and being in the world.

Model 2: 'high trust' societies and authoritarian communitarianism

The second model of social control is based on the statist promotion of collective compliance within a conservative, moralizing culture as an antidote to the risks and uncertainties of individualism. A mix of state authoritarianism and conservative communitarianism, emphasizing family and community obligation enforced by the state, thus offers another possible scenario of crime control for the future. Such trends are to the fore in some of the group of nations popularly known as the 'Asian Tigers'. In passing, I would also point out the popular attraction of a communitarian authoritarianism from a paternalistic state, particularly Singapore, to contemporary Western politicians such as Tony Blair in the UK. It is important to note that countries like Japan, Taiwan, South Korea and Singapore are not all 'cut from the same cloth' (Fukuyama, 1996). However, there appear to be certain common features to their social structure that enables their grouping together for the particular purposes of this discussion. In particular, Misztal (1996: 5) has noted a common call across the 'Asian Tigers' for national revival based on 'the recognition of mutual obligation and a more collectivistic culture'. According to John Gray (1995: 16), these East Asian countries are united by Confucian ideas which animate the thought and practice in their 'extraordinary experiments of harnessing the dynamism of market institutions to the needs of strong and enduring communities'.

Japan: culture as a restraining medium against crime?

Japan has one of the developed world's lowest recorded crime rates and possibly the smallest per capita number of police officers. Since the Second World War it has become the second most successful industrialized country in the world and uniquely its official crime rate has declined. How might this be explained? In Chapter 6 I examined in depth the claims made for moral authoritarian communitarian social control. Frank Leishman (1994: 39) confirms the importance of such mechanisms as shaming, and 'the web of expectations to conform' operating in crime prevention in Japan. He also acknowledges that in Japan there is a strong cultural sense of 'home' and 'outside'. However, Leishman does not wish to explain the seeming Japanese success story on crime prevention simply in terms of some rather mystical and unique world view. Instead, he also highlights the existence of important institutional and structural factors in explaining the low crime rate, such as schooling on Saturdays for young people, a highly visible police presence, ubiquitous security systems and tough gun and weapon-control laws (1994: 40). We might also note the relatively small income differentials between occupational classes and the virtual guarantee of lifetime (male) employment in most firms (Fukuyama, 1996). Tadashi Moriyama (1993) has also pointed to the importance of the process of social conditioning to established norms in explaining the comparatively low crime rate in postwar Japan. He specifies four factors which are especially important: the absence of an established class system and the promotion of a 'meritocracy'; strong familial loyalties and duty to the group with a concomitant fear of ostracism; a culture of shame as opposed to that of guilt; and the family model of social control. I would also add that Japan's low or non-reporting of such crimes as rape, other sexual offences and domestic violence, together with high levels of (male) public drunkenness, may reflect the fear of bringing shame to the family as a victim given the patriarchal and hierarchical nature of the society. However, this high degree of constraining cohesion and stability appears to be under threat at the end of the twentieth century given the increasing urbanization, growing economic instability and heightened levels of population mobility at work in Japan.

Cohesive communities, coercive states

This second model of crime control stands opposed to the highly individualized and marketized model of privatism epitomized by the USA. According to some commentators, such as Fukuyama (1996), Japan represents the fullest expression of the 'high trust' society which may offer the risk-obsessed West many important lessons regarding the economic benefits of what he terms 'spontaneous solidarity'. Fukuyama, in common with other conservative moral communitarians, also sees much merit in the existence and acceptance of hierarchical and paternalistic authority: 'The most important social bonds are not horizontal ones between equals (such as, between disciples of a given master) but the vertical ones between senior and junior' (1996: 176). A crucial means of crime prevention in this model would thus appear to be a healthy dose of hierarchical yet paternalistic discipline.

The degree to which this second model of crime control is an expression of 'spontaneous solidarity' in East Asian states may also be questioned. In Singapore, for example, the long-standing People's Action Party government has been actively *dirigiste* in delineating the features of a social programme for its communitarian philosophy (Chua, 1997). The vision of social order sponsored and promoted by the Singapore government since independence from colonial rule has increasingly been that of an anti-liberal democracy where collective well-being is safeguarded by the good government of honourable leaders. According to Beng-Huat Chua (1997: 187):

> Instead of a minimal and neutral state of liberalism, the conflation of state/society justifies state interventions in all spheres of social life, rationalized as pre-emptive interventions which 'ensure' the collective well-being, as measures of good government rather than abuses of individuals' rights.

This conflation of state and society not only legitimizes an interventionist state but also enables the guardians of the state to slip easily into authoritarianism, either because of a genuine belief that they are acting for collective welfare or simply by using this as a self-serving excuse (Chua, 1997: 191). One example of this statist and moral authoritarian communitarianism was the law passed in 1994 which forced children to provide financial support for their elderly parents. This law was passed to signal and enforce community support for the core 'Asian value' of filial piety.

In more general ways it is also possible to question the extent to which specific cultures and social structures such as the hierarchical communalism in Japan are 'transferable' to societies elsewhere who have evolved very different philosophies and practices around the balance of rights and obligations. We may also ask what price to individual freedom or dissident groups' freedoms is paid by social cohesion and low recorded crime and disorder. Furthermore, is the 'pay-off' for such conservative communitarian order the institutionalized subordination of women to men?

Model 3: towards civic and inclusive 'safe' cities?

The third model focuses on what may be viewed as both in part the resurfacing but also the radical reworking of the social democratic project on public safety and security. It is important to note that this project is taking place within the context of the post-welfare state and what Rose (1996) has termed 'the death of the social'. By this latter phrase, Rose means that the notion of a universalistic public whose needs are met by the 'expert' social welfare state has died in contemporary political discourses. What form of governance replaces the 'social' and the centralized social state? Kevin Stenson (1995: 103) describes the new governance as a governmental shift whereby 'the social' and 'the state' have given way to communities, individuals and partnerships, and we now find 'political enemies join combat within the same discursive field' (see also Clarke *et al.*, 1998). Commenting on such developments in the context of policing, O'Malley and Palmer (1996: 138) have noted that 'In this emergent discourse, the community appears as a network of agentive, expert and independent actors who enter "partnerships" with the police'. Nor are such developments all negative, since in the process of such relationships and 'partnerships', competent and skilled agents also get constituted. For example, O'Malley has claimed controversially that the stress on lifestyle, market and enterprise models of freedom may also create a variety of openings or spaces which may be exploited for a reformist politics, such as the possibility of a non-sexist crime prevention geared towards the needs and wishes of women as consumers (O'Malley, 1995: 296).

In contrast to the old social democratic faith shown almost exclusively in the centralized, sovereign nation-state to solve social problems like crime in earlier decades of the century (see Chapter 3), the emergent radical pluralist debates on the public sphere and civil society discussed next also point to the participation of citizens and communities, and to local strategies from cities and regions as a 'way forward' (allied with positive state actions) in the era of late modernity. Taken together, there may be a new politics of crime prevention whose contours are becoming discernible and which may offer a third route in contrast to Models 1 and 2.

Renaissance of the local?

It is now accepted that there is a counter-argument to the claim that globalization is necessarily equated with the decline of community. In particular, there is another line of argument that the social and economic changes of the late twentieth century are leading people in some important ways to become more, rather than less, attached to their locality and immediate community.

More than any other Western European country, the UK since the 1970s witnessed a systematic dismantling of the powers of local authorities by the central state. There now exists a profound 'democratic deficit' in the arena of local democracy. What now seems certain is that the old paternalistic 'welfare state', which to a large extent was synonymous with the local delivery of public services, has now had its day (Hughes and Lewis, 1998). Out of this uncertain scenario, several influential commentators have made attempts to 'imagine' a more participatory and democratic future for local governance beyond the old unresponsive public service bureaucracy model and the recent consumer-driven frameworks of New Right marketization. Put briefly, the alternative is that of a more expansive democracy in which citizens are not empowered by their ability to 'exit' (as in the consumer's option of going elsewhere to 'shop') but rather by the option of 'voice' as citizens making demands on and being heard by their political representatives, and actively participating in the democratic process.

Common to the work of such writers as Burns et al. (1994) Stoker and Young (1993) is the emphasis on constructing a more expansive conception of local government as 'enabling' and even 'constituting' new participatory democracies in specific locales. We also see a reawakening of the concept of civil society as a space to be populated by an active citizenry which also retains particularities (Mouffe, 1992). This admittedly utopian agenda is best captured in Walzer's vision of 'critical associationism' in which citizenship would mediate other associations which individuals have and cut across them in an inclusive yet pluralistic fashion: 'It would appear to be an elementary requirement of social democracy that there exist a *society* of lively, engaged, and effective men and women – where the honour of 'action' belongs to the many and not to the few' (Walzer, 1992: 107).

According to this body of work, a social democracy is thus constituted by local networks and not just by the state, the market and the nation. As Stoker and Young (1993) argue there is a pressing need for local solutions not least in the realm of crime control, often drawing on multi-agency involvement in problem solving. In the context of such multi-agency work, Stoker and Young press the claim of cooperation through the establishment of 'relations premised on solidarity, loyalty, trust and reciprocity rather than through hierarchy' (p. 10). In such a vision, local or city government would be driven by a quest for cooperation and coalition-building. Burns *et al.* make out a case for decentralization as a means of revitalizing local democracy and in turn empowering local communities. Noting the dangers of employing 'naturalistic' notions of the community which can easily stimulate racist and other exclusionist tendencies in the arena of crime prevention, they argue for a politics of pluralism rather than consensus in which the local authority's role is 'one of mediation of interest and the management of complexity rather than the representation of a single community' (1994: 224). Such a role is particularly important in the area of crime prevention and the promotion of community safety where narrow, particularistic conceptions of community often prevail. Finally, Burns *et al.* conclude with a plea for a new communitarian and democratic agenda based on 'voice' in the new governance of diversity:

> Do we not need some kind of social agency (perhaps the kind of state which has not yet been created) which can pressurize adults to respect the needs of children, enable silent voices to be heard, restore a group's capacity to resist the temptation to embark upon the process of inferiorizing other social groups and sustain a commitment to the collective interest which is as vibrant as that to one's self-interest?
>
> (1994: 245)

Such 're-imagining' is in part a response to the narrow legalism of the liberal definition of citizenship but it also constitutes a challenge to the bureaucratic/statist conception of politics which has often been the left's alternative for many years. We see then a reassertion and reaffirmation of the notion of the citizen as having a certain pre-eminence among our identities given its status as the 'democratic political identity *par excellence*' (Mouffe, 1992: 5–7).

It may also be argued that the city as the locale for such social programmes is also being rejuvenated across Western Europe (and beyond).

Manuel Castells (1994, 1997) has emphasized that cities are socially determined in their forms and processes. Some of these determinants are structural, others are historically and culturally specific, 'And all are played out,
and twisted, and the social actions that impose their interests and their
values, to project the city of their dreams and to fight the space of their nightmares' (Castells, 1994: 18–19). Put simply, this line of thinking suggests that
the dreams and nightmares of Los Angeles are not necessarily those of other
cities.

It is also important to realize that there are significant changes in both
inter-governmental relations and forms of local autonomy as we approach
the millennium. Indeed, according to Castells, 'In this troubled world, Western Europe has, in fact, become a fragile island of prosperity, peace, democracy, culture, science, welfare and civil rights' (1994: 24). This said, Castells
does recognize the dangers of the selfish reflex of trying to preserve this
'heaven' by erecting 'walls' which would undermine the very fundamentals
of European culture namely the appeal of 'Fortress Europe'. Castells is confident that the basic prerogatives of the nation-state will be shifted to European institutions by the end of the century. Accepting this premise of
Europeanization, it is then argued that the expression of specific interests
will be shifted to the regional and local levels and away from the national.
Castells sees a crucial and difficult role for local (city) governments both in
managing the new urban contradictions and conflicts and in avoiding the
danger of the American style 'dual city' (of haves and have-nots, insiders and
outsiders). The fostering of citizenship participation is seen as one of the key
policies for such a politics of managing cities alongside the promotion of the
interconnection and cooperation between local governments throughout
Europe. Finally, Castells holds out the following hope: 'Because European
cities have strong civil societies, rooted in an old history and a rich, diversi-
fied culture, they could stimulate citizen participation as a fundamental antidote against tribalism and alienation' (1994: 32).

Such a hope or vision appears particularly important in any contemporary debate on crime control and, more broadly, social justice. As the abolitionist criminologist, René van Swaaningen (1997: 180) notes, Europe is
characterized by a 'stronger social democratic communitarian tradition'
than the USA but it is a tradition that is under grave threat given the current
importation by politicians across Europe of 'US' ideas of deregulation, privatization, 'consumer choice' and the criminalization of those unable to
'choose'.

Regenerating the public sphere in debates on crime and safety

Ian Taylor (1997) has recently contended that it is crucial that we try and
connect global developments to local expressions of concern about risks and
(in)security. Taylor's own research focuses on the role of secondary

associations in regenerating a sense of democratic participation and making sense of politics as such: in the process, such developments will also quickly show up competing interests at work. For Taylor, we need to see crime prevention work in specific localities as 'one of the fastest growing areas of a new civic politics':

> In the sitting rooms of the suburbs, as well as in the estates, the ideological and political struggle seems currently to be poised somewhere between oriental despotism and various different attempts to think through the basis of a new Social Contract, in a society which, for all the denials of the free-market theologians, feels itself to be in a deep crisis over its economic and social future.
>
> (1997: 70)

To unpack this passage: Taylor recognizes the potential dangers of moral despotism in crime prevention/community safety work 'on the ground', which he obscurely refers to as 'oriental despotism' and which may be more productively called neo-conservative moralizing. However, the politics of local community safety is recognized also as a space which has opened up new questions about the common good and *shared* risks and opportunities, beyond that of the free market or neo-liberal discourse.

Andy Merrifield (1996) has argued for the possibilities of cities with inclusive public spaces in contrast to the 'doom and gloom' visions of the 'fortress city' thesis. According to Merrifield, it is important to acknowledge that a society with inclusive public spaces might not be more stable and conflict-free. Indeed, if such spaces bring people together to debate and argue, it could well be more conflictual, but will probably be a fairer and more democratic society (Merrifield, 1996: 59). This resonates with Davis' yearning from Los Angeles for real public places 'with their democratic intoxifications, risks and unscented odours' (Davis, 1990: 26). A visible presence in public is particularly vital for those stigmatized, criminalized and marginalized groups struggling for recognition. As Merrifield notes, during the 1990s in the UK, the magazine *The Big Issue*, produced and sold by homeless people, both problematized and raised awareness over the ideological divide separating supposed 'normality' and 'deviance' and was part of a process of 're-dignification' for homeless people in our cities (Merrifield, 1996: 64). Such processes of 're-dignification' may be a crucial component in progressive projects of community safety. As an alternative to the 'fortress city' mentality in the USA, Merrifield argues that 'cities should comprise a broad range of public spaces with multiple publics, each having, unless otherwise justified, open entrances and exits' (p. 68). He cites one particular example of how this strategy of inclusion may be adapted to meet the 'community safety' needs of particular vulnerable groups; in other words, exceptions that prove the general (inclusive) rule. Corans Field in Holborn, London has been preserved as a public site for the welfare of children since the 1920s. The park excludes all adults unless they are accompanied by a child. Here then is an example of a safe public space for children which is also policed and exclusionary.

Programmes for social defence

A specific illustration of the new social politics of community safety is evident in Massimo Pavarini's work on 'secure cities' in Emilia-Romagna in Italy. Pavarini recognizes that there is an obsession with security and risk in most late modern societies, including Italy. This obsession (exemplified in Model 1 above) often results in making security a commodity to be purchased on the private security market. Its most likely effect in Pavarini's eyes is 'a strong tendency towards the re-feudalization of social relations' (1997: 80) by which I take it he means the destruction of any sense of civil society and of universal laws and their replacement by small, mutually exclusive and hostile micro-societies led by politicians or 'bosses' of any type (as latter-day barons) offering protection and security to their fiefs. As an alternative to this scenario, Pavarini argues for the need for new conditions of legality in the future 'social state' which must be sought in political, social, cultural and economic strategies which, more than legal norms, will meet society's demands for security without involving the criminal justice system. The key task of such a project is thus to ensure that social conditions are able to provide alternative answers to problems that are (in Italy) currently the exclusive terrain of criminal justice (Pavarini, 1997: 79). According to Pavarini, the crime question must be confronted in terms of political and economic democracy, in what he admits is 'a project as ambitious as it is uncertain' (p. 87). In other words, the 'solution' to the problems of insecurity and fear of crime necessarily lie outside the criminal justice system and by implication beyond criminology. For example, Pavarini contends that situational crime prevention is not the answer since it is only feasible in contained, physical social spaces and for a limited time. 'Technically-based prevention is therefore both illusory and politically dangerous' contends Pavarini (p. 89) in that it is impossible to turn modern metropolises into the neo-medieval fortified city; instead displacement onto other areas necessarily takes place and technically-based prevention is counter-productive since it augments collective feelings of insecurity. As an alternative community safety strategy, Pavarini points to local prevention initiatives that appeal to social participation. Even if such collective campaigns and networks do not prevent crime, Pavarini sees a positive public and civic 'pay-off' by producing 'social representations of greater security' (p. 90). Such prevention policies are thus to be seen as part of social action in the wider sense of the word (see Chapters 5 and 6).

The above discussion has presented various arguments and analyses which suggest that there are alternatives to the privatism of the neo-liberal discourse on crime prevention and to the authoritarian communitarianism of the 'Asian Tiger' states. It has been argued that there are contested spaces opened up by current debates on crime prevention and public safety which may enable a progressive agenda of social inclusion and pluralism to develop. Much of this discussion has necessarily led us to examine debates on 'social security' in the generic sense of the term and issues around democracy and participation which fall beyond the traditionally narrow frontiers of crime prevention (and criminology). However, it may also be wise to preach caution with regard to the 'civic cities' discourse of inclusion and plurality given the powerful countervailing forces of both conservative moral communitarianism and neo-liberal privatism which occupy the centre-stage of current debates on law and order across late modern societies. Localism, and the related appeals to 'community', are often achieved through the power to exclude and demonize 'the other' (Young, 1990). Nor should we assume that 'the local' is the answer to the problems facing particular cities, regions or localities 'beneath' the national. It must be acknowledged that local authorities are often impotent when it comes to the most structural determinants of community safety (such as macroeconomic policies). Instead, local and national politics should be geared to one another. As van Swaaningen (1997: 215) observes, the radical project on 'safety politics' must be to 're-moralize the social, facilitative role of the state, which ultimately legitimizes its very existence'.

Having looked at three contrasting models of the possible future for crime control, it is important to note that elements from all three are likely to resurface and converge in specific situations and locales. It is beyond the remit of this book to suggest which scenario, if any, will come to the fore. Indeed it may be that no one unadulterated model will prevail. However, if nothing else, the discussion will have alerted you both to the open-ended nature of future trends in social control and to the impossibility of adequately understanding the changing modes of crime prevention without a close and critical engagement with the wider politics of social order in late modernity.

Summary

In this chapter I began with an overview of the influential sociological thesis on late modern risk society. Following this exposition, I examined how these broad trends might be connected to current comparative developments in crime prevention. The chapter then presented three possible scenarios of the future of crime prevention, associated with the model of privatism and social exclusion, the model of authoritarian communitarianism, and the model of inclusive cities and local democratic programmes of community safety. In the Postscript the general implications of these broad trends for both the practices of and theorizing about crime prevention are addressed.

Further reading

Giddens, A. (1990) *The Consequences of Modernity*. Cambridge: Polity.
Nelken, D. (ed.) (1994) *The Futures of Criminology*. London: Sage.
van Swaaningen, R. (1997) *Critical Criminology: Visions from Europe*. London: Sage.

Postscript: Beyond crime prevention?

Introduction
A new paradigm beyond crime prevention?

Introduction

In this brief Postscript I speculate on the directions in which crime prevention strategies, and the analysis of them by social scientists, may go in the future. Hudson (1996: 3) has acutely observed that 'Some theorists claim that this period of modernity is now over . . . If this is so, then we can expect considerable implications for conceptions of justice and systems of punishment'. A similar tale of change is likely in the mercurial field of relations that is termed crime prevention. On a more cautionary note, Esping-Andersen (1990: 223) remarks that:

> The proliferation of labels, such as 'post-modernist', 'post-materialist', 'post-Fordist ' or 'post-industrial', often substitutes for analysis. But it mirrors the recognition that we are leaving behind us a social order that was pretty much understood, and entering another the contours of which can be only dimly recognised.

The current situation, according to the theorist of post-modernity, Zygmunt Bauman (1993: 245) is even more uncertain:

> What the post-modern mind is aware of is that there are problems in human and social life with no good solutions, twisted trajectories that cannot be straightened up, ambivalences that are more than linguistic blunders yelling to be corrected, doubts which cannot be legislated out

of existence, moral agonies which no reason-dictated recipes can soothe, let alone cure.

In other words the messiness of the human predicament is here to stay.

In the present historical context, it is clear that there is a plurality of competing strategies on crime control, with 'old' philosophies and models often running parallel with more recent ones. The history of crime and its prevention or control is not one of cumulative and linear progress. Much of the discussion in this book has pointed to the complex, open-ended situation facing us. In particular, this wide-ranging study of specific contexts, localities and initiatives has shown the persistent but creative tension between the detailed empirical investigation of crime prevention and globalizing, theoretical frameworks of social theory. Both attention to empirical detail and engagement with the big issues in modern social theory are surely the lifeblood of the study of crime, its control and its prevention.

A new paradigm beyond crime prevention?

At the risk of generalizing, it does appear that late modern societies may be moving beyond a crime prevention paradigm to that of risk management. Garland's (1996) diagnosis of the crisis of penal modernism provides a valuable overview of some of the master patterns of crime control at the end of the twentieth century. According to Garland, crime can no longer be seen as an aberration but rather is viewed as 'an everyday risk to be managed like air pollution and road traffic' and high rates of crime are viewed as normal. Increasingly, there is little confidence in the capacity of the state to solve, prevent or fight the problem of crime. The result of all this is the 'erosion of one of the foundational myths of modern society: that the sovereign state is capable of providing security, law and order and crime control' (Garland, 1996: 4). Out of this crisis new modes of governing crime have developed, namely:

- the increasing involvement of the private sector (especially the selling of policing and security as commodities);
- the model of crime as a risk 'condition' to be calculated or an accident to be avoided versus a moral aberration needing special explanation;
- the development of a 'supply-side' policy which seeks to modify the routines of everyday life;
- a strategy of making citizens responsible for crime;
- the managerial ethos of 'performance indicators' which judges criminal justice agencies by self-referential measures that have nothing to do with reducing crime.

Commenting on Garland's (1996) thesis, Cohen (1996: 10) notes that 'the message is that crime control is beyond the state'. Is it then the end of crime prevention as we have known it? It is ironic that Garland also notes that the state simultaneously swings into episodes of hysterical and populist denial of these very limitations (as reflected in the currently exploding prison population and the burgeoning custodial crime control industry). 'State sovereignty over crime is simultaneously denied (transferred to private security corporations or "responsible citizens") and symbolically reasserted' (Garland, 1996: 19). A note of caution is perhaps worthwhile at this juncture. There are problems with such a sweeping if elegant scenario as that offered by Garland. We still need to ask ourselves what of the messy complexities of the global-local mix and the countervailing forces which may resist this seemingly new 'master pattern' of crime control? Not least among the countervailing forces, and hidden in Garland's pessimistic account, is the radical potential of local community safety strategies in Europe and beyond which Chapters 5 and 6 highlighted.

That noted, it may be that the field of practices described in this book may be neither widely-known in twenty years time as that of 'crime prevention' nor located in the province of the discipline of criminology. It may be that new knowledges will be privileged over sociology and criminology, such as forensic psychology and geography combined together in a pseudo-science of 'risk management studies'. Should this be the case, however, I would contend there will still be the urgent need for a critical social science which is able to relate such new discourses to wider questions of social order, social justice and social control in late modern societies.

Whatever intellectual developments occur, the challenge for social scientists remains that of combining relevant engagement with both the detailed policies and practices of crime prevention/risk management and the theoretical and practical knowledge of the broader conditions of their existence. As Sutton and O'Malley (1997: 10) have noted, crime prevention brings criminologists into contact with practice and may thus be the area where challenges to criminology are most acute: 'As a result, crime prevention is moving rapidly into place as one of the most central and dynamic areas of contemporary criminology'. Such a prediction will be worth bearing in mind during the coming years.

Perhaps a more radical break with the dominant agenda around 'prevention' is required than that implied by Sutton and O'Malley. As Muncie *et al.* (1994: 356) point out, few attempts, even by radical critics, have been made to go beyond the intrinsically limited boundaries of the discourse of crime prevention. This continuing emphasis on *crime* prevention thus acts to systematically exclude other readings of the relationship between social problems and social order. In a similar way, van Swaaningen (1997: 174) has argued that the negative politics of law enforcement and exclusion is one of the key political strategies of risk society. This strategy is oriented towards the negative rationale of limiting risk rather than producing positive ideas (such as social justice and empowerment). As a consequence of this logic, solidarity is not based on the positive feeling of connectedness but on the negative communality of fear. Radical critics thus need to develop a positive 'replacement discourse' (to that of penal interventionism and prevention through exclusion) in which the demand for social justice and human rights may provide the normative touchstone of a progressive criminal justice politics (van Swaaningen, 1997: 190). Indeed, the meta-narrative of human rights is crucial to this project, further illustrating the dangerous political naiveté of post-modernists who deny the existence of the old truths of collective struggles against misery and oppression. As Cohen (1990: 31) notes in support of the discourse of human rights and justice, 'For most of the world, the old truths of racism, naked injustice, mass starvation and brutal physical repression still apply'. These old truths surely lie at the heart of any radical agenda for a socially just 'safety politics'. Such an agenda moves beyond the technicism of administrative criminology and cannot avoid the messy, normative questions of what constitutes the 'good society' and how relations between people and major institutions may be re-figured. The discourse of human rights and social justice also raises the key issue of how solidarity in the contemporary world is to be understood (see Clarke *et al.*, 1998). Bauman (1997: 63) argues for a new vision of solidarity, namely 'the recognition of the other person's misery and suffering as one's responsibility, and the alleviation and eventually the removal of misery as one's task'.

It has been noted in the preceding chapters that the last decades of the twentieth century across neo-liberal societies have seen the 'criminalization of social policy', not least through the burgeoning trade in crime prevention techniques. It is of course crucial that social theorists critique existing crime prevention policies. However, it is also vital that attempts are made to see beyond the present and imagine another possible politics. It is surely crucial then to begin a debate about the possible shift from the criminalization of social policy towards the socialization of criminal justice and crime prevention policies. The subordination of questions of crime control to those of social justice and human rights may open up a new discourse of possibilities beyond the current one.

The great sociologist Émile Durkheim (1895) argued what at the time was an outrageously radical case for the 'normality' of deviance and crime and for the limits of crime prevention and control in the 'good society'. In line with this viewpoint, an orderly, conforming, highly regulated society is not necessarily a 'healthy' democratic society and so we need to be wary of the ramifications of demanding a crime-free society through effective prevention and control. It is now evident that the modernist 'dream of purity', such as 'eradicating' crime and deviance, may have terrible consequences. As Bauman (1997: 5) notes, 'Great crimes often start from great ideas'. In the context of late modernity's culture of uncertainty, there is now both less optimism and less arrogance among social scientists about solving the 'crime problem' in a supposedly pure, scientific manner. This is an important lesson for our times.

Glossary of key terms

Abolitionism The movement in criminology and criminal justice reform which seeks to abolish all or part of the penal and criminal justice system.

Actuarial justice The approach to crime control and risk management which is organized around the principles of social utility and efficient management rather than classical criminal justice principles of legality and due process, responsibility and culpability. The policy objective associated with this emergent discourse is the clear categorization of 'risky' people to identify and manage.

Administrative criminology The term used to describe the development of a body of technical and politically pragmatic knowledge, linked to the Home Office in Britain since the 1970s. According to critics (such as 'Left Realists'), it represents a body of criminological research aimed at helping those in power to put their ideas into practice by the employment of technical evaluations.

Aetiology A term derived from biomedical science which suggests that the original and specific causes of crime can be identified and 'diagnosed' in the same way as the causes of disease and illness.

Anomie A term originally used by the sociologist Durkheim to capture the state of 'pathological normlessness' induced when aspirations are incapable of being met due to restricted opportunities or due to lack of regulation over behaviour.

Classicism The school of criminology which views both criminality and the administration of criminal justice as premised upon principles of rationality, choice, and the deterrent, preventive power of punishment.

Communitarianism The broad philosophical and sociological tradition in which there is an emphasis on the centrality of informal, communal bonds and networks for the maintenance of social order. It is critical of individualistic theories of social behaviour and 'society' such as 'neo-liberalism' (see below), invoking notions of 'social beings' and 'community' rather than 'atomized individuals'. It is characterized by both conservative moralistic and radical left variants.

Community safety The strategy which seeks to move beyond a police-driven crime prevention agenda, to involve greater participation from all sections of the 'community'. It has been particularly associated with local authority strategies of crime prevention and urban regeneration.

Corporate crime Offences committed by business corporations in the pursuit of their own profits and interests.

Corporatism   The term used to describe the tendencies to be found in advanced welfare societies whereby the capacity for conflict and disruption is reduced by means of the increased centralization of policy, central intervention and the cooperation of previously separate professional agencies and interest groups into a collective whole with common aims and objectives. In criminal justice, it leads to a focus on 'successful' policy outcomes rather than a concern with justice and due process and is associated with the rise of 'multi-agency crime prevention'.

Criminalization   The application of the label 'criminal' to specific 'deviant' behaviours or social groups.

Critical criminology   A perspective emerging in the 1970s which focuses on deficiencies, absences and closures in existing theories and ways of understanding the concept of 'crime'.

Discourse   Discourse describes how social knowledge is organized in particular ways. A discourse is about how knowledge is institutionalized in social policies and the organizations through which they are carried out. Discourse draws our attention to the minute arrangements of, for example, how criminals have certain things done to them. Thus discourses are about relations of power, about organized positions and places in the field of power. Finally a discourse defines 'what the problem is' and 'what is to be done about it'.

Diversion   Strategies developed to prevent (young) people from either committing crime or to ensure they avoid formal court or custodial action if they are prosecuted.

Eugenics   The supposed 'science' of 'human races' which demanded that 'undesirables' and 'defectives' be isolated or sterilized. Selective breeding was seen as the key to the production of healthy populations.

Globalization   This concept refers to the intensification of worldwide relations which link distant localities in such a way that local happenings are shaped by events occurring many miles away and vice versa (Giddens, 1990).

Governance   The notion, associated with Foucault, that social order is achieved through dispersed relations of power and knowledge (i.e. discourses) rather than by centralized state coercion.

Late modernity   The late modernity thesis has emerged out of recent sociological theorizing on the major social transformations in the late twentieth century. In the work of Giddens, it focuses on both the growth of new forms of trust, new risks and critical reflexivity and the decline of old certainties such as tradition and deference to 'experts'. The thesis also points to the consequences of the processes of 'globalization' for social relations (see above).

Left realism   The school of criminology which came to the fore in the UK in the 1980s. Its chief claim was that it took people's fears of crime and victimization seriously (unlike 'critical criminology', see above).

Managerialism   The discourse which suggests that the organization and coordination of public services are best realized by means of the processes of marketization and the replacement of professionals and bureaucrats by managers. It assumes that better management will prove an effective and economical solution for a wide range of economic and social problems.

Modernity   According to sociologists, the period from industrialization to the 1970s (approximately). In the West it was a period characterized by capitalist industrialization and imperialism, urbanization, secularization, a limited form of democracy and the welfare state. In this period it was assumed that social and 'natural' problems could be addressed through positivist science and rationality. It was characterized by belief in progress.

Multi-agency crime prevention Coordinated response of several social agencies to the problems of 'crime' and 'incivilities'. Supporters argue for the 'success' of such corporate and managerial approaches over traditional, single-agency prevention approaches. The movement to 'multi-agency' prevention implies that probation, education, employment, social work and other family services, health and housing, private bodies such as charities and business and members of the 'community', as well as the police, all have a role to play in crime prevention.

Neo-liberalism The dominant political discourse in countries like the UK and the USA in the last two decades of the twentieth century. Its project has been to selectively 'roll back' the (welfare) state and privilege the operation of 'free', unregulated markets.

Penality The complex of ideas, institutions, rules and practices pertaining to punishment.

Positivism A paradigm first emerging in the nineteenth century, based on the belief that social behaviour can be studied scientifically by using the methods of the natural sciences and that such study can lead to predictive laws and 'cures'.

Postmodernism An intellectual movement which challenges the claims of rational and scientific (positivist) thought to incorporate universal truths. Unlike modernism, it embraces uncertainty, doubt and profound relativism.

Radical totalitarianism The thesis associated with authors of a radical disposition (see 'Critical criminology', above). It suggests that we have witnessed broad trends in social control whereby the late twentieth-century period is characterized by an evermore penetrative, 'panoptical' system of surveillance.

Rehabilitation The strategy and technique to reform offenders through various 'treatment' regimes as a result of which they can be retrained and re-socialized.

Retribution The idea that punishment as vengeance is a justified response to the wrong already committed by the offender.

Risk society The thesis (associated with the work of Beck) that in the era of late modernity, the certainties of industrialism, class society and rational science have been undermined. The latter in turn have been replaced by a series of global, local and individualized risks defined as the probabilities of physical harm due to given technological or other processes. The dominant culture is one obsessed with fears of risks and the quest for safety and security.

Sceptical pluralism A term used to describe most mainstream research on crime prevention. It is sceptical about the achievements of such policy and practice initiatives as multi-agency and 'community' crime prevention. It also avoids any adherence to a monocausal theory, preferring a pluralist approach.

Situational crime prevention The discourse of preventing crime by environmental modification, such as target-hardening and 'natural' surveillance.

Social contract theory The idea that the power and authority of government and state are derived from an unwritten but binding contract entered into by members of a society, associated with the school of classicism.

Social control The broad term used to describe all the means available in society through which conformity and regulation might be achieved.

Social crime prevention The strategy of preventing crime by targeting antisocial behaviour and those 'at risk' as well as known offenders. It also includes programmes aimed at improving the opportunities of 'at risk' groups through 'community mobilization'.

Social exclusion   A broad and politically popular idea in the 1990s which refers to the ways in which the poor are marginalized from the economic, political and cultural mainstream of society.

Statism   The theory and practice of concentrating power in the state resulting in a 'weak' position for the individual or community with respect to government.

Technicism   (see 'Administrative criminology', above).

Underclass   The term used to describe 'non-working' and economically marginalized groups. It has often been used to depict those who are dependent on state benefits as 'undeserving', 'criminal' and 'dangerous'.

Utilitarianism   The theory that people are motivated by the desire to maximize happiness and minimize pain and that the duty of the state is to promote the maximum amount of happiness and well-being in society.

References

Audit Commission (1996) *Misspent Youth*. London: Audit Commission.

Barr, R. and Pease, K. (1990) 'Crime, Placement, Displacement and Deflection', in M. Tonry (ed.) *Criminal Justice: A Review of Research*. Chicago: University of Chicago Press.

Bauman, Z. (1993) *Postmodern Ethics*. Oxford: Blackwell.

Bauman, Z. (1997) *Postmodernity and its Discontents*. Cambridge: Polity.

Beccaria, C. (1764) *On Crimes and Punishment* (reprinted 1963). New York: Bobbs-Merrill.

Beck, U. (1992) *Risk Society*. London: Sage.

Beck, U. (1996) 'Risk Society and the Provident State', in S. Lasch, B. Szerszynski and B. Wynne (eds), *Risk, Environment and Modernity: Towards a New Ecology*. London: Sage.

Becker, H. (1963) *Outsiders*. London: Macmillan.

Bennett, T. (1990) *Evaluating Neighbourhood Watch*. Aldershot: Gower.

Blagg, H. (1997) 'A Just Measure of Shame: Aboriginal Youth and Conferencing in Australia', *British Journal of Criminology*, 37, 4: 481–501.

Blagg, H., Pearson, G., Sampson, A., Smith, D. and Stubbs, P. (1988) 'Inter-agency Co-ordination: Rhetoric and Reality', in T. Hope and M. Shaw (eds), *Communities and Crime Reduction*. London: HMSO.

Bloch, M. (1961) *Feudal Society*. London: Routledge & Kegan Paul.

Bottomley, A.K. (1979) *Criminology in Focus*. Oxford: Martin Robertson.

Bottoms, A. (1980) 'Nothing Works', in A. Bottoms and R. H. Preston (eds), *The Coming Penal Crisis*. Edinburgh: Scottish Academic Press.

Bottoms, A. and Wiles, P. (1996) 'Crime Prevention and Late Modernity', in T. Bennett (ed.), *Crime Prevention: The Cropwood Papers*. Cambridge: Cropwood.

Bowring, B. (1997) 'Law and Order in the "New" Britain', *Soundings*, special edition, 'The Next Ten Years': 100–10.

Box, S. (1983) *Power, Crime and Mystification*. London: Tavistock.

Braithwaite, J. (1989) *Crime, Shame and Reintegration*. Oxford: Oxford University Press.

Braithwaite, J. (1992) 'Reducing the crime problem: a not so dismal criminology', *Australian and New Zealand Journal of Criminology*, 25: 1–10.

Braithwaite, J. (1993) 'Shame and Modernity', British Journal of Criminology, 33, 1: 1–18.

Braithwaite, J. (1995) 'Inequality and Republican Criminology', in J. Hagan and J. Peterson (eds), Crime and Inequality. Stanford, CA: Stanford University Press.

Braithwaite, J. (1996) 'The Implications of the Globalization of Business for the Regulation of the Abuse of Corporate Power'. Paper delivered at the Australian and New Zealand Criminology Conference, Wellington, February.

Braithwaite, J. and Daly, K. (1994) 'Masculinities, Violence and Communitarian Control', in T. Newburn and B. Stanko (eds), Just Boys Doing Business. London: Routledge.

Braithwaite, J. and Mugford, S. (1994) 'Conditions of Successful Reintegration Ceremonies', British Journal of Criminology, 34, 2: 131–71.

Braithwaite, J. and Pettit, P. (1990) Not Just Desserts: A Republican Theory of Justice. Oxford: Oxford University Press.

Brantingham, P. and Brantingham, P. (1991) Environmental Criminology (2nd edn). Prospect Heights, IL: Waterland Press.

Bright, J. (1987) 'Community safety, crime prevention and the local authority', in P. Wilmott (ed.), Policing and the Community. London: Policy Studies Institute.

Bright, J. (1991) 'Crime Prevention: The British Experience', in D. Cowell and K. Stenson (eds), The Politics of Crime Control. London: Sage.

Burns, T., Hambleton, R. and Hoggett, P. (1994) The Politics of Decentralisation. Basingstoke: Macmillan.

Burt, C. (1925) The Young Delinquent. London: University of London Press.

Caldeira, T. (1996) 'Fortified Enclaves: The New Urban Segregation', Public Culture, 8: 303–28.

Campbell, B. (1993) Goliath: Britain's Dangerous Places. London: Methuen.

Campbell, B. (1995) 'Old Fogeys and Angry Young Men', Soundings, 1: 47–64.

Castells, M. (1994) 'European Cities, the Informational Society, and the Global Economy', New Left Review, 204: 18–32.

Castells, M. (1997) The Power of Identity. Oxford: Blackwell.

Chevalier, L. (1973) Labouring Classes and Dangerous Classes. London: Routledge & Kegan Paul.

Christie, N. (1977) 'Conflicts as property', British Journal of Criminology, 17, 1: 1–19.

Christie, N. (1993) Crime Control as Industry: Towards Gulags Western style? London: Routledge.

Chua, B.-H. (1997) Communitarian Ideology and Democracy in Singapore. London: Routledge.

Clarke, J. (1996a) 'The Problem of the State after the Welfare State', in M. May, E. Brunsdon and G. Craig (eds), Social Policy Review 8. London: Social Policy Association.

Clarke, J. (1996b) 'Public Nightmares and Communitarian Dreams: The Crisis of the Social in Social Welfare', in S. Edgell, K. Hetherington and A. Warde (eds), Consumption Matters. Oxford: Blackwell.

Clarke, J., Hughes, G., Lewis, G. and Mooney, G. (1998) 'Reinventing the Public', in G. Hughes (ed.), Imagining Welfare Futures. London: Routledge.

Clarke, R. (1992) Situational Crime Prevention: Successful Case Studies. New York: Harrow & Heston.

Clarke, R. (1995) 'Situational Crime Prevention', in M. Tonry and D. Farrington (eds), *Building a Safer Society: Strategic Approaches to Crime*. Chicago: University of Chicago Press.

Clarke, R. and Cornish, D. (1983) *Crime Control in Britain: A Review of Policy Research*. Albany, NY: State University of New York Press.

Clarke, R. and Mayhew, P. (eds) (1980) *Designing Out Crime*. London: HMSO.

Cochrane, A. (1986) 'Community Politics and Democracy', in D. Held and C. Pollitt (eds), *New Forms of Democracy*. London: Sage.

Cohen, S. (1974) 'Criminology and the Sociology of Deviance in Britain', in P. Rock and M. MacIntosh (eds), *Deviance and Social Control*. London: Tavistock.

Cohen, S. (1985) *Visions of Social Control*. Cambridge: Polity.

Cohen, S. (1990) *Intellectual Scepticism and Political Commitment: The Case of Radical Criminology*. Amsterdam: Bonger Institute.

Cohen, S. (1993) 'Human Rights and Crimes of the State: The Culture of Denial', *Australian and New Zealand Journal of Criminology*, 26, 1: 87–115.

Cohen, S. (1996) 'Crime and Politics: Spot the Difference', *British Journal of Sociology*, 47:1.

Coleman, A. (1985) *Utopia on Trial*. London: Hilary Shipman.

Coleman, C. and Moynihan, J. (1996) *Understanding Crime Data*. Buckingham: Open University Press.

Comedia (1991) *Out of Hours: Summary Report*. London: Calouste Gulbenkion Foundation.

Conservative Party (1979) *Conservative Party Manifesto*. London: Conservative Party.

Coote, A. (1995) 'A bit of a prig and a prude', *Independent*, 3 July.

Cornish, D. and Clarke, R. (1986) 'Situational Crime Prevention, Displacement of Crime and Rational Choice Theory', in K. Heal and G. Laycock (eds), *Situational Crime Prevention: From Theory into Practice*. London: HMSO.

Crawford, A. (1994) 'The Partnership Approach to Community Crime Prevention: Corporatism at the Local Level', *Social and Legal Studies*, 3: 497–519.

Crawford, A. (1995) 'Appeals to Community and Crime Prevention', *Crime, Law and Social Change*, 22: 97–126.

Crawford, A. (1997) *The Local Governance of Crime*. Oxford: Clarendon Press.

Crawford, A. and Jones, M. (1995) 'Inter-agency Cooperation and Community-based Crime Prevention', *British Journal of Criminology*, 35, 1: 17–33.

Crawford, A. and Jones, M. (1996) 'Kirkholt Revisited: Some Reflections on the Transferability of Crime Prevention Initiatives', *Howard Journal*, 35, 1: 21–39.

Cullen, F. and Gilbert, K. (1982) *Reaffirming Rehabilitation*. Cincinnati, OH: Anderson.

Currie, E. (1985) *Confronting Crime: An American Challenge*. New York: Pantheon Books.

Currie, E. (1993) *Reckoning: Drugs, the Cities and the American Future*. New York: Hill & Wang.

Currie, E. (1996) *Is America Really Winning the War on Crime and Should Britain Follow its Example?* NACRO 30th annual lecture. London: NACRO.

Currie, E. (1997) 'Market, Crime and Community', *Theoretical Criminology*, 1, 2: 147–72.

Davis, M. (1990) *City of Quartz: Excavating the Future of Los Angeles*. London: Verso.

de Haan, W. (1990) *The Politics of Redress*. London: Unwin Hyman.

Dennis, N. (1993) *Rising Crime and the Dismembered Family*. London: IEA.

Dennis, N. (1997a) *The Invention of Permanent Poverty*. London: IEA.

Dennis, N. (ed.) (1997b) *Zero Tolerance Policing*. London: IEA.

Dennis, N. and Erdos, G. (1992) *Families Without Fatherhood*. London: IEA.

Downes, D. and Morgan, R. (1994) ' "Hostages to Fortune?" The Politics of Law and Order in Post-War Britain', in M. Maguire, R. Morgan and R. Reiner (eds), *Oxford Handbook of Criminology* (1st edn). Oxford: Clarendon Press.

Durkheim, E. (1893) *The Division of Labour in Society* (reprinted 1964). New York: Free Press.

Durkheim, T. (1895) *The Rules of Sociological Method*, (reprinted 1964). New York: Free Press.

Ekblom, P. (1996) 'Towards a Discipline of Crime Prevention: A Systematic Approach to its Nature, Range and Concepts', in T. Bennett (ed.), *Crime Prevention: The Cropwood Papers*. Cambridge: Cropwood.

Ekblom, P. and Pease, K. (1995) 'Evaluating Crime Prevention', in M. Tonry and D. Farrington (eds), *Building a Safer Society: Strategic Approaches to Crime*. Chicago: University of Chicago Press.

Elias, N. (1956) 'Problems of Involvement and Detachment', *British Journal of Sociology*, 7, 3: 226–52.

Elmsley, C. (1994) 'The History of Crime and Crime Control Institutions, c.1770–c.1945', in M. Maguire, R. Morgan and R. Reiner (eds), *Oxford Handbook of Criminology* (1st edn). Oxford: Clarendon Press.

Etzioni, A. (1994) *The Spirit of Community: The Reinvention of American Society*. New York: Touchstone.

Etzioni, A. (1995) *The Spirit of Community*. London: Fontana.

Etzioni, A. (1997) *The New Golden Rule; Community and Morality in a Democratic Society*. London: Profile Books.

Farrell, G. (1995) 'Preventing Repeat Victimization', in M. Tonry and D. Farrington (eds) *Building a Safer Society: Strategic Approaches to Crime*. Chicago: University of Chicago Press.

Farrington, D. (1992) 'Criminal Career Research: Lessons for Crime Prevention', *Studies on Crime and Crime Prevention*, 1, 1: 7–29.

Farrington, D. (1994) 'Human Development and Criminal Careers', in M. Maguire, R. Morgan and R. Reiner (eds), *Oxford Handbook of Criminology* (1st edn). Oxford: Clarendon Press.

Feeley, M. and Simon, J. (1992) 'The New Penology: Notes on the Emerging Strategy of Corrections and its Implications', *Criminology*, 30, 4: 452–74.

Feeley, M. and Simon, J. (1994) 'Actuarial Justice: The Emerging New Criminal Law', in D. Nelken (ed.), *Futures of Criminology*. London: Sage.

Felson, M. (1986) 'Linking Criminal Choices, Routine Activities, Informal Control and Criminal Outcomes', in D. Cornish and R. Clarke (eds), *The Reasoning Criminal: Rational Choice Perspectives on Offending*. New York: Springer-Verlag.

Forrester, D., Chatterton, M. and Pease, K. (1988) 'The Kirkholt Burglary Prevention Project', *CPU Paper no. 13*. London: HMSO.

Foucault, M. (1977) *Discipline and Punish*. Harmondsworth: Penguin.

Frazer, E. and Lacey, N. (1993) *The Politics of Community*. London: Harvester Wheatsheaf.

Fukuyama, F. (1996) *Trust*. Harmondsworth: Penguin.

Furedi, F. (1997) *Culture of Fear*. London: Cassell.

Gabor, T. (1990) 'Crime Prevention: The Agenda', *Canadian Journal of Criminology*, 32, 1: 2–35.

Galbraith, J. (1996) *The Good Society*. New York: Sinclair Stevenson.

Garland, D. (1985) *Punishment and Welfare*. Aldershot: Gower.

Garland, D. (1990) *Punishment and Society*. Oxford: Clarendon Press.

Garland, D. (1994) 'Of Crimes and Criminals: The Development of Criminology in Britain', in M. Maguire, R. Morgan and R. Reiner (eds), *Oxford Handbook of Criminology* (1st edn). Oxford: Clarendon Press.

Garland, D. (1996) 'The Limits of the Sovereign State: Strategies of Crime Control in Contemporary Society', *British Journal of Criminology*, 36, 4: 445–71.

Garland, D. and Young, P. (eds) (1983) *The Power to Punish*. London: Heinemann.

Gattrell, V. (1996) 'Crime, Authority and the Police-man State', in J. Muncie, E. McLaughlin and M. Langan (eds), *Criminological Perspectives*. London: Sage.

Giddens, A. (1990) *The Consequences of Modernity*. Cambridge: Polity.

Giddens, A. (1991) *Modernity and Self-identity*. Cambridge: Polity.

Gilling, D. (1993) 'Crime Prevention Discourses and the Multi-Agency Approach', *International Journal of the Sociology of Law*, 21: 145–57.

Gilling, D. (1994) 'Multi-Agency Crime: Some Barriers to Collaboration', *Howard Journal*, 33, 3: 246–57.

Gilling, D. (1996) 'Policing, Crime Prevention and Partnerships', in F. Leishman, S. Savage and B. Loveday (eds), *Core Issues in Policing*. London: Longman.

Gilling, D. and Barton, A. (1997) 'Crime Prevention and Community Safety: A New Home for Social Policy', *Critical Social Policy*, 17, 1: 63–83.

Glueck, S. and Glueck, E. (1936) *Preventing Crime: A Symposium*. New York: McGraw-Hill.

Gold, M. (1977) 'Crime and Delinquency: Treatment and Prevention', in J. B. Turner (ed.), *Encyclopaedia of Social Work*. Washington: National Association of Social Workers.

Gordon, P. (1987) 'Community Policing', in P. Scraton (ed.), *Law, Order and the Authoritarian State*. Milton Keynes: Open University Press.

Gorz, A. (1992) 'On the Difference Between Society and Community; and Why Basic Income Cannot by Itself Confer Full Membership of Either', in P. van Parijs (ed.), *Arguing for Basic Income*. London: Verso.

Gottfredson, M. and Hirshi, T. (1990) *A General Theory of Crime*. Palo Alto: Stanford University Press.

Gough, I. (1994) 'Economic Interests and the Satisfaction of Human Needs', *Journal of Economic Issues*, 28: 25–66.

Graham, J. and Bennett, T. (1995) *Crime Prevention Strategies in Europe and North America*. Helsinki: Helsinki United Nations Institute.

Gray, J. (1995) *Enlightenment's Wake*. London: Routledge.

Green, D. (1995) *Community without Politics*. London: IEA.

Hart, H. L. A. (1968) *Punishment and Responsibility*. Oxford: Oxford University Press.

Harvey, L., Grimshaw, P. and Pease, K. (1989) 'Crime Prevention Delivery: The Work of CPOs', in R. Morgan and D. Smith (eds), *Coming to Terms with Policing*. London: Routledge.

Hay, D. (ed.) (1975) *Albion's Fatal Tree*. Harmondsworth: Penguin.

Himmelfarb, G. (1995) The Demoralization of Society. London: IEA.

Hindelang, M., Gottfredson, M. and Garafalo, J. (1978) *Victims of Personal Crime: An Empirical Foundation for a Theory of Personal Victimisation*. Cambridge, MA: Ballinger.

Hirshi, T. (1969) *The Causes of Crime*. Berkeley, CA: University of California Press.

Hirst, P. (1994) *Associative Democracy: New Forms of Social Governance*. Cambridge: Polity.

Holmes, R. and Holmes, S. (1996) *Profiling Violent Criminals*. Thousands Oaks, CA: Sage.

Home Office (1984) *Circular 8/84: Crime Prevention*. London: Home Office.

Home Office (1989) *Tackling Crime*. London: Home Office.

Home Office (1990) *Circular 44/1990: Crime Prevention. The Success of the Partnership Approach*. London: Home Office.

Home Office (1991) *Safer Communities: The Local Delivery of Crime Prevention through the Partnership Approach*. London: Home Office.

Home Office (1994) *Partners Against Crime*. London: Home Office.

Home Office (1997) *Getting to Grips with Crime*. London: Home Office.

Hope, T. (1995) 'Community Crime Prevention', in M. Tonry and D. Farrington (eds), *Building a Safer Society: Strategic Approaches to Crime*. Chicago: University of Chicago Press.

Hope, T. and Shaw, M. (1988) *Communities and Crime Reduction*. London: HMSO.

Hudson, B. (1996) *Understanding Justice*. Buckingham: Open University Press.

Hughes, G. (1994) 'Talking Cop Shop: A Case-study of Police Community Consultation in Transition', *Policing and Society*, 4: 253–70.

Hughes, G. (1996a) 'Communitarianism and Law and Order', *Critical Social Policy*, 16, 4: 17–41.

Hughes, G. (1996b) 'Strategies of Crime Prevention and Community Safety in Contemporary Britain', *Studies on Crime and Crime Prevention*, 5: 221–44.

Hughes, G. (1996c) 'The Politics of Criminological Research', in R. Sapsford (ed.), *Researching Crime and Criminal Justice*. Milton Keynes: The Open University.

Hughes G. (1997a) 'Policing Late Modernity: Crime Management in Contemporary Britain', in N. Jewson and S. Macgregor (eds), *Transforming Cities: Contested Governance and New Spatial Divisions*. London: Routledge.

Hughes, G. (1997b) 'Radical Communitarianism, Community Safety and Social Justice', in J. Stanyer and G. Stoker (eds), *Contemporary Political Studies*, Vol. 1. Political Studies Association: Nottingham.

Hughes, G. (1997c) 'What Works in Multi-agency Crime Prevention: A Critical Perspective'. Key-note address, Home Office Conference 'What Works in Crime Prevention', Leeds, September.

Hughes, G. (1998a) 'A Suitable Case for Treatment? Social Constructions of Disability', in E. Saraga (ed.) *Embodying the Social*. London: Routledge.

Hughes, G. (1998b) ' "Picking Over the Remains": The Welfare State Settlements in the Post-War UK', in G. Hughes and G. Lewis (eds), *Unsettling Welfare*. London: Routledge.

Hughes, G. (ed.) (1998c) *Imagining Welfare Futures*. London: Routledge.

Hughes, G. and Lewis, G. (eds) (1998) *Unsettling Welfare*. London: Routledge.

Hughes, G. and Mooney, G. (1998) 'Community', in G. Hughes (ed.) *Imagining Welfare Futures*. London: Routledge.

Hughes, G., Mears, R. and Winch, C. (1997) 'An Inspector Calls: Regulation and Accountability in Three Public Services', *Policy and Politics*, 25, 3: 299–313.

Hughes, G., Pilkington, A. and Leisten, R. (1998) 'Diversion in a Culture of Severity', *Howard Journal of Criminal Justice*, 37, 1: 16–33.

Hulsman, L. (1986) 'Critical Criminology and the Concept of Crime', *Contemporary Crises*, 10, 1: 63–80.

Hutton, W. (1995) *The State We're In*. London: Jonathan Cape.

Iadicola, P. (1986) 'Community Crime Control Strategies', *Crime and Social Justice*, 25.

Ignatieff, M. (1978) *A Just Measure of Pain*. London: Macmillan.

Jacobs, J. (1962) *The Life and Death of Great American Cities*. New York: Vintage Books.

Jenkins, P. (1984) 'Varieties of Enlightenment Criminology', *British Journal of Criminology*, 24, 2: 112–30.

Johnson, E. (ed.) (1987) *Handbook on Crime and Delinquency*. New York: Greenwood Press.

Jones, T ., Newburn, T. and Jones, T. (1994) *Democracy and Policing*. London: PSI.

Jordan, B. (1992) 'Basic Income and Common Good', in P. van Parijs (ed.), *Arguing for Basic Income*. London: Verso.

Jordan, B. (1996) *A Theory of Poverty and Social Exclusion*. Cambridge: Polity.

Jordan, B. and Arnold, J. (1995) 'Democracy and Criminal Justice', *Critical Social Policy*, 44/45: 171–80.

Keane, J. (1996) *Reflections on Violence*. London: Verso.

Kelly, G. (1995) 'Off the shelf Sociology', *Times Higher Educational Supplement*, 24 March.

Kerr, P. (1992) *A Philosophical Investigation*. London: Arrow.

King, M. (1989) 'Social crime prevention à la Thatcher', *Howard Journal*, 28: 291–312.

King, M. (1991) 'The political construction of crime prevention: a contrast between the French and the British experience', in K. Stenson and D. Cowell (eds), *The Politics of Crime Control*. London: Sage.

Kumar, K. (1978) *Prophecy and Progress*. Harmondsworth: Penguin.

Lasch, C. (1995) *The Revolt of the Elites and the Betrayal of Democracy*. New York: Norton.

Lea, J. and Young, J. (1984) *What is to be done about Law and Order?* Harmondsworth: Penguin.

Leadbetter, C. (1996) *The self-policing Society*. London: Demos.

Leishman, F. (1994) 'Under Western Eyes: Perspectives on Policing and Society in Japan', *Policing and Society*, 4: 33–51.

Liddle, M. and Gelsthorpe, L. (1994a) 'Inter-agency Crime Prevention: Organising Local Delivery', CPU Paper 53. London: HMSO.

Liddle, M. and Gelsthorpe, L. (1994b) 'Crime Prevention and Inter-agency Cooperation', CPU Paper 52. London: HMSO.

Liddle, M. and Gelsthorpe, L. (1994c) 'Inter-agency Crime Prevention: Further Issues', CPU Paper 52, 53. London: HMSO.

Lilly, J., Cullen, F. and Ball, R. (1995) *Criminological Theory: Context and Consequences*. London: Sage.

Little, A. (1998) *Post-industrial Socialism: Towards a New Politics of Welfare*. London: Routledge.

Lombroso, C. (1968) *Crime and its Remedies*. Montclair, NJ: Patterson Smith.

Loveday, B. (1994) 'Government Strategies for Community Crime Prevention Programmes in England and Wales: A Study in Failure?', *International Journal of the Sociology of Law*, 22: 181–202.

Lowman, J., Menzies, R. and Palys, T. (1987) *Transcarceration: Essays in the Sociology of Social Control*. Aldershot: Gower.

McGuire, J. (ed.) (1995) *What Works: Reducing Reoffending, Guidelines from Research and Practice*. Chichester: John Wiley & Sons Ltd.

McLaughlin, E. (1994) *Community, Policing and Accountability*. Avebury: Aldershot.

McLaughlin, E. (1996) 'Political Violence, Terrorism and the Crimes of the State', in J. Muncie and E. McLaughlin (eds), *The Problem of Crime*. London: Sage.

McLaughlin, E. (1998) 'Probation Work: Social Work or Social Control?', in G. Hughes and G. Lewis (eds), *Unsettling Welfare*. London: Routledge.

McLaughlin, E. and Muncie, J. (1994) 'Managing criminal justice', in J. Clarke, A. Cochrane and E. McLaughlin (eds), *Managing Social Policy*. London: Sage.

McLaughlin, E. and Muncie, J. (eds) (1996) *Controlling Crime*. London: Sage.

McMahon, M. (1990) 'Net-widening: Vagaries in the Use of a Concept', *British Journal of Criminology*, 30, 2: 121–49.

Maguire, M. (1994) 'Crime Statistics, Patterns and Trends: Changing Perceptions and their Implications' in M. Maguire, R. Morgan and R. Reiner (eds), *Oxford Handbook of Criminology* (1st edn). Oxford: Clarendon Press.

Martinson, R. (1974) 'What Works? Questions and Answers about Prison Reform', *The Public Interest*, 35: 22–54.

Marx, G. (1995) 'The Engineering of Social Control: The Search for the Silver Bullet', in J. Hagan and R. Peterson (eds), *Crime and Society*. Stanford, CA: Stanford University Press.

Massey, D. (1997) 'Problems with Globalization', *Soundings*, 7: 7–12.

Matza, D. (1964) *Delinquency and Drift*. New York: Wiley.

Mednick, S., Moffitt T. and Stark S. (eds) (1987) *The Causes of Crime: New Biological Approaches*. New York: Cambridge University Press.

Melossi, D. and Pavarini, M. (1981) *The Prison and the Factory*. London: Macmillan.

Merrifield, A. (1996) 'Integration and Exclusion in Urban Life', *City*, 5/6: 57–72.

Misztal, B. (1996) *Trust in Modern Societies*. Cambridge: Polity.

Morgan, R. (1992) 'Talking Policing', in D. Downes (ed.), *Unravelling Criminal Justice*. London: Macmillan.

Morgan, R. and Swift, P. (1988) 'The Future of Police Authorities', *Public Administration*, 65, 20: 259–76.

Moriyama, T. (1993) 'Crime, Criminal Justice and Social Control: Why Do We Enjoy a Low Crime Rate?'. Paper presented at the British Criminology Conference, Cardiff, July.

Morris, J. (1991) *Pride Versus Prejudice*. London: Women's Press.

Morrison, W. (1995) *Theoretical Criminology: From Modernity to Post-modernism*. London: Cavendish Publishing Ltd.

Mouffe, C. (ed.) (1992) *Dimensions of Radical Democracy*. London: Verso.

Muncie, J. (1998) *Youth and Crime: A Critical Introduction*. London: Sage.

Muncie, J., Coventry, G. and Walters, R. (1994) 'Politics of Youth Crime Prevention: Developments in Australia and England and Wales', in L. Noaks, M. Levi and M. Maguire (eds), *Contemporary Issues in Criminology*. Cardiff: University of Wales Press.

Muncie, J., McLaughlin, E. and Langan, M. (1996) *Criminological Perspectives: A Reader*. London: Sage.

Murray, C. (1990) *Losing Ground*. New York: Arrow.

Murray, C. (1996) 'The Underclass', in J. Muncie and E. McLaughlin (eds), *Criminological Perspectives*. London: Sage.

Nelken, D. (1985) 'Community Involvement in Crime Control', *Contemporary Legal Problems*, 85: 259–67.

Nelken, D. (1994) *The Futures of Criminology*. London: Sage.

Newman, O. (1972) *Defensible Space: People and Design in the Violent City*. London: Architectural Press.

Norris, C. and Armstrong, S. (1997) 'Categories of Control: The Social Construction of Suspicion and Intervention in CCTV Systems', in C. Norris and S. Armstrong (eds), *Images of Control: CCTV and the Rise of Surveillance Societies*. Berg.

O'Malley, P. (1992) 'Risk, Power and Crime Prevention', *Economy and Society*, 21, 3: 251–68.

O'Malley, P. (1994) 'Responsibility and Crime Prevention: A Response to Adam Sutton', *Australian and New Zealand Journal of Criminology* (special edition): 21–4.

O'Malley, P. (1995) 'Neo-liberal Crime Control: Political Agendas and the Future of Crime Prevention in Australia', in D. Chappell and P. Wilson (eds), *The Australian Criminal Justice System: The Mid-1990s*. Adelaide: Butterworths.

O'Malley, P. (1997) 'The Politics of Crime Prevention', in P. O'Malley and A. Sutton (eds), *Crime Prevention in Australia: Issues in Policy and Research*. Sydney: Federation Press.

O'Malley P. and Palmer, D. (1996) 'Post-Keynesian Policing', *Economy and Society*, 25, 5: 137–55.

Offe, C. (1992) 'A New Non-productive Design for Social Policies', in P. van Parijs (ed.), *Arguing for Basic Income*. London: Verso.

Oldfield, A. (1990) *Citizenship and Community: Civic Republicanism and the Modern World*. London: Routledge.

Palmer, D. (1997) 'When Tolerance is Zero', *Alternative Law Journal*, 22, 5: 232–6.

Pavarini, M. (1997) 'Controlling Social Panic: Questions and Answers About Security in Italy at the End of the Millennium', in R. Bergalli and C. Sumner (eds), *Social Control and Political Order*. London: Sage.

Pearson, G. (1975) *The Deviant Imagination*. London: Macmillan.

Pearson, G., Blagg, H., Smith, D., Sampson, A. and Stubbs, P. (1992) 'Crime, Community and Conflict: The Multi-agency Approach', in D. Downes (ed.), *Unravelling Criminal Justice*. London: Macmillan.

Pease, K. (1994) 'Crime Prevention', in M. Maguire, R. Morgan and R. Reiner (eds), *Oxford Handbook of Criminology* (1st edn). Oxford: Clarendon Press.

Pease, K. (1997) 'Crime Prevention', in M. Maguire, R. Morgan and R. Reiner (eds), *Oxford Handbook of Criminology* (2nd edn). Oxford: Clarendon Press.

Phillips, M. (1996) *All Must Have Prizes*. London: Little, Brown

Pitts, J. (1996) 'The Politics and Practice of Youth Justice', in E. McLaughlin and J. Muncie (eds), *Controlling Crime*. London: Sage.

Pollitt, C. (1993) *Managerialism and the Public Services*. Oxford: Blackwell.

Polk, K. (1997) 'A Community and Youth Development Approach to Crime Prevention', in P. O. Malley and A. Sutton (eds), *Crime Prevention in Australia: Issues in Policy and Research*. Sydney: Federation Press.

Poster, M. (1990) *The Mode of Information: Poststructuralism and Social Context*. Cambridge: Polity.

Pratt, J. (1989) 'Corporatism: The Third Model of Juvenile Justice', *British Journal of Criminology*, 29, 3: 236–54.

Proctor, R. (1988) *Racial Hygiene: Medicine Under The Nazis*. Cambridge, MA: Harvard University Press.

Radzinowicz, L. and Wolfgang, M. (eds) (1971) *Crime and Justice*, Vol. 2. New York: Basic Books.

Reiner, R. (1992) *The Politics of the Police*. Hemel Hempstead: Harvester Wheatsheaf.

Reiner, R. (1994) 'Policing and the Police', in M. Maguire, R. Morgan and R. Reiner (eds), *Oxford Handbook of Criminology* (1st edn). Oxford: Clarendon Press.

Ritzer, G. (1993) *The Macdonaldization of Society*. Newbury Park, CA: Pine Forge Press.

Roberts, J. and Grossman, M. (1990) 'Crime prevention and public opinion', *Canadian Journal of Criminology*, 32, 1.

Rock, P. (1989) 'New Directions in Criminological Theory', *Social Studies Review*, 5, 1: 2–6.

Rose, N. (1989) *Governing the Soul*. London: Routledge.

Rose, N. (1996) 'The Death of the Social? Refiguring the Territory of Government', *Economy and Society*, 25, 3: 321–56.

Rosenbaum, D. (1988) Community Crime Prevention: A Review and Synthesis of the Literature', *Justice Quarterly*, 5: 323–95.

Roshier, B. (1989) *Controlling Crime*. Milton Keynes: Open University Press.

Rutherford, A. (1993) *Criminal Justice and the Pursuit of Decency*. Oxford: Oxford University Press.

Sampson, A., Stubbs, P., Pearson, G. and Blagg, H. (1988) 'Crime, Localities and the Multi-agency Approach', *British Journal of Criminology*, 28: 478–93.

Schwendinger, H. and Schwendinger, J. (1993) 'Giving Crime Prevention Top Priority', *Crime and Delinquency*, 38, 4: 425–45.

Sennett, R. (1977) *Fall of Public Man*. Cambridge: Cambridge University Press.

Shaw, C. and McKay, H. (1969) *Juvenile Delinquency and Urban Areas*. Chicago: University of Chicago Press.

Shearing, C. and Stenning, P. (1981) 'Private security: its growth and implications', in M. Tonry and N. Morris (eds) *Crime and Justice: An Annual Review of Research*, Vol. 3. Chicago: University of Chicago Press.

Shearing, C. and Stenning, P. (1985) 'From the Panopticon to Disney World: The

Development of Discipline', in A. Dobb and E. Greenspan (eds), *Perspectives in Criminal Law*. Aurora, Ontario: Canada Book Co.

Sheptycki, J. (1997) 'Insecurity, Risk, Suppression and Segregation: Some Reflections on Policing in the Transnational Age', *Theoretical Criminology*, 1, 3: 303–15.

Sparks, R. (1997) 'Recent Social Theory and the Study of Crime and Punishment', in M. Maguire, R. Morgan and R. Reiner (eds), *Oxford Handbook of Criminology* (2nd edn). Oxford: Clarendon Press.

Spicker, P. (1994) 'Understanding particularism', *Critical Social Policy*, 39: 5–20.

Stanko, E. (1990) 'When Precaution is Normal: A Feminist Critique of Crime Prevention', in L. Gelsthorpe and A. Morris (eds), *Feminist Perspectives in Criminology*. Buckingham: Open University Press.

Stenson, K. (1991) 'Making Sense of Crime Control', in D. Cowell and K. Stenson (eds), *The Politics of Crime Control*. London: Sage.

Stenson, K. (1995) 'Community Security as Government: The British Experience', in W. Hammerschicht, I. Karazman-Marawetz and W. Staagl (eds), *Jahrbuch fur Rechtsand Kriminalsoziologie*. Baden-Baden: Nomos.

Stoker, G. and Young, P. (1993) *Cities in the 1990s*. London: Longman.

Sutton A. (1994) 'Crime Prevention: Promise or Threat?', *Australian and New Zealand Journal of Criminology*, 27: 5–20.

Sutton, A. (1997) 'Crime Prevention: The Policy Dilemma – A Personal Account', in P. O'Malley and A. Sutton (eds), *Crime Prevention in Australia: Issues in Policy and Research*. Sydney: Federation Press.

Sutton, A. and O'Malley, P. (1997) 'Introduction', in P. O'Malley and A. Sutton (eds), *Crime Prevention in Australia: Issues in Policy and Research*. Sydney: Federation Press.

Taylor, I. (1997) 'Crime, Anxiety and Locality: Responding to the "Condition of England" at the end of the century', *Theoretical Criminology*, 1, 1: 53–75.

Taylor, I., Walton, P. and Young, J. (1973) *The New Criminology*. London: Routledge.

Tilley, N. (1994) 'Crime Prevention and the Safer Cities Story', *Howard Journal*, 32, 1: 40–57.

Tilley, N. and Pawson, R. (1994) 'What Works in Evaluation Research', *British Journal of Criminology*, 34: 291–306.

Tonry, M. and Farrington, D. (1995) 'Strategic Approaches to Crime Prevention', in M. Tonry and D. Farrington (eds), *Building a Safer Society: Strategic Approaches to Crime*. Chicago: University of Chicago Press.

Trembliss, R. and Craig, W. (1995) 'Developmental Crime Prevention', in M. Tonry and D. Farrington (eds), *Building a Safer Society: Strategic Approaches to Crime*. Chicago: University of Chicago Press.

Unger, R. (1972) *Law and Modern Society: Toward a Critique of Social Theory*. New York: Free Press.

United Nations (1991) *8th Congress on the Prevention of Crime and the Treatment of Offenders*, Havana, 27 August–7 September, New York: United Nations Secretariat.

Van Dijk, J. and De Waard J. (1991) 'A Two-dimensional Typology of Crime Prevention Projects', *Criminal Justice Abstracts*, September: 483–503.

van Swaaningen, R. (1997) *Critical Criminology: Visions from Europe*. London: Sage.

von Hirsch, A. (1976) *Doing Justice: The Choice of Punishments*. New York: Hill and Wang.

Walklate, S. (1996) 'Community and Crime Prevention', in E. McLaughlin and J. Muncie (eds), *Controlling Crime*. London: Sage.

Walzer, M. (1992) 'The Civil Society Argument', in C. Mouffe (ed.), *Dimensions of Radical Democracy*. London: Verso.

Weatheritt, M. (1986) *Innovations in Policing*. Beckenham: Croom Helm.

Weber, M. (1949) *The Methodology of the Social Sciences*, trans. E. Shils and M. Rheinstein. Massachusetts: Harvard University Press.

Weiss, R. (1987) 'The Community and Crime Prevention', in E. Johnson (ed.), *Handbook on Crime and Delinquency Prevention*. New York: Greenwood Press.

Wiener, M. (1990) *Reconstructing the Criminal: Culture, Law and Policy in England, 1830–1914*. Cambridge: Cambridge University Press.

Wilson, J. (1975) *Thinking about Crime*. New York: Basic Books.

Wilson, J. and Kelling, G. (1982) 'Broken Windows', *Atlantic Monthly*, March: 29–38.

Wolfe, T. (1997) 'Sorry, but your soul just died', *Independent On Sunday*, 2 February.

Young, I. (1990) 'The Idea of Community and the Politics of Difference', in L. Nicholson (ed.) *Feminism/Postmodernism*. New York: Routledge.

Young, J. (1991) 'Left Realism and the Priorities of Crime Control', in D. Cowell and K. Stenson (eds), *The Politics of Crime Control*. London: Sage.

Young, J. (1994) 'Incessant Chatter: Recent Paradigms in Criminology, in M. Maguire, R. Morgan and R. Reiner (eds), *Oxford Handbook of Criminology* (1st edn). Oxford: Clarendon Press.

Index

socialized risk management, 72
sociological positivism, 45–6, 55
Stanko, Betsy, 68
state
  authoritarian statist-communitarian
    model, 144–6
  central government policy on multi-
    agency crime prevention, 79–86,
    101–2
  changing modalities of power, 78
  crime committed by, 68–9
  institutionalization of classical
    theory, 32–5
  institutionalization of positivist
    discourse, 43–4, 45, 46–7
  role in crime control and prevention,
    16–17, 146–7, 155–6
  role in radical left
    communitarianism, 117–18
  use of communitarian crime
    prevention, 127–8
Stenning, Philip, 141–2
Stoker, G., 148
street crime, 118
street watch, 84
surveillance, 61
Sutton, Adam, 16, 102, 156

target hardening, 61
Taylor, Ian, 149–50
technicist orientation, 4
technology, impact of, 70
tertiary crime prevention, 21
Tilley, Nicholas, 92–4
Tonry, M., 2, 16, 21–2, 52–3
treatment
  in positivist paradigm, 39, 42–3, 45,
    47, 48
  see also rehabilitative ideal in
    positivism

Trembliss, R., 52
trust, in late modern risk society thesis,
  134

underclass, 110, 114, 119, 140, 141
utilitarianism, 28

van Swaaningen, R., 156–7
victim precipitation, 69
victims, initiatives targeting, 88
vigilantism, 98

Walklate, Sandra, 18–19, 106
Weatheritt, M., 17
welfare state, institutionalization of
  positivism in, 46–7
Wiles, P., 22, 33–4, 127, 136–8
Wolfe, Tom, 49–50
Wolfgang, Marvin, 15
women
  and communitarian crime
    prevention, 114, 124–5
  crimes against, 68
  multi-agency crime prevention
    initiatives for, 100

Young, Jock, 20, 59, 61, 67, 68, 118
Young, P., 148
youth crime
  community safety approach and, 84f
  response of justice system to, 16
youth offenders
  Chicago school theory of, 45–6
  developmental theory of, 51–4, 55
  positivist approach to delinquency,
    46–7, 48
  rehabilitation of, 44

zero-tolerance, 112–13